ASPEN PUBLISH

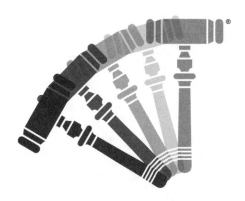

Casenote™ *Legal Briefs*

EMPLOYMENT DISCRIMINATION

Keyed to Courses Using

Zimmer, Sullivan, and White's
Cases and Materials on Employment Discrimination

Seventh Edition

Wolters Kluwer
Law & Business

AUSTIN   BOSTON   CHICAGO   NEW YORK   THE NETHERLANDS

© 2008 Aspen Publishers, Inc. All Rights Reserved.
a Wolters Kluwer business
http://lawschool.aspenpublishers.com

No part of this publication may be reproduced or transmitted in any form or by any means, electronic or mechanical, including photocopy, recording, or any information storage and retrieval system, without permission in writing from the publisher. Requests for permission to make copies of any part of this publication should be mailed to:

Aspen Publishers
Attn: Permissions Dept.
76 Ninth Avenue, 7th Floor
New York, NY 10011-5201

To contact Customer Care, e-mail customer.care@aspenpublishers.com, call 1-800-234-1660, fax 1-800-901-9075, or mail correspondence to:

Aspen Publishers
Attn: Order Department
P.O. Box 990
Frederick, MD 21705

Printed in the United States of America.

1 2 3 4 5 6 7 8 9 0

ISBN 978-0-7355-7175-4

About Wolters Kluwer Law & Business

Wolters Kluwer Law & Business is a leading provider of research information and workflow solutions in key specialty areas. The strengths of the individual brands of Aspen Publishers, CCH, Kluwer Law International and Loislaw are aligned within Wolters Kluwer Law & Business to provide comprehensive, in-depth solutions and expert-authored content for the legal, professional and education markets.

CCH was founded in 1913 and has served more than four generations of business professionals and their clients. The CCH products in the Wolters Kluwer Law & Business group are highly regarded electronic and print resources for legal, securities, antitrust and trade regulation, government contracting, banking, pension, payroll, employment and labor, and health-care reimbursement and compliance professionals.

Aspen Publishers is a leading information provider for attorneys, business professionals and law students. Written by preeminent authorities, Aspen products offer analytical and practical information in a range of specialty practice areas from securities law and intellectual property to mergers and acquisitions and pension/benefits. Aspen's trusted legal education resources provide professors and students with high-quality, up-to-date and effective resources for successful instruction and study in all areas of the law.

Kluwer Law International supplies the global business community with comprehensive English-language international legal information. Legal practitioners, corporate counsel and business executives around the world rely on the Kluwer Law International journals, loose-leafs, books and electronic products for authoritative information in many areas of international legal practice.

Loislaw is a premier provider of digitized legal content to small law firm practitioners of various specializations. Loislaw provides attorneys with the ability to quickly and efficiently find the necessary legal information they need, when and where they need it, by facilitating access to primary law as well as state-specific law, records, forms and treatises.

Wolters Kluwer Law & Business, a unit of Wolters Kluwer, is headquartered in New York and Riverwoods, Illinois. Wolters Kluwer is a leading multinational publisher and information services company.

Format for the Casenote Legal Brief

Nature of Case: This section identifies the form of action (e.g., breach of contract, negligence, battery), the type of proceeding (e.g., demurrer, appeal from trial court's jury instructions) or the relief sought (e.g., damages, injunction, criminal sanctions).

Fact Summary: This is included to refresh your memory and can be used as a quick reminder of the facts.

Rule of Law: Summarizes the general principle of law that the case illustrates. It may be used for instant recall of the court's holding and for classroom discussion or home review.

Facts: This section contains all relevant facts of the case, including the contentions of the parties and the lower court holdings. It is written in a logical order to give the student a clear understanding of the case. The plaintiff and defendant are identified by their proper names throughout and are always labeled with a (P) or (D).

Party ID: Quick identification of the relationship between the parties.

Concurrence/Dissent: All concurrences and dissents are briefed whenever they are included by the casebook editor.

Analysis: This last paragraph gives you a broad understanding of where the case "fits in" with other cases in the section of the book and with the entire course. It is a hornbook-style discussion indicating whether the case is a majority or minority opinion and comparing the principal case with other cases in the casebook. It may also provide analysis from restatements, uniform codes, and law review articles. The analysis will prove to be invaluable to classroom discussion.

Issue: The issue is a concise question that brings out the essence of the opinion as it relates to the section of the casebook in which the case appears. Both substantive and procedural issues are included if relevant to the decision.

Holding and Decision: This section offers a clear and in-depth discussion of the rule of the case and the court's rationale. It is written in easy-to-understand language and answers the issue presented by applying the law to the facts of the case. When relevant, it includes a thorough discussion of the exceptions to the case as listed by the court, any major cites to the other cases on point, and the names of the judges who wrote the decisions.

Quicknotes: Conveniently defines legal terms found in the case and summarizes the nature of any statutes, codes, or rules referred to in the text.

Palsgraf v. Long Island R.R. Co.

Injured bystander (P) v. Railroad company (D)

N.Y. Ct. App., 248 N.Y. 339, 162 N.E. 99 (1928).

NATURE OF CASE: Appeal from judgment affirming verdict for plaintiff seeking damages for personal injury.

FACT SUMMARY: Helen Palsgraf (P) was injured on R.R.'s (D) train platform when R.R.'s (D) guard helped a passenger aboard a moving train, causing his package to fall on the tracks. The package contained fireworks which exploded, creating a shock that tipped a scale onto Palsgraf (P).

🏛 RULE OF LAW
The risk reasonably to be perceived defines the duty to be obeyed.

FACTS: Helen Palsgraf (P) purchased a ticket to Rockaway Beach from R.R. (D) and was waiting on the train platform. As she waited, two men ran to catch a train that was pulling out from the platform. The first man jumped aboard, but the second man, who appeared as if he might fall, was helped aboard by the guard on the train who had kept the door open so they could jump aboard. A guard on the platform also helped by pushing him onto the train. The man was carrying a package wrapped in newspaper. In the process, the man dropped his package, which fell on the tracks. The package contained fireworks and exploded. The shock of the explosion was apparently of great enough strength to tip over some scales at the other end of the platform, which fell on Palsgraf (P) and injured her. A jury awarded her damages, and R.R. (D) appealed.

ISSUE: Does the risk reasonably to be perceived define the duty to be obeyed?

HOLDING AND DECISION: (Cardozo, C.J.) Yes. The risk reasonably to be perceived defines the duty to be obeyed. If there is no foreseeable hazard to the injured party as the result of a seemingly innocent act, the act does not become a tort because it happened to be a wrong as to another. If the wrong was not willful, the plaintiff must show that the act as to her had such great and apparent possibilities of danger as to entitle her to protection. Negligence in the abstract is not enough upon which to base liability. Negligence is a relative concept, evolving out of the common law doctrine of trespass on the case. To establish liability, the defendant must owe a legal duty of reasonable care to the injured party. A cause of action in tort will lie where harm,

though unintended, could have been averted or avoided by observance of such a duty. The scope of the duty is limited by the range of danger that a reasonable person could foresee. In this case, there was nothing to suggest from the appearance of the parcel or otherwise that the parcel contained fireworks. The guard could not reasonably have had any warning of a threat to Palsgraf (P), and R.R. (D) therefore cannot be held liable. Judgment is reversed in favor of R.R. (D).

DISSENT: (Andrews, J.) The concept that there is no negligence unless R.R. (D) owes a legal duty to take care as to Palsgraf (P) herself is too narrow. Everyone owes to the world at large the duty of refraining from those acts that may unreasonably threaten the safety of others. If the guard's action was negligent as to those nearby, it was also negligent as to those outside what might be termed the "danger zone." For Palsgraf (P) to recover, R.R.'s (D) negligence must have been the proximate cause of her injury, a question of fact for the jury.

▶ ANALYSIS
The majority defined the limit of the defendant's liability in terms of the danger that a reasonable person in defendant's situation would have perceived. The dissent argued that the limitation should not be placed on liability, but rather on damages. Judge Andrews suggested that only injuries that would not have happened but for R.R.'s (D) negligence should be compensable. Both the majority and dissent recognized the policy-driven need to limit liability for negligent acts, seeking, in the words of Judge Andrews, to define a framework "that will be practical and in keeping with the general understanding of mankind." The Restatement (Second) of Torts has accepted Judge Cardozo's view.

Quicknotes

FORESEEABILITY A reasonable expectation that change is the probable result of certain acts or omissions.

NEGLIGENCE Conduct falling below the standard of care that a reasonable person would demonstrate under similar conditions.

PROXIMATE CAUSE The natural sequence of events without which an injury would not have been sustained.

Aspen Publishers is proud to offer *Casenote Legal Briefs*—continuing thirty years of publishing America's best-selling legal briefs.

Casenote Legal Briefs are designed to help you save time when briefing assigned cases. Organized under convenient headings, they show you how to abstract the basic facts and holdings from the text of the actual opinions handed down by the courts. Used as part of a rigorous study regimen, they can help you spend more time analyzing and critiquing points of law than on copying bits and pieces of judicial opinions into your notebook or outline.

Casenote Legal Briefs should never be used as a substitute for assigned casebook readings. They work best when read as a follow-up to reviewing the underlying opinions themselves. Students who try to avoid reading and digesting the judicial opinions in their casebooks or online sources will end up shortchanging themselves in the long run. The ability to absorb, critique, and restate the dynamic and complex elements of case law decisions is crucial to your success in law school and beyond. It cannot be developed vicariously.

Casenote Legal Briefs represents but one of the many offerings in Aspen's Study Aid Timeline, which includes:

- *Casenote Legal Briefs*
- *Emanuel Law Outlines*
- *Examples & Explanations* Series
- *Introduction to Law* Series
- Emanuel *Law in a Flash* Flashcards
- Emanuel *CrunchTime* Series

Each of these series is designed to provide you with easy-to-understand explanations of complex points of law. Each volume offers guidance on the principles of legal analysis and, consulted regularly, will hone your ability to spot relevant issues. We have titles that will help you prepare for class, prepare for your exams, and enhance your general comprehension of the law along the way.

To find out more about Aspen Study Aid publications, visit us online at *http://lawschool.aspenpublishers.com* or email us at *legaledu@wolterskluwer.com*. We'll be happy to assist you.

Free access to Briefs online!

Download cases from this Casenote Legal Brief. Simply fill out this form for full access to this useful feature provided by Loislaw. Learn more about Loislaw services on the inside front cover of this book or visit *www.loislawschool.com*.

Name	Phone ( )
Address	Apt. No.
City	State	ZIP Code
Law School	Graduation Date

Cut out the UPC found on the lower left-hand corner of the back cover of this book. Staple the UPC inside this box.
Only the original UPC from the book cover will be accepted. No photocopies or store stickers are allowed.

**Attach UPC
inside this box.**

Email (Print legibly or you may not get access!)
Title of this book (course subject)
Used with which casebook (provide author's name)

Mail the completed form to: Aspen Publishers, Inc.
Legal Education Division
Casenote Online Access
130 Turner Street, Building 3, 4th Floor
Waltham, MA 02453-8901

I understand that online access is granted solely to the purchaser of this book for the academic year in which it was purchased. Any other usage is not authorized and will result in immediate termination of access. Sharing of codes is strictly prohibited.

Signature _____

Upon receipt of this completed form, you will be emailed codes with which to access the briefs for this Casenote Legal Brief. Online briefs are not available for all titles. For a full list of Casenote Legal Brief titles, please visit *http://lawschool.aspenpublishers.com*.

A. Decide on a Format and Stick to It

Structure is essential to a good brief. It enables you to arrange systematically the related parts that are scattered throughout most cases, thus making manageable and understandable what might otherwise seem to be an endless and unfathomable sea of information. There are, of course, an unlimited number of formats that can be utilized. However, it is best to find one that suits your needs and stick to it. Consistency breeds both efficiency and the security that when called upon you will know where to look in your brief for the information you are asked to give.

Any format, as long as it presents the essential elements of a case in an organized fashion, can be used. Experience, however, has led *Casenotes* to develop and utilize the following format because of its logical flow and universal applicability.

NATURE OF CASE: This is a brief statement of the legal character and procedural status of the case (e.g., "Appeal of a burglary conviction").

There are many different alternatives open to a litigant dissatisfied with a court ruling. The key to determining which one has been used is to discover *who is asking this court for what.*

This first entry in the brief should be kept as *short as possible.* Use the court's terminology if you understand it. But since jurisdictions vary as to the titles of pleadings, the best entry is the one that addresses who wants what in this proceeding, not the one that sounds most like the court's language.

RULE OF LAW: A statement of the general principle of law that the case illustrates (e.g., "An acceptance that varies any term of the offer is considered a rejection and counteroffer").

Determining the rule of law of a case is a procedure similar to determining the issue of the case. Avoid being fooled by red herrings; there may be a few rules of law mentioned in the case excerpt, but usually only one is *the* rule with which the casebook editor is concerned. The techniques used to locate the issue, described below, may also be utilized to find the rule of law. Generally, your best guide is simply the chapter heading. It is a clue to the point the casebook editor seeks to make and should be kept in mind when reading every case in the respective section.

FACTS: A synopsis of only the essential facts of the case, i.e., those bearing upon or leading up to the issue.

The facts entry should be a short statement of the events and transactions that led one party to initiate legal proceedings against another in the first place. While some cases conveniently state the salient facts at the beginning of the decision, in other instances they will have to be culled from hiding places throughout the text, even from concurring and dissenting opinions. Some of the "facts" will often be in dispute and should be so noted. Conflicting evidence may be briefly pointed up. "Hard" facts must be included. Both must be *relevant* in order to be listed in the facts entry. It is impossible to tell what is relevant until the entire case is read, as the ultimate determination of the rights and liabilities of the parties may turn on something buried deep in the opinion.

Generally, the facts entry should not be longer than three to five *short* sentences.

It is often helpful to identify the role played by a party in a given context. For example, in a construction contract case the identification of a party as the "contractor" or "builder" alleviates the need to tell that that party was the one who was supposed to have built the house.

It is always helpful, and a good general practice, to identify the "plaintiff" and the "defendant." This may seem elementary and uncomplicated, but, especially in view of the creative editing practiced by some casebook editors, it is sometimes a difficult or even impossible task. Bear in mind that the *party presently* seeking something from this court may not be the plaintiff, and that sometimes only the cross-claim of a defendant is treated in the excerpt. Confusing or misaligning the parties can ruin your analysis and understanding of the case.

ISSUE: A statement of the general legal question answered by or illustrated in the case. For clarity, the issue is best put in the form of a question capable of a "yes" or "no" answer. In reality, the issue is simply the Rule of Law put in the form of a question (e.g., "May an offer be accepted by performance?").

The major problem presented in discerning what is *the* issue in the case is that an opinion usually purports to raise and answer several questions. However, except for rare cases, only one such question is really the issue in the case. Collateral issues not necessary to the resolution of the matter in controversy are handled by the court by language known as *"obiter dictum"* or merely *"dictum."* While dicta may be included later in the brief, they have no place under the issue heading.

To find the issue, ask *who wants what* and then go on to ask *why did that party succeed or fail in getting it.* Once this is determined, the "why" should be turned into a question.

The complexity of the issues in the cases will vary, but in all cases a single-sentence question should sum up the issue. *In a few cases,* there will be two, or even more rarely, three issues of equal importance to the resolution of the case. Each should be expressed in a single-sentence question.

Since many issues are resolved by a court in coming to a final disposition of a case, the casebook editor will reproduce the portion of the opinion containing the issue or issues most relevant to the area of law under scrutiny. A noted law professor gave this advice: "Close the book; look at the title on the cover." Chances are, if it is Property, you need not concern yourself with whether, for example, the federal government's treatment of the plaintiff's land really raises a federal question sufficient to support jurisdiction on this ground in federal court.

The same rule applies to chapter headings designating sub-areas within the subjects. They tip you off as to what the text is designed to teach. The cases are arranged in a casebook to show a progression or development of the law, so that the preceding cases may also help.

It is also most important to remember to *read the notes and questions* at the end of a case to determine what the editors wanted you to have gleaned from it.

HOLDING AND DECISION: This section should succinctly explain the rationale of the court in arriving at its decision. In capsulizing the "reasoning" of the court, it should always include an application of the general rule or rules of law to the specific facts of the case. Hidden justifications come to light in this entry; the reasons for the state of the law, the public policies, the biases and prejudices, those considerations that influence the justices' thinking and, ultimately, the outcome of the case. At the end, there should be a short indication of the disposition or procedural resolution of the case (e.g., "Decision of the trial court for Mr. Smith (P) reversed").

The foregoing format is designed to help you "digest" the reams of case material with which you will be faced in your law school career. Once mastered by practice, it will place at your fingertips the information the authors of your casebooks have sought to impart to you in case-by-case illustration and analysis.

B. Be as Economical as Possible in Briefing Cases

Once armed with a format that encourages succinctness, it is as important to be economical with regard to the time spent on the actual reading of the case as it is to be economical in the writing of the brief itself. This does not mean "skimming" a case. Rather, it means reading the case with an "eye" trained to recognize into which "section" of your brief a particular passage or line fits and having a system for quickly and precisely marking the case so that the passages fitting any one particular part of

the brief can be easily identified and brought together in a concise and accurate manner when the brief is actually written.

It is of no use to simply repeat everything in the opinion of the court; record only enough information to trigger your recollection of what the court said. Nevertheless, an accurate statement of the "law of the case," i.e., the legal principle applied to the facts, is absolutely essential to class preparation and to learning the law under the case method.

To that end, it is important to develop a "shorthand" that you can use to make margin notations. These notations will tell you at a glance in which section of the brief you will be placing that particular passage or portion of the opinion.

Some students prefer to underline all the salient portions of the opinion (with a pencil or colored underliner marker), making marginal notations as they go along. Others prefer the color-coded method of underlining, utilizing different colors of markers to underline the salient portions of the case, each separate color being used to represent a different section of the brief. For example, blue underlining could be used for passages relating to the rule of law, yellow for those relating to the issue, and green for those relating to the holding and decision, etc. While it has its advocates, the color-coded method can be confusing and time-consuming (all that time spent on changing colored markers). Furthermore, it can interfere with the continuity and concentration many students deem essential to the reading of a case for maximum comprehension. In the end, however, it is a matter of personal preference and style. Just remember, whatever method you use, underlining must be used sparingly or its value is lost.

If you take the marginal notation route, an efficient and easy method is to go along underlining the key portions of the case and placing in the margin alongside them the following "markers" to indicate where a particular passage or line "belongs" in the brief you will write:

N (NATURE OF CASE)
RL (RULE OF LAW)
I (ISSUE)
HL (HOLDING AND DECISION, relates to the RULE OF LAW behind the decision)
HR (HOLDING AND DECISION, gives the RATIONALE or reasoning behind the decision)
HA (HOLDING AND DECISION, APPLIES the general principle(s) of law to the facts of the case to arrive at the decision)

Remember that a particular passage may well contain information necessary to more than one part of your brief, in which case you simply note that in the margin. If you are using the color-coded underlining method instead of margin notation, simply make asterisks or checks in the margin next to the passage in question in the colors that indicate the additional sections of the brief where it might be utilized.

The economy of utilizing "shorthand" in marking cases for briefing can be maintained in the actual brief writing process itself by utilizing "law student shorthand" within the brief. There are many commonly used words and phrases for which abbreviations can be substituted in your briefs (and in your class notes also). You can develop abbreviations that are personal to you and which will save you a lot of time. A reference list of briefing abbreviations can be found on page xii of this book.

C. Use Both the Briefing Process and the Brief as a Learning Tool

Now that you have a format and the tools for briefing cases efficiently, the most important thing is to make the time spent in briefing profitable to you and to make the most advantageous use of the briefs you create. Of course, the briefs are invaluable for classroom reference when you are called upon to explain or analyze a particular case. However, they are also useful in reviewing for exams. A quick glance at the fact summary should bring the case to mind, and a rereading of the rule of law should enable you to go over the underlying legal concept in your mind, how it was applied in that particular case, and how it might apply in other factual settings.

As to the value to be derived from engaging in the briefing process itself, there is an immediate benefit that arises from being forced to sift through the essential facts and reasoning from the court's opinion and to succinctly express them in your own words in your brief. The process ensures that you understand the case and the point that it illustrates, and that means you will be ready to absorb further analysis and information brought forth in class. It also ensures you will have something to say when called upon in class. The briefing process helps develop a mental agility for getting to the *gist* of a case and for identifying, expounding on, and applying the legal concepts and issues found there. The briefing process is the mental process on which you must rely in taking law school examinations; it is also the mental process upon which a lawyer relies in serving his clients and in making his living.

Abbreviations for Briefs

acceptance	acp	offer	O
affirmed	aff	offeree	OE
answer	ans	offeror	OR
assumption of risk	a/r	ordinance	ord
attorney	atty	pain and suffering	p/s
beyond a reasonable doubt	b/r/d	parol evidence	p/e
bona fide purchaser	BFP	plaintiff	P
breach of contract	br/k	prima facie	p/f
cause of action	c/a	probable cause	p/c
common law	c/l	proximate cause	px/c
Constitution	Con	real property	r/p
constitutional	con	reasonable doubt	r/d
contract	K	reasonable man	r/m
contributory negligence	c/n	rebuttable presumption	rb/p
cross	x	remanded	rem
cross-complaint	x/c	res ipsa loquitur	RIL
cross-examination	x/ex	respondeat superior	r/s
cruel and unusual punishment	c/u/p	Restatement	RS
defendant	D	reversed	rev
dismissed	dis	Rule Against Perpetuities	RAP
double jeopardy	d/j	search and seizure	s/s
due process	d/p	search warrant	s/w
equal protection	e/p	self-defense	s/d
equity	eq	specific performance	s/p
evidence	ev	statute of limitations	S/L
exclude	exc	statute of frauds	S/F
exclusionary rule	exc/r	statute	S
felony	f/n	summary judgment	s/j
freedom of speech	f/s	tenancy in common	t/c
good faith	g/f	tenancy at will	t/w
habeas corpus	h/c	tenant	t
hearsay	hr	third party	TP
husband	H	third party beneficiary	TPB
in loco parentis	ILP	transferred intent	TI
injunction	inj	unconscionable	uncon
inter vivos	I/v	unconstitutional	unconst
joint tenancy	j/t	undue influence	u/e
judgment	judgt	Uniform Commercial Code	UCC
jurisdiction	jur	unilateral	uni
last clear chance	LCC	vendee	VE
long-arm statute	LAS	vendor	VR
majority view	maj	versus	v
meeting of minds	MOM	void for vagueness	VFV
minority view	min	weight of the evidence	w/e
Miranda warnings	Mir/w	weight of authority	w/a
Miranda rule	Mir/r	wife	W
negligence	neg	with	w/
notice	ntc	within	w/i
nuisance	nus	without prejudice	w/o/p
obligation	ob	without	w/o
obscene	obs	wrongful death	wr/d

Table of Cases

A   Adams v. City of Chicago........................... 36
Albemarle Paper Co. v. Moody................. 38, 94
Albertson's, Inc. v. Kirkingburg..................... 87
Arbor Hill Concerned Citizens Neighborhood
   Association v. County of Albany............... 107
Ash v. Tyson Foods, Inc. 12

B   Baylie v. FRB... 42
Bragdon v. Abbott.................................. 71
Bryant v. City of Chicago 39
Buckhannon Board & Care Home, Inc. v.
   West Virginia Department of Health and
   Human Resources 105
Burlington Industries, Inc. v. Ellerth................ 56
Burlington Northern and Santa Fe Railway
   Co. v. White...................................... 67

C   California Federal Savings & Loan Association v.
   Guerra 52
Cassino v. Reichhold Chemicals, Inc................ 99
Chevron U.S.A., Inc. v. Echazabal 85
Christiansburg Garment Co. v. EEOC............. 104
Circuit City Stores, Inc. v. Adams................ 113
Clark County School District v.
   Breeden... 65
Connecticut v. Teal 33

D   Desert Palace, Inc. v. Costa 6
Dothard v. Rawlinson............................... 34
Dukes v. Wal-Mart, Inc. 91

E   EEOC v. Dial Corporation.......................... 43
EEOC v. Schneider National, Inc................... 77
EEOC v. Sears, Roebuck & Co...................... 23
El v. Southeastern Pennsylvania Transportation
   Authority 35

F   Ford Motor Co. v. EEOC............................ 97
Franks v. Bowman Transportation Co............... 95

G   Gambini v. Total Renal Care, Inc................... 84
Gilmer v. Interstate/Johnson Lane Corp. 111
Griggs v. Duke Power Co............................ 28

H   Harris v. Forklift Systems, Inc. 55
Hazelwood School District v. United States......... 20
Hazen Paper Co. v. Biggins 3, 103
Hishon v. King & Spalding........................... 4
Huber v. Wal-Mart................................. 82

I   International Union, UAW v. Johnson
   Controls, Inc..................................... 24

J   Jespersen v. Harrah's Operating
   Company, Inc..................................... 50

Johnson v. Transportation Agency of Santa Clara
   County 25

K   Kolstad v. American Dental Association........... 102

L   Laughlin v. Metropolitan Washington Airports
   Authority 66
Ledbetter v. The Goodyear Tire & Rubber
   Company, Inc...................................... 90
Lerohl v. Friends of Minnesota Sinfonia............. 47
Los Angeles Department of Water & Power v.
   Manhart... 18

M   Maldonado v. U.S. Bank and
   Manufacturers Bank.............................. 51
Matvia v. Bald Head Island Management, Inc....... 59
McDonald v. Santa Fe Trail Transportation Co. 13
McDonnell Douglas Corp. v. Green 10
McKennon v. Nashville Banner Publishing Co....... 98
Meritor Savings Bank v. Vinson 54
Minor v. Centocor, Inc. 5

O   Oncale v. Sundowner Offshore Services, Inc. 48
Oubre v. Entergy Operations, Inc.................. 110

P   Patterson v. McLean Credit Union 11
Pennsylvania State Police v. Suders 57
Personnel Administrator v. Feeney 22
Pollard v. E.I. du Pont de Nemours & Co.......... 101
Price Waterhouse v. Hopkins........................ 8

R   Rachid v. Jack in the Box, Inc. 15
Reed v. Great Lakes Cos. 61
Reeves v. Sanderson Plumbing Products, Inc. 14
Rehrs v. The Iams Company......................... 79

S   Slack v. Havens..................................... 2
Smith v. City of Jackson 31
Sutton v. United Air Lines, Inc................... 74, 76

T   Teamsters v. United States 19, 96
Toyota Motor Manufacturing, Kentucky, Inc. v.
   Williams 72
Turic v. Holland Hospitality, Inc. 100

U   U.S. Airways, Inc. v. Barnett....................... 80

V   Vande Zande v. State of Wisconsin Department of
   Administration.................................... 83
Vickers v. Fairfield Medical Center 49

W   Wards Cove Packing Co. v. Atonio................. 29
Watson v. Forth Worth Bank & Trust............... 32
Wilson v. U.S. West Communications 62

Z   Zamora v. Elite Logistics, Inc...................... 63

CHAPTER 1

Individual Disparate Treatment Discrimination

Quick Reference Rules of Law

PAGE

1. **The Elements: Intent to Discriminate.** In cases under Title VII, the discriminatory intent required by the statute may be inferred from the defendant's conduct. (Slack v. Havens) — 2

2. **The Elements: Intent to Discriminate.** In an ADEA-case based on disparate treatment, liability depends on whether age actually motivated the employer's decision. (Hazen Paper Co. v. Biggins) — 3

3. **The Elements: Terms, Conditions, or Privileges of Employment.** A benefit that is part and parcel of the employment relationship may not be doled out in a discriminatory fashion, even if the employer is free not to provide the benefit under the employment contract. (Hishon v. King & Spalding) — 4

4. **The Elements: Terms, Conditions, or Privileges of Employment.** An increase in workload can be a material difference in the terms and conditions of employment, and therefore may constitute an adverse employment action for purposes of a disparate-treatment action. (Minor v. Centocor) — 5

5. **The Elements: Linking Discriminatory Intent to the Employer's Treatment of Plaintiff.** Direct evidence of sex discrimination is unnecessary in a mixed-motive sex-bias case when both impermissible and permissible reasons played a role in an employment decision. (Desert Palace, Inc. v. Costa) — 6

6. **Proving the Discrimination Element.** Once a plaintiff in a Title VII action shows that gender played a motivating part in an employment decision, the employer may avoid liability only by proving by a preponderance of the evidence that it would have made the same decision if it had not allowed gender to play a part in the decision. (Price Waterhouse v. Hopkins) — 8

7. **Proving the Discrimination Element.** If a prima facie case of racial discrimination is rebutted by the defendant, the complainant must then show that the reason given for rejection was a pretext for discrimination. (McDonnell Douglas Corp. v. Green) — 10

8. **Proving the Discrimination Element.** The court cannot limit the type of evidence a complainant may offer to show that an employer's reasons for disparate treatment were a pretext. (Patterson v. McLean Credit Union) — 11

9. **Proving the Discrimination Element.** Pretext can be inferred from evidence of an employee's qualifications. (Ash v. Tyson Foods, Inc.) — 12

10. **Proving the Discrimination Element.** Title VII and § 1981 prohibit discrimination against all races, white as well as nonwhite. (McDonald v. Santa Fe Trail Transportation Co.) — 13

11. **Proving the Discrimination Element.** A prima facie age discrimination case, combined with sufficient evidence to find that an employer's asserted justification is false, may permit the trier of fact to conclude that an employer unlawfully discriminated. (Reeves v. Sanderson Plumbing Products, Inc.) — 14

12. **Implementing *Desert Palace* and *Reeves*.** Employees claiming to have been fired because of their age, in violation of ADEA, can use indirect evidence to prove age discrimination under a mixed-motive theory. (Rachid v. Jack in the Box, Inc.) — 15

Slack v. Havens

Black employee (P) v. Industrial-plant employer (D)

7 FEP 885 (S.D. Cal. 1973), *aff'd as modified*, 522 F.2d 1091 (9th Cir. 1975).

NATURE OF CASE: Action for violation of the Title VII Civil Rights Act of 1964.

FACT SUMMARY: Slack (P) and three other black female employees were fired when they refused to do heavy cleaning, which their white co-worker was not required to do.

🏛 RULE OF LAW
In cases under Title VII, the discriminatory intent required by the statute may be inferred from the defendant's conduct.

FACTS: Four female employees (P) at Havens's (D) plant were asked by their supervisor to do heavy cleanup work, which was not included in their job descriptions. A white female co-worker with less seniority in the same department was not asked to do this work but instead was transferred to another department when the work was to take place. The four black employees (P) refused to do the work and were fired because of their refusal. During these women's (P) meetings with their supervisor, Pohasky, he stated that "colored people should stay in their places" and that they had been assigned the work because "colored people clean better." Havens (D) contended that the women were fired over a disagreement over their job description and that Pohasky's conduct could not be attributed to top management of Havens (D).

ISSUE: Under Title VII, may the discriminatory intent required by the statute be inferred from the defendant's conduct?

HOLDING AND DECISION: (Thompson, J.) Yes. In cases under Title VII, the discriminatory intent may be inferred from the defendant's conduct. Title VII does not require the intent to discriminate, merely the intent to carry out a practice that had a discriminatory effect. The principal purpose of the Act is to address the discriminatory effect of employment practices. To this end, whether or not Havens's (D) top management intended to discriminate against its black employees is irrelevant. Pohasky did intend to force these employees (P) to undertake activities that he did not require of white employees of the same rank and seniority. He enforced this discriminatory job assignment by requiring these employees (P) to choose to take the work or lose their jobs. Title VII expressly includes "any agent" of an employer within the definition of employer. Pohasky was an agent of Havens (D). Thus, regardless of intent, the consequences of Havens's (D) conduct, through its supervisor, was racial discrimination.

▶ ANALYSIS

Slack v. Havens changes the common-law rule regarding at-will employment contracts, making the employment terminable for any reason other than race. While insubordination is a valid reason for termination, if the employee is refusing to accept a discriminatory work assignment, insubordination is no longer good cause.

■=■

Quicknotes

AT-WILL EMPLOYMENT The rule that an employment relationship is subject to termination at any time, or for any cause, by an employee or an employer in the absence of a specific agreement otherwise.

DISCRIMINATION Unequal treatment of a class of persons.

■=■

Hazen Paper Co. v. Biggins

Employer (D) v. Fired employee (P)

507 U.S. 604 (1993).

NATURE OF CASE: Appeal from jury verdict finding liability for violations of the Age Discrimination in Employment Act (ADEA) and the Employee Retirement Income Security Act (ERISA).

FACT SUMMARY: Biggins (P) contended that he was fired by Hazen Paper Co. (Hazen) (D) at the age of 62 in order to prevent his pension benefits from vesting.

🏛 RULE OF LAW

In an ADEA-case based on disparate treatment, liability depends on whether age actually motivated the employer's decision.

FACTS: At the age of 62, Biggins (P) was fired from his job at Hazen Paper Co. (D) a few weeks before his pension was due to vest. Hazen (D) claimed that Biggins (P) was fired for doing business with competitors. Biggins (P) filed claims under the Age Discrimination in Employment Act (ADEA) and the Employee Retirement Income Security Act (ERISA). A jury found in Biggins's (P) favor. The lower courts denied Hazen's (D) motion for a judgment n.o.v., and Hazen (D) appealed to the Supreme Court.

ISSUE: In an ADEA case based in disparate treatment, does liability depend on whether age actually motivated the employer's decision?

HOLDING AND DECISION: (O'Connor, J.) Yes. In an ADEA case based in disparate treatment, liability depends on whether age actually motivated the employer's decision. Congress enacted the ADEA to address the problem of inaccurate and stigmatizing stereotypes applied to older workers. The ADEA is not implicated if an employer's decision is wholly motivated by factors other than age, even if the factor, like pension status, is correlated with age. In this case, Hazen's (D) decision to fire Biggins (P) because he was close to vesting does not constitute discriminatory treatment on the basis of age. Its decision was not a result of denigrating generalizations about age. Of course, Hazen (D) may not legally fire an employee in order to prevent his pension benefits from vesting. That conduct is actionable under ERISA, as the lower courts correctly found. Reversed in part and remanded to reconsider whether the jury had sufficient evidence to find an ADEA violation.

▌ ANALYSIS

Proof of "intent to discriminate," that is, a discriminatory motive, is absolutely required for a successful disparate-treatment case. Disparate treatment simply means that an employer treats some people less favorably than others because of their race, color, religion, or some other protected characteristic. By contrast, a disparate-impact claim involves facially neutral employer practices that, in fact, fall more harshly on one group than another and cannot be justified by business necessity. A complainant who files an employment discrimination claim based on disparate impact is not required to prove intent to discriminate.

Quicknotes

DISPARATE IMPACT Effect of a practice that appears neutral but, in fact, falls more harshly on one group of people because of the group's race, sex, national origin, age, or disability and that cannot be justified by business necessity.

DISPARATE TREATMENT Unequal treatment of employees or of applicants for employment without justification.

EMPLOYEE RETIREMENT INCOME SECURITY ACT OF 1974 (ERISA) Federal law of employee benefits which establishes minimum standards to protect employees from breach of benefit promises made by employers.

Hishon v. King & Spalding

Associate lawyer (P) v. Law-firm employer (D)

467 U.S. 69 (1984).

NATURE OF CASE: Appeal from dismissal of a Title VII complaint for declaratory, compensatory, and injunctive relief.

FACT SUMMARY: When Hishon (P), an associate with King & Spalding (D), brought a Tittle VII action after being rejected as a candidate for partner, King & Spalding (D) argued that the Civil Rights Act did not apply to the selection of partners by a partnership.

RULE OF LAW
A benefit that is part and parcel of the employment relationship may not be doled out in a discriminatory fashion, even if the employer is free not to provide the benefit under the employment contract.

FACTS: Hishon (P) was an associate in the law firm of King & Spalding (D). After being considered and rejected for partnership, Hishon (P) brought an action, alleging that King & Spalding (D) was an employer within the meaning of Title VII and that consideration for partnership was one of the terms, conditions, or privileges of employment as an associate. Hishon (P) also alleged that King & Spalding (D) made a contract to consider her for partnership, that this was a key provision that induced her to accept employment, and that, by rejecting her as a partner, King & Spalding (D) discriminated against her on the basis of sex. The lower courts dismissed the case for failure to state a claim, and Hishon (P) appealed.

ISSUE: May a benefit that is part and parcel of the employment relationship be doled out in a discriminatory fashion, where the employer is free not to provide the benefit under the employment contract?

HOLDING AND DECISION: (Burger, C.J.) No. A benefit that is part and parcel of the employment relationship may not be doled out in a discriminatory fashion, even if the employer is free not to provide the benefit under the employment contract. If the evidence at trial establishes that the parties contracted to have Hishon (P) considered for partnership, that promise clearly was a term, condition, or privilege of her employment. Title VII would then bind King & Spalding (D) to consider Hishon (P) for partnership without regard to her sex. An employer may also provide its employees with many benefits that it is under no obligation to furnish by an express or implied contract. Such a benefit may qualify as a privilege of employment. The importance of the partnership decision to a lawyer's status as an associate is underscored by the allegation that associates' employment is terminated if they are not elected to become partners. These allegations, if proved at trial, would suffice to show that partnership consideration was a term, condition, or privilege of an associate's employment at King & Spalding (D). Thus, partnership consideration must be without regard to sex. Reversed and remanded.

CONCURRENCE: (Powell, J.) The Court's opinion should not be read as extending Title VII to the management of a law firm by its partners. Under the Court's reasoning, the relationship among partners does not have to be characterized as an "employment" relationship to which Title VII would apply. The relationship among law partners differs markedly from that between employer and employee—including that between the partnership and its associates.

ANALYSIS

Presumably, once advanced to the status of partner, a lawyer would no longer be an employee for the purposes of Title VII. However, in *Caruso v. Peat, Marwick, Mitchell & Co.*, 664 F. Supp. 144 (S.D.N.Y.), the argument was made that even partners in large organizations may be employees within the meaning of Title VII and the Age Discrimination in Employment Act (ADEA). The court in *Caruso* held that, under these circumstances, a partner was an employee.

Quicknotes

DISCRIMINATION Unequal treatment of a class of persons.

Minor v. Centocor

Employee (P) v. Employer (D)

457 F.3d 632 (7th Cir. 2006).

NATURE OF CASE: Action against employer for disparate treatment based on age and sex.

FACT SUMMARY: A sales representative whose new supervisor required her to work longer hours with no salary increase brought an action for disparate treatment based on her age and sex.

RULE OF LAW
An increase in workload can be a material difference in the terms and conditions of employment, and therefore may constitute an adverse employment action for purposes of a disparate-treatment action.

FACTS: M. Jane Minor (P) worked for Centocor (D) as a sales representative. When Antonio Siciliano became her new supervisor, he required her to visit all of her accounts twice a month, and major accounts more frequently, resulting in an increase from approximately 55 hours per week to between 70 and 90 hours. She began to experience atrial fibrillation and depression after working at that pace for 2 months, and eventually stopped working. The district court found that Minor (P) failed to show that Centocor (D) took an adverse employment action against her, and therefore she failed to establish a prima facie case of age and sex discrimination.

ISSUE: Can an increase in workload be a material difference in the terms and conditions of employment, and therefore constitute an adverse employment action for purposes of a disparate-treatment action?

HOLDING AND DECISION: (Easterbrook, J.) Yes. An increase in workload can be a material difference in the terms and conditions of employment, and therefore may constitute an adverse employment action for purposes of a disparate-treatment action. Minor (P) was required to work 25 percent longer to earn the same income as before, which is functionally the same as a 25 percent reduction in hourly pay. But Minor (P) failed to show that Centocor (D) required women or older workers to work longer hours than men or younger workers in order to receive the same pay, and despite the adverse employment action, she was not discriminated against.

ANALYSIS

The significance of this case is the rule that longer hours can constitute an adverse employment action for purposes of proving a case of discrimination under both Title VII of the 1964 Civil Rights Act (covering gender and race bias) and the Age Discrimination and Employment Act (covering age bias).

Quicknotes

DISPARATE TREATMENT Unequal treatment of employees or of applicants for employment without justification.

PRIMA FACIE CASE An action where the plaintiff introduces sufficient evidence to submit the issue to the judge or jury for determination.

Desert Palace, Inc. v. Costa

Employer (D) v. Fired employee (P)

539 U.S. 90 (2003).

NATURE OF CASE: Appeal U.S. Appeals Court judgment for employee.

FACT SUMMARY: Catharina Costa (P) was fired from her job as a forklift operator. She filed suit, and wanted to introduce circumstantial evidence supporting her claim that her discharge was the result of sex discrimination. The district court allowed it; a three-judge panel of the U.S. Court of Appeals for the Ninth Circuit reversed. A full panel of the Ninth Circuit then reversed the panel.

🏛 RULE OF LAW
Direct evidence of sex discrimination is unnecessary in a mixed-motive sex-bias case when both impermissible and permissible reasons played a role in an employment decision.

FACTS: Catharina Costa (P) was fired from her job as a forklift operator at Desert Palace Casino (D), ostensibly for poor performance and her involvement in a physical altercation with an alleged sexual harasser. She filed a lawsuit alleging that she was fired as a result of sex discrimination, in violation of Title VII of the 1964 Civil Rights Act. Jurors during the trial were instructed to rule for Costa (P) if they determined that sex was a motivating factor in the firing, even if other legal factors, like disciplinary issues, were present as well. The jury found for Costa (P), and that sex was a motivating factor in her termination. Because Desert Palace (D) failed to show that she would have been fired anyway, without consideration of her sex, the jury awarded backpay and compensatory damages. Desert Palace (D) appealed, saying that the instructions incorrectly shifted the burden of proof to the defendant in the case. A three-judge panel of the U.S. Court of Appeals for the Ninth Circuit reversed, holding that by giving a mixed-motive jury instruction, the lower court prejudiced Desert Palace (D) because it erroneously shifted the burden of proof to the Desert Palace (D) when Costa (P) had not presented direct evidence of discrimination. A year later, the full Ninth Circuit vacated the panel decision and agreed to review the case, ultimately rejecting the arguments of the panel and finding that direct evidence was unnecessary.

ISSUE: Is direct evidence of sex discrimination necessary in a mixed-motive sex bias case when both impermissible and permissible reasons played a role in an employment decision?

HOLDING AND DECISION: (Thomas, J.) No. Direct evidence of sex discrimination is unnecessary in a mixed-motive sex bias case when both impermissible and permissible reasons played a role in an employment decision. Costa (P) should have been able to present circumstantial evidence of discrimination in her case against Desert Palace (D) even though Desert Palace (D) produced evidence that there were performance issues that may have led to its decision to fire Costa (P). Title VII, on its face, does not state that a plaintiff must make a heightened showing through direct evidence. Therefore, Costa (P) needed only to present sufficient evidence for a reasonable jury to conclude, by a preponderance of the evidence, that "race, color, religion, sex, or national origin was a motivating factor for any employment practice." Because direct evidence of discrimination is not required in mixed-motive cases, the court of appeals correctly concluded that the district court did not abuse its discretion in giving a mixed-motive instruction to the jury. Affirmed.

CONCURRENCE: (O'Connor, J.) Prior to the Civil Rights Act of 1991, the evidentiary rule developed by the court required direct evidence that "an illegitimate factor played a substantial role" in an employment decision. That direct evidence supported the statute's purpose of deterring such employment decisions by permitting a reasonable factfinder to conclude that absent further explanation, the employer's discriminatory motivation caused the employment decision. The rule changed, however, with the 1991 amendments to Title VII, when Congress passed a new evidentiary rule.

▶ ANALYSIS

In affirming the en banc Ninth Circuit, the Supreme Court resolved a debate between the circuit courts over the meaning of the plurality decision in *Price Waterhouse v. Hopkins*, 490 U.S. 228 (1989), which most courts had interpreted to mean that direct evidence was required in mixed-motive cases. After *Price Waterhouse*, a number of circuit courts, including the First, Fourth, Eighth, and Eleventh, had found that a concurrence in the case written by Justice O'Connor was actually the rule in the case and that her opinion said direct evidence was necessary. Only the Ninth Circuit had ruled that plaintiffs in both mixed-motive and traditional bias cases were permitted to provide either circumstantial or direct evidence when saying discrimination took place in the workplace. In this case, the justices sided with the Ninth Circuit in finding that *Price Waterhouse* should not prevent plaintiffs from using circumstantial evidence in mixed-motive cases and that the Civil Rights Act of 1991, which amended Title VII of the 1964 Civil Rights Act, had not created a more rigid standard of proof.

■=■

Continued on next page.

Quicknotes

CIRCUMSTANTIAL EVIDENCE Evidence that, though not directly observed, supports the inference of principal facts.

COMPENSATORY DAMAGES Measure of damages necessary to compensate victim for actual injuries suffered.

PREPONDERANCE OF THE EVIDENCE A standard of proof requiring the trier of fact to determine whether the fact sought to be established is more probable than not.

TITLE VII OF THE CIVIL RIGHTS ACT OF 1964 Law prohibiting discrimination in employment on the basis of race, color, religion, sex, and national origin.

■━■

Price Waterhouse v. Hopkins

Employer (D) v. Employee seeking partnership (P)

490 U.S. 228 (1989).

NATURE OF CASE: Appeal from a judgment of liability in a Title VII action.

FACT SUMMARY: Hopkins (P) contended that she was denied partnership in Price Waterhouse (D) because of sex discrimination.

🏛 RULE OF LAW
Once a plaintiff in a Title VII action shows that gender played a motivating part in an employment decision, the employer can avoid liability only by proving by a preponderance of the evidence that it would have made the same decision if it had not allowed gender to play a part in the decision.

FACTS: Hopkins (P) was a senior manager at Price Waterhouse (D) in 1982 and sought a promotion to partner. According to company policy, partners submitted written comments and recommendations on each candidate, and the Policy Board made the final decision. The written comments regarding Hopkins (P) included indications that some partners disliked her personality because of her gender. Hopkins (P) was denied the partnership although she was the only one of eighty-eight candidates who had secured a major contract for Price Waterhouse (D). Hopkins (P) was informed that she should act and dress more femininely in order to improve her chances for partnership. Hopkins (P) filed suit under Title VII against Price Waterhouse (D) for sex discrimination. The district court found that Price Waterhouse (D) legitimately used interpersonal skills as one of the factors in partnership decisions. However, the district court held that Price Waterhouse (D) had also relied on comments resulting from sex stereotyping in making the decision regarding Hopkins (P) and ruled against Price Waterhouse (D) on the liability issue. The court of appeals affirmed the judgment but held that an employer could avoid liability by proving by clear and convincing evidence that the same employment decision would have been made absent the impermissible consideration of gender. Price Waterhouse (D) appealed.

ISSUE: In order to avoid liability, must an employer prove by a preponderance of the evidence that it would have made the same employment decision without regard to gender after the plaintiff has showed that gender was a motivating part of the decision?

HOLDING AND DECISION: (Brennan, J.) Yes. Once a plaintiff in a Title VII action shows that gender played a motivating part in an employment decision, the employer may avoid liability only by proving by a preponderance of the evidence that it would have made the same decision if it had not allowed gender to play a part in the decision. Title VII was enacted to make sex and race irrelevant in employment decisions but did not limit the other qualities that employers may legitimately consider. The language used in Title VII suggests that employment decisions based on a mixture of legitimate and illegitimate considerations are prohibited. In order to balance the employer's right to make employment decisions free of interference, the employer is not liable under Title VII if the decision regarding a particular person would have been the same without the consideration of sex or race. Therefore, once a plaintiff has shown that sex or race has played a motivating part in an employment decision, an employer must prove that the same decision would have been made based on legitimate reasons standing alone in order to avoid liability. This burden is most appropriately deemed an affirmative defense and must be proved by a preponderance of the evidence. The district court found that sex stereotyping was permitted to play a part in Price Waterhouse's (D) decision on Hopkins's (P) promotion. Therefore, Price Waterhouse (D) had the burden to prove, by a preponderance of the evidence, that Hopkins's (P) interpersonal skills alone, apart from the sex stereotyping, were the basis for the denial of the partnership. Since the court of appeals held that the standard was clear and convincing evidence, its judgment is reversed and the case is remanded.

CONCURRENCE: (O'Connor, J.) Where uncertainty as to causation has been created by an employer's consideration of an illegitimate criterion, placing the risk of nonpersuasion on the defendant is appropriate. However, this should be limited to cases such as this one in which the plaintiff has shown by direct evidence that an illegitimate criterion was a substantial factor in the decision.

DISSENT: (Kennedy, J.) The plurality adopts a but-for standard, the implication of which is that in certain cases it is not the plaintiff in a Title VII case who must prove the causation, but the defendant who must prove its absence. Also, Dr. Fiske discerned stereotyping in comments that were gender-neutral without knowing whether the comments had a basis in reality or really applied to their speaker. Thus, following Dr. Fiske's analysis, no woman could ever be overbearing, abrasive, or arrogant, because to characterize a woman as such would necessarily be the product of stereotyping. The result of such analysis would be that an employer could never base any adverse action as to a woman on such attributes.

▶ ANALYSIS

Justice Brennan's decision differs from Justice O'Connor's opinion in that he suggests that if the decision process is

Continued on next page.

tainted by awareness of sex or race in any way, the burden of justification shifts to the employer, whereas O'Connor specifically would shift the burden only if discrimination is proven by direct evidence. In plurality decisions where a rationale is not adopted by at least five justices, the holding is considered to be the position taken by concurrence on the narrowest grounds. In this case, some circuits have interpreted O'Connor's restriction to direct evidence as the holding of the Court.

■≡■

Quicknotes

AFFIRMATIVE DEFENSE A manner of defending oneself against a claim not by denying the truth of the charge, but by the introduction of some evidence challenging the plaintiff's right to bring the claim.

CIRCUMSTANTIAL EVIDENCE Evidence that, though not directly observed, supports the inference of principal facts.

PREPONDERANCE OF THE EVIDENCE A standard of proof requiring the trier of fact to determine whether the fact sought to be established is more probable than not.

■≡■

McDonnell Douglas Corp. v. Green

Former employer (D) v. Laid-off employee (P)

411 U.S. 792 (1973).

NATURE OF CASE: Appeal from remand of action under Title VII of the Civil Rights Act of 1964.

FACT SUMMARY: Green (P), a former employee of McDonnell Douglas (D), was denied re-employment based on his participation in illegal protests of McDonnell Douglas's (D) discriminatory employment practices.

🏛 RULE OF LAW
If a prima facie case of racial discrimination is rebutted by the defendant, the complainant must then show that the reason given for rejection was a pretext for discrimination.

FACTS: Green (P), a black man, had been employed by McDonnell Douglas (D) as a mechanic for eight years prior to being laid off during a reduction of McDonnell Douglas's (D) workforce. In protest of this layoff, and McDonnell Douglas's (D) discriminatory hiring practices, Green (P) participated in illegal demonstrations against McDonnell Douglas (D), for which he was arrested and fined. When McDonnell Douglas (D) began to solicit applicants for Green's (P) previous position, Green (P) applied but was rejected because of his activities against the company. The district court rejected Green's (P) Title VII claim, stating that nothing in the Act prevented an employer from refusing to rehire a person who undertook illegal actions against them. The Eighth Circuit affirmed that unlawful protests were not protected by Title VII but remanded for trial on Green's (P) claims relating to discriminatory hiring practices. McDonnell Douglas (D) appealed, and the Supreme Court granted review.

ISSUE: If a prima facie case of racial discrimination is rebutted by the defendant, must the complainant then show that the reason given for rejection of the complainant was a pretext for discrimination?

HOLDING AND DECISION: (Powell, J.) Yes. If a prima facie case of racial discrimination is rebutted by the defendant, the complainant must then show that the reason given for rejection of complainant was a pretext for discrimination. The purpose of Title VII is to eliminate employment procedures that have a discriminatory effect. The Act does not require an employer to rehire an employee who has undertaken illegal activities against the company. However, the employee should be given the opportunity to show that the apparently legitimate reason for rejecting the applicant was merely an excuse for discrimination. Here, Green (P) must be permitted to show that the policy of not hiring applicants who have participated in illegal activities against

McDonnell Douglas (D) was either a pretext or exercised discriminatorily. Affirmed.

▶ ANALYSIS

To establish a prima facie case of racial discrimination, a complainant must show that (1) he is a member of a racial minority; (2) he was a qualified applicant for the position the employer was filling; (3) he was not chosen in spite of his qualifications; and (4) the position remained open after his rejection. The burden then shifts to the employer to articulate some legitimate nondiscriminatory reason for the employer's rejection. The burden then shifts a third time, pursuant to *Green*, to the complainant to demonstrate, if possible, that the employer's presumptively valid reason was in fact a cover-up for a racially discriminatory decision.

Quicknotes

DISCRIMINATION Unequal treatment of a class of persons.

PRIMA FACIE CASE An action where the plaintiff introduces sufficient evidence to submit the issue to the judge or jury for determination.

Patterson v. McLean Credit Union

Former black employee (P) v. Employer (D)

491 U.S. 164 (1989).

NATURE OF CASE: Appeal from jury decision in favor of defendant in § 1981 action.

FACT SUMMARY: When Patterson (P) filed a § 1981 claim against McLean (D), her employer, for failing to promote her based on her race, the court instructed the jury that, in order to prevail, Patterson (P) must show that she was better qualified than the white woman hired in her place.

> **RULE OF LAW**
> The court cannot limit the type of evidence a complainant may offer to show that an employer's reasons for disparate treatment were a pretext.

FACTS: Patterson (P) worked for McLean Credit Union (D) for ten years before she was laid off. She claimed that McLean's (D) failure to promote her to a position she was qualified for and her subsequent termination were both based on race. In answer to her prima facie case, McLean (D) contended that Patterson (P) was not promoted because the white woman who succeeded in the position was more qualified. The district court instructed the jury that they could only find for Patterson (P) if she proved discrimination by showing she was more qualified than her successful, white competitor. The jury found for McLean (D). Patterson (P) appealed.

ISSUE: Can the court limit the type of evidence a complainant may offer to show that an employer's reasons for disparate treatment were a pretext?

HOLDING AND DECISION: (Kennedy, J.) No. The court cannot limit the type of evidence a complainant may offer to show an employer's reasons for disparate treatment were a pretext. The burden under § 1981 requires the complainant to show purposeful discrimination. If the employer rebuts the prima facie case, the complainant is still entitled to persuade the jury of intentional discrimination. While, in this case, the most persuasive evidence that discrimination occurred would be for Patterson (P) to show that she was more qualified than the white candidate McLean (D) hired, this was not the only form of proof available to her. She must be allowed to use any means to meet her burden. Reversed.

> **ANALYSIS**

The Court suggested that Patterson (P) could prove discrimination by offering evidence of McLean's (D) previous bad treatment of her, which was based on her race. Also relevant may be McLean's (D) policies and practices with regard to minority employees. A complainant could also dispute an employer's claim that he or she was unqualified by showing that the employer did not apply the stated qualification requirements to the white candidate.

Quicknotes

DISPARATE TREATMENT Unequal treatment of employees or of applicants for employment without justification.

PRIMA FACIE CASE An action where the plaintiff introduces sufficient evidence to submit the issue to the judge or jury for determination.

Ash v. Tyson Foods, Inc.

Parties not identified in casebook excerpt.

546 U.S. 454 (2006).

NATURE OF CASE: Appeal of summary judgment for employer.

FACT SUMMARY: [Facts not stated in casebook excerpt.]

🏛 RULE OF LAW
Pretext can be inferred from evidence of an employee's qualifications.

FACTS: [Facts not stated in casebook excerpt.]

ISSUE: Can pretext be inferred from evidence of an employee's qualifications?

HOLDING AND DECISION: [Judge not identified in casebook excerpt.] Yes. Pretext can be inferred from evidence of an employee's qualifications. The lower court's test—that pretext can be established through comparing qualifications only when "the disparity in qualifications is so apparent as virtually to jump off the page and slap you in the face"—is unhelpful and imprecise as a statement of the standard for inferring pretext from superior qualifications. While the rule established cannot be read to hold that an employee's superior qualifications necessarily show pretext, some formulation taking into consideration an employee's superior qualifications can suffice to show pretext.

▶ ANALYSIS

On remand, the appeals court reinstated its holding that the jury verdict for the two employees could not stand, holding that the court's application of the "jump off the page and slap you in the face" comparative qualifications standard was not crucial to its conclusion that pretext was not shown on the facts of the case. That is, even though the Supreme Court held that the "jump off the page test" was overturned, this was not essential to the appeals court's initial conclusion that the comparative qualifications evidence did not provide sufficient evidence of pretext, especially since the Supreme Court declined to offer a substitution for the test.

■═■

Quicknotes

PRETEXT Ostensible reason or motive assigned or assumed as a color or cover for the real reason or motive.

■═■

McDonald v. Santa Fe Trail Transportation Co.

Dismissed white employee (P) v. Employer (D)

427 U.S. 273 (1976).

NATURE OF CASE: Appeal from dismissal of action under Title VII of the Civil Rights Act of 1964 and under § 1981.

FACT SUMMARY: Two white employees (P) were dismissed from Santa Fe Trail Transportation Co. (D) for misappropriating company property even though a black employee similarly charged was not dismissed.

RULE OF LAW
Title VII and § 1981 prohibit discrimination against all races, white as well as nonwhite.

FACTS: Two white employees (P) and a black employee of Santa Fe Trail Transportation Co. (D) were jointly charged with misappropriating part of Santa Fe's (D) shipment to its customers. Several days after being charged, the two white employees (P) were discharged, but the black employee remained in Santa Fe's (D) employ. The district court dismissed the employees' (P) Title VII and § 1981 actions, finding that no violation was alleged. The employees (P) appealed.

ISSUE: Do Title VII and § 1981 prohibit discrimination against all races, white as well as nonwhite?

HOLDING AND DECISION: (Marshall, J.) Yes. Title VII and § 1981 prohibit discrimination against all races, white as well as nonwhite. The legislative history of Title VII clearly shows that it was Congress's intent to protect the civil rights of all races, including whites. While Title VII does not require an employer to retain an employee who has committed a criminal offense against it, it does require that, if it uses this fact as a criterion for employment, it must apply that criterion to all races equally. In addition, § 1981 affords a federal remedy against discrimination. Despite language in § 1981 insuring the rights as "enjoyed by white citizens" to all races, whites are also entitled to seek § 1981 protection. Thus, the district court erred in dismissing the employees' (P) claims under § 1981 and Title VII. Reversed.

▶ ANALYSIS

The concept of "race" under the law differs from scientific definitions. The Court in *Saint Francis College v. Al-Khazraji*, 481 U.S. 604 (1987), engaged in a long discussion of the meaning of race. It concluded that § 1981 protects those who are subject to differential treatment solely because of their ethnic background or physical characteristics, whether or not such discrimination would be classified as racial in terms of modern scientific theory. Following that reasoning, the *St. Francis* court held that an Arabian complainant could bring suit under § 1981 because Arabs were not considered Caucasians at the time of the enactment of the Civil Rights Act of 1866, from which § 1981 was derived.

Quicknotes

DISCRIMINATION Unequal treatment of a class of persons.

LEGISLATIVE HISTORY The process by which a bill is enacted into law, which reflects the legislature's intention enacting that law.

Reeves v. Sanderson Plumbing Products, Inc.

Employee (P) v. Employer (D)

530 U.S. 133 (2000).

NATURE OF THE CASE: Appeal from a reversal of district court's judgment in an Age Discrimination in Employment Act of 1967 (ADEA) action.

FACT SUMMARY: Reeves (P), 57 years old, had been an employee of Sanderson Plumbing Products, Inc. (D) for 40 years when he was fired in October 1995. Reeves (P) filed suit in June 1996, contending that he had been fired because of his age, in violation of the ADEA. The district court submitted the case to the jury, which found that Reeves (P) had established a prima facie case of discrimination and had introduced enough evidence to show that Sanderson's (D) stated reasons for Reeves's discharge were not the real reasons and that age discrimination was the real reason. The court of appeals overturned the verdict.

> ## 🏛 RULE OF LAW
> A prima facie age discrimination case, combined with sufficient evidence to find that an employer's asserted justification is false, may permit the trier of fact to conclude that an employer unlawfully discriminated.

FACTS: Reeves (P), a 57-year-old supervisor, had spent 40 years in the employ of Sanderson Plumbing Products, Inc. (D). In October 1995 the company president of Sanderson Plumbing Products, Inc. (D) discharged Reeves and his manager, Caldwell, based on an audit that revealed timekeeping misrepresentations and errors on the part of Reeves, Caldwell, and another supervisor. In June 1996, Reeves filed suit in district court contending that he had been fired because of his age, in violation of the Age Discrimination in Employment Act of 1967 (ADEA). At trial, Sanderson (D) argued that it had fired Reeves (P) due to his failure to maintain accurate attendance records. Reeves (P) then attempted to demonstrate that Sanderson's (D) explanation was a pretext for age discrimination, based on evidence that he had kept accurate attendance records of employees under his supervision. Furthermore, the director of manufacturing and the husband of the company president had demonstrated age-based animus in his dealings with Reeves (P). The district court twice denied oral motions by Sanderson (D) for judgment as a matter of law under Rule 50 of the Federal Rules of Civil Procedure, and the case went to the jury. The district court entered judgment for Reeves (P) based on the jury's verdict in favor of Reeves, finding that Sanderson's (D) discrimination was willful. The court of appeals reversed, holding that Reeves (P) had not introduced sufficient evidence for a rational jury to conclude that he had been discharged because of his age. The Supreme Court granted certiorari, to resolve a conflict among the courts of appeals.

ISSUE: Is an employee's prima facie case of discrimination, combined with sufficient evidence for a reasonable factfinder to disbelieve an employer's nondiscriminatory explanation for its decision, adequate to sustain a finding of liability for intentional discrimination?

HOLDING AND DECISION: (O'Connor, J.) Yes. Reeves (P) established a prima facie case of discrimination, introduced enough evidence to create a jury issue as to the falsity of Sanderson's (D) explanation, and even produced additional evidence of age-based animus to find that Sanderson (D) had intentionally discriminated. The district court was correct to submit the case to the jury, and the court of appeals erred in overturning its verdict. Reversed.

CONCURRENCE: (Ginsburg, J.): The court of appeals erroneously required the plaintiff to offer additional evidence. An employment discrimination plaintiff may survive judgment as a matter of law by submitting evidence establishing a prima facie case and evidence from which a rational factfinder could conclude that the employer's explanation for its actions was false. The Court's opinion appropriately leaves room in the event that further elaboration is needed for a case in which plaintiffs will be required to submit additional evidence in order to survive a motion for judgment as a matter of law.

▌ ANALYSIS

The circuit courts have generally read *Reeves* as requiring no more than a prima facie case and evidence of employer pretext in order to go to trial. However, uncertainty continues over the circumstances in which an employee must produce enough evidence to survive summary judgment or judgment as a matter of law.

■▬■

Quicknotes

PRIMA FACIE CASE An action where the plaintiff introduces sufficient evidence to submit the issue to the judge or jury for determination.

■▬■

Rachid v. Jack in the Box, Inc.

Employee (P) v. Employer (D)

376 F.3d 305 (5th Cir. 2004).

NATURE OF CASE: Appeal of summary judgment for employer.

FACT SUMMARY: A 52-year-old restaurant manager filed an age-discrimination claim after he was fired from his job by a supervisor who had made disparaging comments about his age.

🏛 RULE OF LAW
Employees claiming to have been fired because of their age, in violation of ADEA, can use indirect evidence to prove age discrimination under a mixed-motive theory.

FACTS: Ahmed P. Rachid (P) was a restaurant manager for Jack in the Box, Inc. (D) between October 1995 and February 2001. He was 52 years old, and one of his supervisors repeatedly commented negatively about Rachid's (P) age. When Rachid (P) was fired for failing to follow procedures for changing time cards when employees took breaks, he was fired and replaced by a manager five years younger. Rachid (P) filed a lawsuit under the Age Discrimination in Employment Act, claiming that he was terminated from his position because of his age. To establish a prima facie case, Rachid (P) did not offer direct evidence, but showed through indirect evidence that he was terminated, he was qualified for the job, and that he was in a protected class. The parties disputed whether he demonstrated the fourth element— that he was either replaced by someone outside the protected class, replaced by someone younger, or otherwise discharged because of his age. The trial court granted summary judgment for Jack in the Box (D), holding that Rachid (P) could not use indirect evidence to prove a mixed-motive theory of age discrimination.

ISSUE: Can employees claiming to have been fired because of their age, in violation of ADEA, use indirect evidence to prove age discrimination under a mixed-motive theory?

HOLDING AND DECISION: (Clement, J.) Yes. Employees claiming to have been fired because of their age, in violation of ADEA, can use indirect evidence to prove age discrimination under a mixed-motive theory. Generally, an employee can show age discrimination through direct evidence or indirect evidence. Where an employee shows discrimination through direct evidence, and the employer claims that the same adverse employment decision would have been made regardless of discrimination, the *Price Waterhouse* mixed-motives theory of discrimination comes into play. Under *Price Waterhouse*, once an employee presents direct evidence of discrimination, the burden of proof shifts to the employer to show that the same adverse employment

decision would have been made regardless of discriminatory animus. Discrimination can also be shown indirectly, by following the "pretext" method set forth in *McDonnell Douglas*. If the employee shows a prima facie case, and the employer meets its burden of producing a legitimate, nondiscriminatory reason for firing the employee, the employee must then offer enough evidence to create a genuine issue of material fact either that the employer's reason is not true, but is instead a pretext for discrimination, or that the employer's reason, while true is only one of the reasons for the employer's conduct, and another motivating factor is the employee's protected characteristic. The *Desert Palace* case created a modified *McDonnell Douglas* approach by which an employee can use indirect evidence to prove a mixed-motive theory of discrimination. Under this new approach, the employee must still demonstrate a prima facie case of discrimination, and the employer must then state a legitimate, nondiscriminatory reason for its decision. If the employer meets its burden of production, the employee must then offer enough evidence to create a genuine issue of material fact either that the employer's reason is not true but is instead a pretext for discrimination (pretext alternative), or the employer's reason is true, but the reason is only one reason for its conduct, and another "motivating factor" is the employee's protected characteristic (mixed-motives alternative). Because Rachid (P) raised disputed material issues of fact as to whether Jack in the Box's (D) stated reason for discharging him might be only one reason for its conduct, and another "motivating factor" might be his age, summary judgment was inappropriate. Although he acknowledged that he occasionally changed timecards without filling out proper forms, he claimed the request by his supervisor to fill out certain forms in such cases was not company policy. Even if it had been policy, he argued, he did not violate the policy because forms were only required when an employee challenged an alteration in a timecard. In addition, Rachid's (P) assertions that his supervisor "continually" made ageist comments were supported by other managers. Rachid (P) had also complained to the company's human resources department about his fears that the supervisor would fire him because of his age. A rational finder of fact could conclude that age played a role in the supervisor's decision to fire Rachid (P).

▌ ANALYSIS

Applying *Desert Palace* to the ADEA was an apparent issue of first impression for the Fifth Circuit Court of Appeals. The court noted that the ADEA was silent with respect to

Continued on next page.

the mixed-motives theory of analysis, but found that the statute's silence on the matter was not dispositive.

■══■

Quicknotes

PRETEXT Ostensible reason or motive assigned or assumed as a color or cover for the real reason or motive.

PRIMA FACIE CASE An action where the plaintiff introduces sufficient evidence to submit the issue to the judge or jury for determination.

PROTECTED CLASS A class sought to be protected by Title VII of the Civil Rights Act; includes race, sex, national origin and religion.

■══■

Systemic Disparate Treatment Discrimination

Quick Reference Rules of Law

PAGE

1. **Formal Policies of Discrimination.**   Sex-differentiated employee contributions to a   18
pension plan, even if based on valid actuarial tables, are prohibited by Title VII.
(Los Angeles Dept. of Water & Power v. Manhart)

2. **Patterns and Practices of Discrimination.**   A prima facie case of systemic employment   19
discrimination may be established by statistical evidence. (Teamsters v. United States)

3. **Patterns and Practices of Discrimination.**   When gross statistical disparities exist   20
between the composition of a work force and that of the general population, this alone
may constitute prima facie proof of a pattern or practice of discrimination. (Hazelwood School
District v. United States)

4. **Rebutting the Inference of Discriminatory Intent.**   A law can have an intentional   22
discriminatory effect without having an illegal discriminatory purpose. (Personnel
Administrator v. Feeney)

5. **Rebutting the Inference of Discriminatory Intent.**   Proof of women's low interest in   23
and qualifications for certain positions may provide a defense to a systemic disparate
treatment claim. (EEOC v. Sears, Roebuck & Co.)

6. **Bona Fide Occupational Qualifications.**   Employers may not exclude fertile females   24
from certain jobs merely because of concern for the health of the fetus the woman might
conceive. (International Union, UAW v. Johnson Controls, Inc.)

7. **Voluntary Affirmative Action.**   Affirmative-action policies adopted by public employers   25
that make gender a factor on a flexible, case-by-case approach are not prohibited by Title VII.
(Johnson v. Transportation Agency of Santa Clara County)

Los Angeles Department of Water & Power v. Manhart

Municipal employer (D) v. Female employee (P)

435 U.S. 702 (1978).

NATURE OF CASE: Appeal from summary judgment in a class action for injunction and restitution for gender discrimination.

FACT SUMMARY: The Department of Water and Power (D) required its female employees to make larger contributions to the pension fund than its male employees, based on women's longer life expectancy.

RULE OF LAW
Sex-differentiated employee contributions to a pension plan, even if based on valid actuarial tables, are prohibited by Title VII.

FACTS: Based on longevity studies showing that, as a class, women live longer then men, the Department of Water and Power (D) required its female employees to make larger contributions to its pension fund than it required of its male employees. Manhart (P) brought this suit on behalf of a class of women employed or formerly employed by the Department (D), seeking an injunction and restitution of excess contributions. While this action was pending, the California legislature enacted a law prohibiting this practice by certain municipal agencies, and the Department (D) amended its plan. The district court granted Manhart's (P) motion for summary judgment and ordered a refund of all excess contributions made before amendment of the plan. The court of appeals affirmed, and this appeal followed.

ISSUE: Are sex-differentiated employee contributions to a pension plan, even if based on valid actuarial tables, prohibited by Title VII?

HOLDING AND DECISION: (Stevens, J.) Yes. Sex-differentiated employee contributions to a pension plan, even if based on valid actuarial tables, are prohibited by Title VII. Section 703(a)(1) of the Civil Rights Act focuses unambiguously on the "individual." In this case, there is no assurance that any individual woman working for the Department (D) will actually fit the class generalization on which the Department's (D) policy is based. Many women will not live as long as the average man. Thus, the Department's (D) policy is in direct conflict with both the language and the policy of § 703(a)(1) of Title VII. However, retroactive liability could be devastating for a pension fund. The harm would fall in large part on innocent third parties. Therefore, it was error to grant retroactive relief in this case. Vacated.

▶ **ANALYSIS**

The majority's discussion distinguished *General Electric Co. v. Gilbert*, 429 U.S. 125 (1976), because the plan in *General Electric* was permitted to discriminate on the basis of a special physical disability, pregnancy, whereas the present case discriminated on the basis of sex. The present case was decided in 1978, and at that time the majority was obviously not yet ready to overrule its decision in *General Electric*. However, in its 1983 decision in *Newport News Shipbuilding & Dry Dock Co. v. EEOC*, 462 U.S. 669, the Court unhesitatingly declared that, with the 1978 amendments to Title VII, Congress had unambiguously disapproved of both the holding and the reasoning of the *General Electric* decision.

■■■

Quicknotes

GENDER DISCRIMINATION Unequal treatment of individuals without justification on the basis of their sex.

■■■

Teamsters v. United States

Union employer (D) v. Government (P)

431 U.S. 324 (1977).

NATURE OF CASE: Appeal from grant of injunctive relief against an employer for Title VII violations.

FACT SUMMARY: The Government (P) brought an action against T.I.M.E.-D.C. (D) for systematically discriminating against blacks and Hispanics by not hiring them, not paying equal wages, and failing to promote them.

> ### 🏛 RULE OF LAW
> A prima facie case of systemic employment discrimination may be established by statistical evidence.

FACTS: The Government (P) brought an action for injunctive relief against T.I.M.E.-D.C. (D) for continuously and systematically discriminating against blacks and Hispanics through their hiring and employment policies. The government (P) established their prima facie case by offering statistics showing that of the line drivers, a better paid, more desirable job, only .4 percent were blacks and only .3 percent were Hispanic. Furthermore, 83 percent of blacks and 78 percent of Hispanics employed by the company held low-paying jobs, compared to only 39 percent among non-minorities. The Government (P) also introduced testimony of over 40 incidents of discrimination in hiring and promotions. The district court and court of appeals both found for the Government (P). T.I.M.E.-D.C. (D) appealed.

ISSUE: Can a prima facie case of systemic employment discrimination be established by statistical evidence?

HOLDING AND DECISION: (Stewart, J.) Yes. A prima facie case of systemic employment discrimination may be established by statistical evidence. What the government (P) must show was that there was a pattern or practice of different treatment and that differences were based on race. Statistical evidence can be very useful in cases such as this, where the discrimination is widespread and continuing. Like any evidence, statistical evidence is not irrefutable and must be examined in light of all the evidence presented. T.I.M.E-D.C.'s (D) argument that the statistics reflected the fact that the company's workforce had shrunk does not refute the importance of the statistics. Affirmed.

▶ ANALYSIS

In *Washington v. Davis*, 426 U.S. 229 (1976), the Court refused to apply disparate-impact theory to an Equal Protection Clause discrimination case. It instead maintained the requirement of showing discriminatory intent, as in a Title VII disparate-treatment case. However, showing of disparate impact can lend to the totality of circumstances that establish discriminatory intent.

■■■

Quicknotes

DISCRIMINATORY PURPOSE Intent to discriminate; must be shown to establish an Equal Protection violation.

DISPARATE IMPACT Effect of a practice that appears neutral but, in fact, falls more harshly on one group of people because of the group's race, sex, national origin, age, or disability and that cannot be justified by business necessity.

PRIMA FACIE CASE An action where the plaintiff introduces sufficient evidence to submit the issue to the judge or jury for determination.

■■■

1) Shows particular group underrepresented
→ what % would be employed absent discrimination
→ show under rep was result of intl. discrim

Hazelwood School District v. United States

School district employer (D) v. Government (P)

433 U.S. 299 (1977).

NATURE OF CASE: Appeal from remedial order in Title VII discrimination action.

FACT SUMMARY: The Government (P) relied on undifferentiated work force statistics to establish a pattern or practice of discrimination by the Hazelwood School District (D).

RULE OF LAW
When gross statistical disparities exist between the composition of a work force and that of the general population, this alone may constitute prima facie proof of a pattern or practice of discrimination.

FACTS: In a Title VII action against Hazelwood School District (D), the federal government (P) attempted to show a pattern or practice of discrimination by offering statistical disparities in hiring between black teachers in Hazelwood and black teachers in the relevant labor market area. The Government (P) compared the small percentage—1.4 percent—of black teachers in Hazelwood to the 15.4 percent of black teachers in St. Louis. The district court, however, compared the small percentage of black teachers to the small percentage of black students and concluded that the Government (P) had failed to establish a pattern or practice. The appeals court reversed and entered a remedial order. The Supreme Court granted certiorari.

ISSUE: When gross statistical disparities exist between the composition of a work force and that of the general population, may that alone constitute prima facie proof of a pattern or practice of discrimination?

HOLDING AND DECISION: (Stewart, J.) Yes. When gross statistical disparities exist between the composition of a work force and that of the general population, that alone may constitute prima facie proof of a pattern or practice of discrimination. Here, the proper comparison was between the racial composition of Hazelwood's (D) teaching staff and the racial composition of the qualified public school teacher population in the relevant labor market. However, Hazelwood (D) must be given an opportunity to rebut the Government's (P) prima facie case and show that the discriminatory pattern is a product of pre-Civil Rights Act hiring rather than unlawful post-Act discrimination. The appellate court should have remanded the case to determine whether Hazelwood (D) engaged in a pattern of employment discrimination after March 24, 1972. Vacated and remanded.

CONCURRENCE: (White, J.) In finding a prima facie case, too much emphasis was placed on the disparity between the areawide percentage of black teachers and the percentage of black teachers on Hazelwood's staff. Instead,

the Government (P) should have adduced evidence regarding hiring practices in the applicant pool for 1972-1973 and 1973-1974 before it was entitled to its prima facie presumption. This way, it would have been required to present a ground for believing that the racial composition of Hazelwood's applicant pool was roughly the same as that for the school districts in the general area before relying on workforce data to establish its prima facie case.

DISSENT: (Stevens, J.) Statistical, historical, and acts-of-discrimination evidence establish the Government's (P) prima facie case. As to statistical evidence, one-third of the teachers hired by Hazelwood (D) lived in St. Louis, so it was appropriate to treat that city as part of the relevant labor market. In that market, 15 percent of teachers were black, but less than 2 percent of the teachers in the Hazelwood District (D) were black. After Title VII was made applicable to public schools, only 3.7 percent of new teachers hired by Hazelwood (D) were black. These statistics by themselves are enough to establish a prima facie case. Historically, that is, before 1969, Hazelwood (D) employed no black teachers. However, even after Title VII became applicable to it, Hazelwood (D) continued to use a standardless and subjective hiring process, giving rise to the inference that it continued its pre-Act policy of preferring white teachers. Finally, there was evidence that the Hazelwood School District (D) refused to hire 16 qualified black applicants for racial reasons. Hazelwood (D) failed to rebut the Government's (P) evidence. It has two arguments that are insufficient to overcome the Government's (P) case. First, it argues that St. Louis should be excluded from the relevant labor market. Without including the city, only 5.7 percent of the teachers in the county were black. Second, it argues the city's policy of maintaining a 50 percent black teaching staff diverted teachers from the county to the city. Hazelwood (D) offered no evidence about qualitative factors, e.g., wages, commuting, or working in a city school as opposed to a suburban school, that could explain why the fact that the city was the source of one-third of Hazelwood's teachers should not by itself be enough to make the city a part of the relevant market. Moreover, the city's attempt to maintain a 50-50 ratio does not rebut the conclusion given that there was no shortage of qualified black applicants in the Hazelwood (D) or other suburban districts. Even excluding the city from the market, the statistical evidence still tends to prove discrimination, because instead of hiring 23 black teachers (representing 5.7 percent of the teachers hired by Hazelwood), the district only hired 15 black teachers. This disparity, without further explanation, tends to prove discrimination and does not in any way help carry Hazelwood's (D) burden

Continued on next page.

of overcoming the Government's (P) prima facie case, especially since somewhere between the 15 percent hiring suggested by the Government (P) and the 5.7 percent suggested by Hazelwood (D) would have resulted in 30 to 40 black teachers being hired, not 15.

▶ *ANALYSIS*

As originally enacted, Title VII of the Civil Rights Act of 1964 applied only to private employers. The Act was extended to state and local governmental employers by the Equal Employment Opportunity Act of 1972, passed on March 24. Hence, the focus in this case was on March 24, 1972, the date racial discrimination by public employers was made illegal.

■▬■

Quicknotes

PRIMA FACIE EVIDENCE Evidence presented by a party that is sufficient, in the absence of contradictory evidence, to support the fact or issue for which it is offered.

■▬■

Personnel Administrator v. Feeney

State administration (D) v. Government (P)

442 U.S. 256 (1979).

NATURE OF CASE: Appeal from finding of equal protection violations based on gender.

FACT SUMMARY: Massachusetts (D) passed legislation giving military veterans, who were mostly male, an absolute advantage in gaining state jobs.

RULE OF LAW
A law can have an intentional discriminatory effect without having an illegal discriminatory purpose.

FACTS: Under a Massachusetts (D) law, military veterans would receive first priority for state jobs. The fact that 98 percent of these veterans were men virtually excluded women from competing for state jobs. The district court found the law too obviously discriminatory to be unintentional. Massachusetts (D) appealed.

ISSUE: Can a law have an intentional discriminatory effect without having an illegal discriminatory purpose?

HOLDING AND DECISION: (Stewart, J.) Yes. A law can have an intentional discriminatory effect without having an illegal discriminatory purpose. There is a difference between accepting a practice "in spite of" its discriminatory effect and accepting a practice "at least partially because of" that effect. Massachusetts (D) did not seek to exclude women since the law would apply to female veterans who applied for state jobs. Knowingly accepting discriminatory consequences does not rise to the level of purposely excluding persons based on their sex. This law discriminates in favor of veterans, not in favor of a particular sex. Reversed.

ANALYSIS

There are three ways to rebut a prima facie case of disparate treatment: deny the existence of the policy in question, discredit the inference of discriminatory intent, or assert a defense to the discrimination. The case above exemplifies the second approach. Note that this is an equal protection challenge and not a Title VII action, as Title VII exempts veterans' preference laws from the protection of the statute.

Quicknotes

DISCRIMINATORY PURPOSE Intent to discriminate; must be shown to establish an Equal Protection violation.

DISPARATE TREATMENT Unequal treatment of employees or of applicants for employment without justification.

EEOC v. Sears, Roebuck & Co.

Government (P) v. Company employer (D)

839 F.2d 302 (7th Cir. 1988).

NATURE OF CASE: Appeal from rejection of an employment-discrimination action based on gender.

FACT SUMMARY: When the Equal Employment Opportunity Commission (EEOC) (P) brought suit against Sears (D) for its systemic and persistent failure to hire or promote women into higher paying commission sales positions, Sears (D) countered that women were not interested in those positions.

🏛 **RULE OF LAW**
Proof of women's low interest in and qualifications for certain positions may provide a defense to a systemic disparate treatment claim.

FACTS: The Equal Employment Opportunity Commission (EEOC) (P) contended that Sears (D) had systematically discriminated against women by failing to hire or promote them to commission sales positions. To show discriminatory intent, the EEOC (P) presented regression analyses based on Sears's (D) payroll and applications. Sears (D) rebutted EEOC's (P) statistical presentation by presenting nonstatistical evidence that the disproportionate number of males in such positions was due not to discrimination but instead to differing interests between male and female Sears (D) employees. The district and appellate courts found that the EEOC (P) had not met its burden of persuasion on the issue of intent to discriminate. The EEOC (P) appealed.

ISSUE: May proof of women's low interest in and qualifications for certain positions provide a defense to a systemic disparate treatment claim?

HOLDING AND DECISION: (Wood, J.) Yes. Proof of women's low interest in and qualifications for certain positions provide a defense to a systemic disparate treatment claim. There is no limit on the evidence an employer may use to rebut the statistical evidence of the petitioner. An employer, in his rebuttal, must question the accuracy of the evidence presented by the petitioner. Beyond the burden to do that, the employer is free to choose what evidence it will present to accomplish that goal. In this case, Sears (D) presented surveys and testimony demonstrating that managers had not been successful in persuading women to sell on commission. The district court did not find the EEOC's (P) regression evidence compelling. At the same time, it found Sears's (P) explanation of the lack of women in commission sales positions persuasive. Neither of these findings was clearly erroneous. Affirmed.

CONCURRENCE AND DISSENT: (Cudahy, J.) The Court's uncritical acceptance of Sears's (D) explanation for its disparate treatment allows Sears (D) to prevail by alleging the very stereotypes Title VII was designed to eradicate.

▶ **ANALYSIS**

The EEOC's (P) regression studies took into account the extent to which disparate treatment was caused by female disinterest and still found significant disparate treatment. One wonders if this court would have come to the same result in a race discrimination case if Sears (D) had presented evidence showing that blacks were underrepresented in the executive ranks of the company because they showed a higher interest in doing janitorial work. EEOC's (P) own expert testified that "women have been hired into limited numbers of jobs, and discriminated against in the workforce generally. The resulting profile of 'women's work,' then, is perceived to be what women have 'chosen.'"

Quicknotes

DISCRIMINATORY PURPOSE Intent to discriminate; must be shown to establish an Equal Protection violation.

DISPARATE TREATMENT Unequal treatment of employees or of applicants for employment without justification.

International Union, UAW v. Johnson Controls, Inc.

Union (P) v. Battery-manufacturer employer (D)

499 U.S. 187 (1991).

NATURE OF CASE: Appeal of grant of defense motion for summary judgment in an employment-discrimination action.

FACT SUMMARY: Johnson Controls (D) refused to allow any fertile women to hold jobs involving lead exposure.

RULE OF LAW
Employers may not exclude fertile females from certain jobs merely because of concern for the health of the fetus the woman might conceive.

FACTS: Johnson Controls (D), a battery manufacturer, adopted a policy that excluded any fertile woman, whether or not she planned to become pregnant, from jobs where they might be exposed to lead. This resulted in women losing their jobs, being transferred, or facing sterilization in order to keep their jobs. The UAW (P) filed a class action alleging that the policy constituted sexual discrimination under Title VII of the Civil Rights Act of 1964. The trial court held that Johnson Controls's (D) fetal protection policy was valid under a business-necessity defense and granted its motion for summary judgment. The appellate court affirmed.

ISSUE: May employers exclude fertile females from certain jobs merely because of concern for the health of the fetus the woman might conceive?

HOLDING AND DECISION: (Blackmun, J.) No. Employers may not exclude fertile females from certain jobs merely because of concern for the health of the fetus the woman might conceive. Johnson Controls's (D) policy was facially sexually discriminatory because it required only female employees to produce proof that they were not capable of reproducing. Such sex discrimination is allowed under Title VII only if there is a bona fide occupational qualification (BFOQ) reasonably necessary to the normal operation of the particular business or enterprise. Sex discrimination because of safety is allowed only when sex or pregnancy interferes with the employee's job performance. In this case, Johnson Controls (D) could not establish a BFOQ, as fertile women can manufacture batteries as efficiently as anyone else. Additionally, if Johnson Controls (D) is complying with OSHA standards, it should not have any increased tort liability due to danger to a fetus or newborn child. Reversed.

CONCURRENCE: (White, J.) The Court erroneously holds that the BFOQ defense is so narrow that it could never justify a sex-specific fetal protection policy.

CONCURRENCE: (Scalia, J.) An employer may not discriminate against fertile women at all; it is up to parents to make occupational decisions affecting their families.

ANALYSIS

The Court dismissed the possibility of employer tort liability if the employer has informed employees of the risk and has not acted negligently. However, is it difficult for an employer to determine in advance what will constitute negligence, and compliance with Title VII does not insulate an employer from state tort liability. Also, while warnings may reduce or preclude employee claims, depending on whether the court follows a theory of comparative or contributory negligence, such warnings will not preclude claims by injured children. Finally, if the manufacturing process is labeled "abnormally dangerous," employers may be held strictly liable despite taking all proper precautions.

Quicknotes

BONA FIDE OCCUPATIONAL QUALIFICATION A statutory exception to the prohibition on discrimination in employment if the individual's sex, religion or national origin is a necessary qualification for the operation of the business.

NEGLIGENCE Conduct falling below the standard of care that a reasonable person would demonstrate under similar conditions.

OCCUPATIONAL SAFETY AND HEALTH ADMINISTRATION (OSHA) Oversees safety and health standards in the workplace.

TORT A legal wrong resulting in a breach of duty by the wrongdoer, causing damages as a result of the breach.

Johnson v. Transportation Agency of Santa Clara County

Prospective employee (P) v. County agency employer (D)

480 U.S. 616 (1987).

NATURE OF CASE: Appeal from judgment affirming an affirmative-action plan in Title VII action.

FACT SUMMARY: Johnson (P), a male employee, challenged the validity of Santa Clara's (D) affirmative-action plan that made gender a factor in employment decisions.

RULE OF LAW

Affirmative-action policies adopted by public employers that make gender a factor on a flexible, case-by-case approach are not prohibited by Title VII.

FACTS: In 1978, the Santa Clara County Transportation Agency (D) adopted an affirmative-action plan that authorized the Agency (D) to consider the sex of qualified applicants. Santa Clara (D) had declared that the plan was necessary to permit attainment of equitable representation of women in the work force and to remedy past discrimination. Of the 238 Skilled Craft Worker positions at the Agency (D), not one was held by women. Women were also underrepresented in other positions at the Agency (D), and the affirmative-action plan set long- and short-term hiring goals in order to remedy the inequity. The policy did not set aside a specific number of positions for women. In 1979, a road-dispatcher position, designated as a Skilled Craft Worker by the Agency (D), became vacant and 12 county employees applied. Nine applicants were found to be qualified and were interviewed. Johnson (P), a male applicant, scored a 75 and Joyce, a female applicant scored a 73, while other scores ranged from 70 to 80. After second interviews, a board of supervisors recommended Johnson (P) but the Affirmative-Action Coordinator informed the Agency Director, who was to make the final decision, that Joyce ought to be considered because she was qualified and a woman had never worked as a road dispatcher for the Agency (D). The Director considered all of the qualifications and test scores of Johnson (P) and Joyce and decided to hire Joyce. Johnson (P) filed suit alleging sex discrimination under the Equal Protection Clause and Title VII. The district court ruled for Johnson (P), but the court of appeals reversed, and the Supreme Court granted review.

ISSUE: Are affirmative-action policies adopted by public employers that make sex a factor on a flexible, case-by-case approach prohibited by Title VII?

HOLDING AND DECISION: (Brennan, J.) No. Affirmative-action policies adopted by public employers that make sex a factor on a flexible, case-by-case approach are not prohibited by Title VII. Once a Title VII plaintiff has established that sex has been taken into account in an employment decision, the employer must provide a nondiscriminatory reason for the decision. The existence of an affirmative-action plan qualifies as a rationale. An employer seeking to justify the adoption of an affirmative-action program must only point to a conspicuous imbalance in traditionally segregated job categories. This manifest imbalance does not have to be such that it would support a prima facie case against the employer, since employers would not adopt voluntary affirmative-action plans if they had to compile evidence that could be used against them in a Title VII action. The plan adopted by the Agency (D) did not make explicit statistical findings regarding the percentage of qualified women in the labor market for each position. Thus, a hiring quota set under these conditions could be invalid. However, the Agency (D) plan recognized a manifest imbalance and enacted a flexible, case-by-case approach to allow gender to be considered, among other factors, in hiring decisions regarding qualified applicants in order to attain a balanced work force in the long term. Thus, it was reasonable for the Agency (D) to consider gender in the decision between Johnson (P) and Joyce, given the obvious imbalance among Skilled Craft Workers. Affirmed.

CONCURRENCE: (Stevens, J.) Although I disagree with the decisions that allow states to voluntarily adopt special programs to benefit members of minority groups, they have become an important part of the fabric of the law. Given the public interest in stability and orderly development of the law, they must be upheld as precedent.

CONCURRENCE: (O'Connor, J.) Employers must have a firm basis for believing that remedial action is required before adopting a voluntary affirmative-action program. Since there were no women working as Skilled Craft Workers, the Agency (D) had a sufficient basis for allowing sex to be a factor in the hiring decision.

DISSENT: (Scalia, J.) The clear and unequivocal language of Title VII states that the consideration of sex in employment decisions is prohibited. The Agency's (D) plan could not have been adopted to remedy prior discrimination because the district court found that the Agency (D) had not discriminated in the past. Thus, the majority here permits sex discrimination in order to overcome the effect of societal attitudes, rather than an employer's own discrimination. Furthermore, stare decisis should not be the basis for this decision, because it departs from our consistent path regarding civil rights.

ANALYSIS

Following this decision, some plaintiffs have tried to use the adoption of a voluntary affirmative-action plan as a sword rather than a shield against their employers. In *Liao v. Tennessee Valley Authority*, 867 F.2d 1366 (11th Cir. 1989), a woman hired pursuant to a plan was laid off before male

Continued on next page.

workers. She contended that the failure to provide a preferential layoff scheme was a violation of the plan and of
Title VII, but the appellate court rejected her view, holding
that Title VII permits such plans, but failure to abide by
them does not necessarily trigger a Title VII violation.

■═■

Quicknotes

AFFIRMATIVE ACTION A form of benign discrimination
designed to remedy existing discrimination by favoring
one group over another.

■═■

CHAPTER 3

Systemic Disparate Impact Discrimination

Quick Reference Rules of Law

PAGE

1. **The Concept of Disparate Impact Discrimination.** Practices, procedures, or tests neutral on their face, and even neutral in terms of intent, cannot be maintained if they operate to freeze the status quo of prior discriminatory employment practices. (Griggs v. Duke Power Co.) — 28

2. **The Concept of Disparate Impact Discrimination.** Statistical evidence comparing an employer's practice of hiring nonwhite workers in one position to a low percentage of such workers in other positions does not establish a prima facie case of disparate impact of employer's policies in violation of Title VII. (Wards Cove Packing Co. v. Atonio) — 29

3. **The Concept of Disparate Impact Discrimination.** A disparate-impact claim may be made under the Age Discrimination in Employment Act of 1967. (Smith v. City of Jackson) — 31

4. **Plaintiff's Proof of a Prima Facie Case: A Particular Employment Practice.** Disparate-impact analysis may be applied to Title VII cases in which subjective or discretionary criteria are used to make employment decisions. (Watson v. Fort Worth Bank & Trust) — 32

5. **Plaintiff's Proof of a Prima Facie Case: A Particular Employment Practice.** A racially balanced work force is not a defense to a Title VII violation. (Connecticut v. Teal) — 33

6. **Plaintiff's Proof of a Prima Facie Case: The Employer Uses the Practice.** There is no requirement that the statistics used in establishing a prima facie case of sex discrimination reflect the characteristics of the actual applicant pool. (Dothard v. Rawlinson) — 34

7. **Defendant's Options: Business Necessity and Job Relatedness.** Discriminatory hiring policies that include requirements aimed at reducing the risk that an applicant will endanger the employer's patrons may be justified by business necessity if they accurately—if not perfectly—ascertain an applicant's ability to perform successfully the job in question. (El v. Southeastern Pennsylvania Transportation Authority) — 35

8. **Alternative Employment Practices.** An exam that must be taken in order to receive a job promotion that has a disparate impact on minority applicants does not violate Title VII of the 1964 Civil Rights Act if the examination is job related, consistent with business necessity, and there is no other available method of evaluation that is equally valid and less discriminatory. (Adams v. City of Chicago) — 36

9. **Professionally Developed Tests.** Discriminatory employment tests are impermissible unless they are predictive of or correlated with behavior relevant to the job. (Albemarle Paper Co. v. Moody) — 38

10. **Professionally Developed Tests.** The use of a test to determine promotions within a city police department does not violate Title VII if, despite its adverse impact on African-American and Latino applicants, the test is a reasonable measure of job performance. (Bryant v. City of Chicago) — 39

Griggs v. Duke Power Co.

Government (P) v. Employer (D)

401 U.S. 424 (1971).

NATURE OF CASE: Appeal from decision upholding employment-testing requirements.

FACT SUMMARY: Griggs (P) and others challenged the hiring requirements and testing practices of Duke Power Co. (D) as violative of the Civil Rights Act of 1964, alleging that they rendered a disproportionate number of blacks ineligible for hiring or promotion.

🏛 RULE OF LAW
Practices, procedures, or tests neutral on their face, and even neutral in terms of intent, cannot be maintained if they operate to freeze the status quo of prior discriminatory employment practices.

FACTS: Duke Power (D) had a policy of requiring a high school education for initial assignment to any department except labor, the only department employing blacks. When Duke (D) abandoned its policy of restricting blacks to the labor department in 1965, completion of high school also was made a prerequisite to transfer from labor to any other department. Starting on the date on which Title VII of the Civil Rights Act of 1964 became effective, Duke (D) made it necessary for new employees to register satisfactory scores on two professionally prepared aptitude tests, as well as to have a high school education, for placement in any department other than labor. In September 1965, Duke (D) began to permit incumbent employees who lacked a high school education to qualify for transfer from labor or coal handling to an "inside" job by passing two tests, general intelligence and comprehension. The court of appeals (1) held that, in the absence of a discriminatory purpose, use of such requirements was permitted by the Act and (2) rejected the claim that the requirements' effect of rendering ineligible a markedly disproportionate number of blacks was unlawful under Title VII unless shown to be job related.

ISSUE: Can practices, procedures, or tests neutral on their face, and even neutral in terms of intent, be maintained if they operate to freeze the status quo of prior discriminatory employment practices?

HOLDING AND DECISION: (Burger, C.J.) No. Practices, procedures, or tests neutral on their face, and even neutral in terms of intent, cannot be maintained if they operate to freeze the status quo of prior discriminatory employment practices. In this case, whites did far better on Duke's (D) alternative requirements than blacks. This consequence would appear to be directly traceable to race. Basic intelligence must have the means of articulation to manifest itself fairly in a testing process. Because they are blacks, Griggs (P) and the others have long received inferior education in segregated schools and this Court has expressly recognized these differences. The objective of Congress in the enactment of Title VII was to achieve equality of employment opportunities and remove barriers that have operated to favor an identifiable group of white employees over other employees. Congress did not intend by Title VII, however, to guarantee a job to every person regardless of qualifications. What Congress required is the removal of artificial, arbitrary, and unnecessary employment barriers that operate invidiously to discriminate on the basis of racial or other impermissible classification. The Act proscribes not only overt discrimination but also practices that are fair in form, but discriminatory in operation. If an employment practice that operates to exclude blacks cannot be shown to be related to job performance, the practice is prohibited. On the record in this case, the high school completion requirement and the general intelligence test were adopted, as the court of appeals noted, without meaningful study of their relationship to job-performance ability. While the Act does not preclude the use of testing or measuring procedures, Congress has forbidden giving them controlling force unless they are demonstrably a reasonable measure of job performance. Reversed.

▶ ANALYSIS

The Court explained that the requisite scores used for both initial hiring and transfer approximated the national median for high school graduates. Thus, the test standards were more stringent than the high school requirement, since they would screen out approximately half of all high school graduates. Moreover, 1960 census statistics in North Carolina show that while 34 percent of white males had completed high school, only 12 percent of black males had done so. Similarly, with respect to standardized tests, the Equal Employment Opportunity Commission in one case found that use of a battery of tests, including the Wonderlic and Bennett tests used by Duke (D) in the instant case, resulted in 58 percent of whites, as compared with only 6 percent of blacks, passing the tests.

▬▬■

Quicknotes

DISPARATE IMPACT Effect of a practice that appears neutral but, in fact, falls more harshly on one group of people because of the group's race, sex, national origin, age, or disability and that cannot be justified by business necessity.

▬▬■

Wards Cove Packing Co. v. Atonio

Discriminating employer (D) v. Employee (P)

490 U.S. 642 (1989).

NATURE OF CASE: Appeal from finding that employer's employment practices have a disparate impact on minorities.

FACT SUMMARY: Atonio (P) and others employed at the Wards Cove Packing Co. (Wards Cove) (D) filed a class-action suit against Wards Cove (D), alleging that its hiring/promotion practices were responsible for the racial stratification of the work force, denying them and other nonwhites, on the basis of race, employment as noncannery workers.

> ## RULE OF LAW
> Statistical evidence comparing an employer's practice of hiring nonwhite workers in one position to a low percentage of such workers in other positions does not establish a prima facie case of disparate impact of employer's policies in violation of Title VII.

FACTS: Wards Cove Packing Co. (Wards Cove) (D), which operated a salmon cannery in a remote area during the salmon runs each year, hired employees and transported them to the cannery. Cannery jobs were nonskilled positions filled primarily by nonwhites, while noncannery jobs were skilled positions filled predominantly by white workers. Virtually all of the noncannery jobs paid more than cannery positions. The predominantly white noncannery workers and the predominantly nonwhite cannery employees lived in separate dormitories and ate in separate mess halls. Atonio (P) filed a class-action suit against Wards Cove (D), alleging that a variety of Wards Cove's (D) hiring/promotion practices were responsible for the racial stratification of the work force, denying him and other nonwhites employment as noncannery workers on the basis of race. Atonio (P) also complained of the racially segregated housing and dining facilities. The court of appeals held that Atonio (P) had made out a prima facie case of disparate impact, relying solely on statistics showing a high percentage of nonwhite workers in the cannery jobs and a low percentage of such workers in the noncannery positions. This appeal followed.

ISSUE: Does statistical evidence comparing a high percentage of nonwhite workers in one position to a low percentage of such workers hired in other positions establish a prima facie case of disparate impact of employer's policies in violation of Title VII?

HOLDING AND DECISION: (White, J.) No. Statistical evidence comparing an employer's practice of hiring a high percentage of nonwhite workers in one position to hiring a low percentage of such workers in other positions does not establish a prima facie case of disparate impact of employer's policies in violation of Title VII. However, if an absence of minorities holding skilled positions is due to a lack of qualified nonwhite applicants, an employer's employment practices cannot be said to have had a disparate impact on nonwhites. There can be no doubt that the comparison misconceived the role of statistics in employment-discrimination cases. The proper comparison is between the racial composition of the jobs at issue and the racial composition of the qualified population in the relevant labor market. Such a comparison generally forms the proper basis for the initial inquiry in a disparate-impact case. With respect to the skilled noncannery jobs at issue here, the cannery work force in no way reflected the pool of qualified job applicants or the qualified population in the labor force. Measuring alleged discrimination in the selection of accountants, managers, boat captains, electricians, doctors, and engineers comprising the skilled noncannery positions by comparing the number of nonwhites occupying these jobs to the number of nonwhites filling cannery worker positions is nonsensical. On remand, the courts below must require, as part of Atonio's (P) prima facie case, a demonstration that specific elements of the Wards Cove (D) hiring process had a significantly disparate impact on nonwhites. Meeting that burden of proof with respect to any of Wards Cove's (D) employment practices, the case will shift to any business justification Wards Cove (D) offers for its use of these practices. The court must consider the justifications Wards Cove (D) offers for its use of these practices and also the availability of alternate practices to achieve the same business ends with less racial impact. Reversed and remanded.

DISSENT: (Stevens, J.) The majority's opinion blurs the distinction between an employer's burden in a disparate-treatment case—to come forward with evidence of legitimate business purpose—and in a disparate-impact case—to prove an affirmative defense of business necessity. Common-law pleading principles clarify the distinction. In a disparate-treatment case, the employee has the burden of proving the existence of discriminatory intent at all times, but the employer, who may undermine the employee's evidence, itself has no burden of persuasion. In contrast, in a disparate-impact case, when there is proof of disparate impact, the employer's only recourse is the affirmative defense of business necessity, and it carries the burden of persuasion on this defense. However, the majority fails to make this distinction and finds that the employer's burden respecting business necessity is a burden of production, which is a lighter burden than that of persuasion. Departing from the Court's and other federal courts' prior decisions in this area, the majority moves away from business necessity as the touchstone to an employer's justification for his use of the challenged practice, which practice does not have to be "essential." The majority

Continued on next page.

also redefines the employee's burden of proof in a disparate-impact case, stating that no prima facie case is made unless the employee identifies the specific employment practices that are allegedly responsible for any observed statistical disparities. This is unwarranted, because it goes beyond ordinary principles of fairness that require that a Title VII action be tried like any other lawsuit, where a causal link between injury and an act of the defendant need not constitute the sole or primary cause of harm. The majority should have given more credit than it did to the employees' statistical evidence. The industry involved here is a unique one. The at-issue positions are the skilled noncannery positions, to which there is no promotion from within the cannery ranks. The cannery positions are all unskilled and there is no on-the-job training for the skilled, noncannery positions. Also, employees in the noncannery positions learn of openings by word of mouth, as the jobs are seldom advertised or posted. However, the district court failed to make findings regarding the extent to which the cannery workers were already qualified for the noncannery positions. Some plaintiffs testified persuasively that they were fully qualified for such jobs, but the district court neither credited nor discredited this testimony. The district court did find that nearly all cannery workers are nonwhite, and the parties agreed that the noncannery jobs are held mostly by whites. The employer relies on the district court's findings regarding the relevant labor market, but these findings are ambiguous. At one point the district court specifies "Alaska, the Pacific Northwest, and California" as the geographical area from which the employees are drawn, but then restricts this area to nonskilled jobs; there is no express finding of the relevant labor market for noncannery jobs. Even assuming the district court correctly defines the relevant geographical area, its assumption that the population in that area made up the "available labor supply" is not founded. That is because a critical requirement for either cannery or noncannery work is being available for seasonal work in the far reaches of Alaska. Yet, the record does not show the portion of the general population in Alaska, California, and the Pacific Northwest that would accept this type of employment. This deficiency undermines the employer's statistical evidence. In contrast, the employees' evidence does identify a pool of workers that are familiar with and would accept this type of employment. Accordingly, the employees' evidence is more probative than the employer's evidence. The employees' evidence shows racial stratification. The maintenance of housing and mess halls that separate the mostly white noncannery workers from the cannery workers, coupled with the fact that noncannery positions are obtained through nepotism and word of mouth, are barriers to employment opportunities for the nonwhite cannery workers. Thus, the employees' evidence shows that these practices have discriminatory consequences.

▶ *ANALYSIS*

In this case, the trial court had dismissed for lack of jurisdiction, and the court of appeals affirmed in part, reversed in part, and remanded. On remand, the judgment was for Wards

Cove (D), and the court of appeals again affirmed. The court of appeals, in a rehearing en banc, then reversed and remanded solely on the basis of the statistics Atonio (P) presented. According to the Court here, *Griggs v. Duke Power Co.*, 401 U.S. 424 (1971), construed Title VII to proscribe not only overt discrimination but also practices that were facially neutral. Under this basis for liability, known as the "disparate-impact" theory, a facially neutral employment practice may be deemed violative of Title VII without evidence of the employer's subjective intent to discriminate as required in "disparate-treatment" cases like *Price Waterhouse v. Hopkins*, 490 U.S. 228 (1989).

■═■

Quicknotes

DISPARATE IMPACT Effect of a practice that appears neutral but, in fact, falls more harshly on one group of people because of the group's race, sex, national origin, age, or disability and that cannot be justified by business necessity.

DISPARATE TREATMENT Unequal treatment of employees or of applicants for employment without justification.

■═■

Smith v. City of Jackson

Employees (P) v. Public employer (D)

544 U.S. 228 (2005).

NATURE OF CASE: Appeal of judgment for employer in age-discrimination claim.

FACT SUMMARY: Azel Smith (P), a police department employee in Jackson, Mississippi, argued that the department's policy of giving officers with five or fewer years of tenure with the department bigger raises than those with more than five years of tenure violated the Age Discrimination in Employment Act (ADEA).

🏛 RULE OF LAW
A disparate-impact claim may be made under the Age Discrimination in Employment Act of 1967.

FACTS: Azel Smith (P) and group of other police department employees over the age of 40 sued the police department and the city of Jackson, Miss., alleging that the department salary plan violated the ADEA by giving officers with five or fewer years of tenure with the department larger raises than those with more than five years of tenure. The group made a "disparate-impact" claim under the ADEA, arguing the department and city unintentionally engaged in age discrimination. The district court and the U.S. Court of Appeals for the Fifth Circuit ruled that disparate-impact claims could not be made under the ADEA.

ISSUE: Can a disparate-impact claim be made under the Age Discrimination in Employment Act of 1967?

HOLDING AND DECISION: (Stevens, J.) Yes. A disparate-impact claim may be made under the Age Discrimination in Employment Act of 1967. But even though ADEA authorized recovery in disparate-impact cases, Smith (P) and his co-plaintiffs in this case failed to set forth a valid claim. Disparate-impact claims brought under Title VII of the 1964 Civil Rights Act were first authorized in *Griggs v. Duke Power*, and the ADEA authorized disparate-impact claims in cases similar to *Griggs*, because the language of Title VII and ADEA is virtually identical. However, ADEA is narrower than Title VII and allowed an otherwise prohibited action where the discrimination was based on reasonable factors other than age. The employees in this case failed to identify any specific practice within the pay plan that had an adverse impact on older workers. Further, the city's plan was based on reasonable factors other than age. Affirmed.

CONCURRENCE: (Scalia, J.) This is an absolutely classic case for deference to agency interpretation. Resolving this case only requires deference to the EEOC, which has express authority to promulgate rules and regulations interpreting the ADEA, and its position recognizing disparate-impact claims is "eminently reasonable."

CONCURRENCE: (O'Connor, J.) The ADEA's text, legislative history, and purposes together make clear that Congress did not intend the statute to authorize disparate-impact claims. However, the majority's conclusion that the 30 police officers and dispatchers lost their case is correct.

▶ ANALYSIS

Unlike disparate-treatment claims, disparate-impact claims do not require a showing of discriminatory intent. They focus instead on whether employer policies and practices adversely affect one or more protected groups. As a result of this case, older workers may recover against employers if they can show that a practice or policy has a disparate impact on them, even though the practice or policy may have been adopted with no discriminatory intent or motivation.

■=■

Quicknotes

AGE DISCRIMINATION IN EMPLOYMENT ACT (29 U.S.C. § 621) 1967 act prohibiting age discrimination and retaliation in employment.

DISPARATE IMPACT Effect of a practice that appears neutral but, in fact, falls more harshly on one group of people because of the group's race, sex, national origin, age, or disability and that cannot be justified by business necessity.

DISPARATE TREATMENT Unequal treatment of employees or of applicants for employment without justification.

EEOC Equal Employment Opportunity Commission; an agency created by Title VII to institute nondiscriminatory employment practices pursuant to that statute.

TITLE VII OF THE CIVIL RIGHTS ACT OF 1964 Law prohibiting discrimination in employment on the basis of race, color, religion, sex, and national origin.

■=■

Watson v. Forth Worth Bank & Trust

Employee denied promotion (P) v. Employer (D)

487 U.S. 977 (1988).

NATURE OF CASE: Appeal from defense verdict in Title VII race-discrimination action.

FACT SUMMARY: Watson (P) argued that Fort Worth Bank's (D) subjective selection methods were as likely to have discriminatory effects as the objective tests struck down in disparate-impact cases.

> ### 🏛 RULE OF LAW
> Disparate-impact analysis may be applied to Title VII cases in which subjective or discretionary criteria are used to make employment decisions.

FACTS: Watson (P), a black bank teller, applied unsuccessfully for four promotions; the Bank (D) promoted white employees instead. She filed a Title VII lawsuit against the Bank (D). The trial court concluded that Watson (P) had established a prima facie case of employment discrimination but that the Bank (D) had met its rebuttal burden by presenting legitimate, not pretextual, reasons for each of the four promotion decisions. Dismissal of the action was affirmed by the Fifth Circuit, which concluded that a Title VII challenge to a discretionary promotion system is properly analyzed under the disparate-treatment model, not the disparate-impact model, as Watson (P) argued. Watson (P) appealed.

ISSUE: May disparate-impact analysis be applied to Title VII cases in which subjective or discretionary criteria are used to make employment decisions?

HOLDING AND DECISION: (O'Connor, J.) Yes. Disparate-impact analysis may be applied to Title VII cases in which subjective or discretionary criteria are used to make employment decisions. In the typical Title VII "disparate-treatment" case, the plaintiff has the ultimate burden of persuading the trier of fact that the defendant intentionally discriminated. Some cases, however, involve facially neutral employment practices that significantly and adversely affect protected groups. In those cases, "disparate-impact" analysis focuses on statistical disparities, rather than specific incidences of discrimination, exempting the plaintiff from the need to prove intentional discrimination. Disparate-impact analysis rests on the assumption that some facially neutral and objective employment practices may in operation be functionally equivalent to intentional discrimination. Up until now, disparate-impact analyses were confined to employers who used objective criteria and standardized selection practices. But a promotion process based on subjective decision-making may have precisely the same effects as a system pervaded by impermissible intentional discrimination. An employer should not be allowed to insulate itself from liability by merely delegating employment decisions to the discretion of lower-level supervisors. In this case, the lower courts have not evaluated the statistical evidence to determine whether Watson (P) has made out a prima facie case of discriminatory promotion practices under disparate-impact theory. Vacated and remanded for that analysis.

▶ ANALYSIS

Statistical proof under Title VII varies depending on the available data. If general population data has been collected about the employment procedure, then the disparate impact can be demonstrated by comparison to that data. Where no general population data is available, the sample data is analyzed to determine whether the disparate pattern could have occurred by chance.

■━■

Quicknotes

DISPARATE IMPACT Effect of a practice that appears neutral but, in fact, falls more harshly on one group of people because of the group's race, sex, national origin, age, or disability and that cannot be justified by business necessity.

DISPARATE TREATMENT Unequal treatment of employees or of applicants for employment without justification.

PRIMA FACIE CASE An action where the plaintiff introduces sufficient evidence to submit the issue to the judge or jury for determination.

■━■

Connecticut v. Teal

State employer (D) v. Employee (P)

457 U.S. 440 (1982).

NATURE OF CASE: Appeal from reversal of the dismissal of a claim for racial discrimination in an employer's promotion policy.

FACT SUMMARY: After Teal (P) and three other black employees of the State of Connecticut (D) failed to pass the written exam for supervisors, they filed this suit for discrimination, even though the State's (D) overall promotion policy compensated for the lower scoring of black employees on the exam.

🏛 RULE OF LAW
A racially balanced work force is not a defense to a Title VII violation.

FACTS: Four black employees (P) of the State of Connecticut (D), including Teal (P), were each provisionally promoted to the position of welfare-eligibility supervisor, serving in that capacity for almost two years. To attain permanent status, however, they had to pass a written examination. None of the four passed. In fact, a disproportionately smaller percentage of all black employees passed in comparison to the pass rates of other ethnic groups. To compensate, the State (D) implemented a selection process more favorable to black employees. Teal (P) and the others filed suit, alleging racial discrimination. The State (D) argued that the "bottom-line" result of its promotion policy should be a complete defense to the suit. The district court dismissed the claim. The court of appeals reversed. The State (D) appealed.

ISSUE: Is a racially balanced work force a defense to a Title VII violation?

HOLDING AND DECISION: (Brennan, J.) No. A racially balanced work force is not a defense to a Title VII violation. The suggestion that disparate impact should be measured only at the "bottom line" ignores the fact that the principal focus of Title VII is the protection of the individual employee, rather than the protection of the minority group as a whole. The State (D) and amici appear to confuse unlawful discrimination with discriminatory intent. But intent is not the issue here. Rather, the State (D) seeks to justify discrimination against Teal (P) and the others on the basis of its favorable treatment of other members of their racial group. Congress never intended to allow an employer to discriminate against some employees on the basis of race or sex merely because it treats other members of the employees' group favorably. The rights of Teal (P) and the others, under Title VII, have been violated. Affirmed and remanded.

DISSENT: (Powell, J.) This Court has previously been sensitive to the difference between cases proving discrimination under Title VII by a showing of disparate treatment or those proving such discrimination by a showing of disparate impact. Today's decision blurs that distinction and results in a holding inconsistent with the very nature of disparate-impact claims. Having pleaded a disparate-impact case, Teal (P) cannot deny the State (D) the opportunity to show there was no such impact.

▶ ANALYSIS

Whatever the discriminatory practice, an employer's treatment of other members of the employees' group can be of little comfort to the victims of discrimination. Every individual employee is protected against both discriminatory treatment and against practices that are fair in form but discriminatory in operation. Requirements and tests that have a discriminatory impact are merely some of the more subtle, but also the more pervasive, of the practices and devices which have fostered racially stratified job environments to the disadvantage of minority citizens.

Quicknotes

DISPARATE IMPACT Effect of a practice that appears neutral but, in fact, falls more harshly on one group of people because of the group's race, sex, national origin, age, or disability and that cannot be justified by business necessity.

DISPARATE TREATMENT Unequal treatment of employees or of applicants for employment without justification.

Dothard v. Rawlinson

State prison employer (D) v. Guard applicant (P)

433 U.S. 321 (1977).

NATURE OF CASE: Appeal from finding of Title VII violation based on sex.

FACT SUMMARY: Rawlinson (P), an otherwise qualified applicant, was rejected for a position as a prison guard because she did not meet the statutory height and weight requirements.

🏛 RULE OF LAW
There is no requirement that the statistics used in establishing a prima facie case of sex discrimination reflect the characteristics of the actual applicant pool.

FACTS: Rawlinson (P), a 22-year-old woman with a college degree in correctional psychology, was rejected for a job as a guard in one of Alabama's (D) correctional facilities. A statutory requirement for such a position was a minimum height of 5 feet 2 inches and a minimum weight of 120 pounds. Rawlinson (P) was denied employment because she did not meet the weight requirement. She brought suit alleging that these requirements had a disproportionate discriminatory effect against women applicants. The State (D) contended that these requirements were necessary for the applicants to properly carry out the job. The district court found for Rawlinson (P). The State (D) appealed, contending that Rawlinson's (P) analysis was based on generalized national statistics, when she should have used statistics concerning the actual applicant pool in Alabama.

ISSUE: Is there a requirement that the statistics used in establishing a prima facie case of sex discrimination reflect the characteristics of the actual applicant pool?

HOLDING AND DECISION: (Stewart, J.) No. There is no requirement that the statistics used in establishing a prima facie case of sex discrimination reflect the characteristics of the actual applicant pool. Rawlinson (P) presented evidence that the height and weight restrictions would exclude 41.13 percent of the national female population but would only exclude less than 1 percent of the national male population. While the applicant pool in Alabama (D) may reflect different characteristics, it may not be a reliable guide since otherwise interested candidates may be discouraged from applying because they knew they would be rejected immediately based on their physical characteristics. Affirmed.

DISSENT: (White, J.) The court should have required statistical evidence reflecting the characteristics of the applicant pool since it is likely that women interested in a prison guard position would meet the physical requirement.

▶ ANALYSIS

Can the standard applied in disparate-treatment cases apply equally in disparate-impact cases? Disparate treatment requires a showing that the individual is being treated differently from the group he or she is functioning in. Disparate impact intends to show that a group is being prevented from competing at all. Therefore, looking at statistics of applicants from which certain minorities are necessarily excluded makes little sense.

■=■

Quicknotes

DISPARATE IMPACT Effect of a practice that appears neutral but, in fact, falls more harshly on one group of people because of the group's race, sex, national origin, age, or disability and that cannot be justified by business necessity.

DISPARATE TREATMENT Unequal treatment of employees or of applicants for employment without justification.

PRIMA FACIE CASE An action where the plaintiff introduces sufficient evidence to submit the issue to the judge or jury for determination.

■=■

El v. Southeastern Pennsylvania Transportation Authority

Employee (P) v. Employer (D)

479 F.3d 232 (3d Cir. 2007).

NATURE OF CASE: Appeal of summary judgment for employer.

FACT SUMMARY: Douglas El (P) claimed that Southeastern Pennsylvania Transportation Authority (SEPTA) (D) unnecessarily disqualifies job applicants who have prior criminal convictions.

🏛 RULE OF LAW
Discriminatory hiring policies that include requirements aimed at reducing the risk that an applicant will endanger the employer's patrons may be justified by business necessity if they accurately—if not perfectly—ascertain an applicant's ability to perform successfully the job in question.

FACTS: King Paratransit Services, Inc. was a contractor for the Southeastern Pennsylvania Transportation Authority (SEPTA) (D). In January 2000, King hired Douglas El (P) as a bus driver for people with mental and physical disabilities, on the condition that he pass a criminal background check. A few weeks after El (P) began work, King discovered that he was convicted for taking part in a gang-related fight when he was 15 years old, more than 40 years ago. The fight resulted in the death of another teenager and that El (P) served a three-and-one-half-year prison sentence. El (P) claimed that the transportation authority (D) unnecessarily disqualifies job applicants who have prior criminal convictions. He argued that the policy has a disparate impact because African Americans and Hispanics were more likely to have a criminal record and were therefore more likely to be excluded by the policy. The transportation authority (D) was granted summary judgment on its affirmative defense of business necessity.

ISSUE: Can discriminatory hiring policies that include requirements aimed at reducing the risk that an applicant will endanger the employer's patrons be justified by business necessity if they accurately—if not perfectly—ascertain an applicant's ability to perform successfully the job in question?

HOLDING AND DECISION: (Ambro, J.) Yes. Discriminatory hiring policies that include requirements aimed at reducing the risk that an applicant will endanger the employer's patrons may be justified by business necessity if they accurately—if not perfectly—ascertain an applicant's ability to perform successfully the job in question. Title VII does not require that employers make a case-by-case determination of whether a person's criminal record merits disqualification for a job. SEPTA (D) provided evidence that paratransit drivers are in close contact and often alone with vulnerable passengers, that disabled people are disproportionately the target of crime, that violent criminals have a high

recidivism rate, that it is impossible to predict which criminals will recidivate, and that its policy is the most accurate way to screen out applicants who pose an unacceptable risk. El (P) failed to present expert testimony to support his position that he was no more likely than the average person to commit a violent crime and failed to conduct depositions of SEPTA's (D) experts to raise doubts about their testimony. A reasonable juror could find that the hiring policy is consistent with the business necessity of reducing the chance that paratransit drivers will attack the elderly and disabled passengers whom they transport. SEPTA's (D) policy barring contractors from employing anyone convicted of a violent crime therefore does not violate Title VII of the 1964 Civil Rights Act's prohibition on race discrimination.

▶ *ANALYSIS*

The court suggested there might have been a different result in this case had El rebutted the SEPTA's expert testimony regarding his propensity to commit another violent crime, given his previous conviction. The judge said that the expert reports were not "ironclad" but pointed out that "El chose neither to hire an expert to rebut SEPTA's experts on the issue of business necessity nor even to depose SEPTA's experts." As a result, "there is nothing in the record that raises any reasonable credibility question about SEPTA's expert evidence, rebuttable as it may be." The mitigating circumstances of the case—that his crime occurred when he was a juvenile, that it occurred more than 40 years ago, that he has been out of trouble since—would have allowed a different result had he addressed the expert testimony.

■=■

Quicknotes

DISCRIMINATION Unequal treatment of a class of persons.

■=■

Adams v. City of Chicago

State employees (P) v. Employer (D)

469 F.3d 609 (7th Cir. 2006).

NATURE OF CASE: Appeal of summary judgment for employer.

FACT SUMMARY: African American and Hispanic police officers (P) in Chicago (D) challenged a promotional exam that had a disparate impact on them.

🏛 RULE OF LAW
An exam that must be taken in order to receive a job promotion that has a disparate impact on minority applicants does not violate Title VII of the 1964 Civil Rights Act if the examination is job related, consistent with business necessity, and there is no other available method of evaluation that is equally valid and less discriminatory.

FACTS: Chicago police officers seeking to be promoted to sergeant had to take a test covering laws, regulations, and department procedures. After the City (D) first made promotions to sergeant based on the 1994 test, approximately 280 minority officers (P) sued the City, alleging that the exam had a disparate impact on them in violation of Title VII. The City (D) agreed that the exam had a disparate impact on the minority officers (P). The City made further promotions based on the list later in March 1996, after which the mayor appointed a task force to examine the promotional process. The task force's report, issued on Jan. 16, 1997, included a recommendation that 30 percent of promotions to sergeant be based on a combination of merit, meaning job performance as rated by supervisors, and performance on the exam. The City (D) again made promotions to sergeant in 1997, based on the 1994 list. The minority officers (P) argued that Chicago (D) could have and should have instituted a merit component before making the 1997 promotions. The officers (P) pointed out that since 1989, the City (D) had used merit to fill 20 percent of D-2 positions—officers who function as detectives, youth officers, and gang crime specialists. They also pointed out that the City (D) implemented the task force's recommendations and beginning in August 1998, made 30 percent of promotions to sergeant and lieutenant based on merit.

The district court excluded evidence of the process used for making the 1998 promotions, finding that it was irrelevant to the earlier promotions and inadmissible under Rule 407 of the Federal Rules of Evidence, which bars evidence of remedial measures taken in response to an injury or harm. The district court later granted summary judgment to the City (D), finding that the minority officers (P) failed to show that a promotional process that considered merit was available to the City (D) in 1994 or that consideration of merit would result in an equally valid but less discriminatory method of selecting officers for promotion to sergeant.

ISSUE: Does an exam that must be taken in order to receive a job promotion that has a disparate impact on minority applicants violate Title VII of the 1964 Civil Rights Act if the examination is job related, consistent with business necessity, and there is no other available method of evaluation that is equally valid and less discriminatory?

HOLDING AND DECISION: (Manion, J.) No. An exam that must be taken in order to receive a job promotion that has a disparate impact on minority applicants does not violate Title VII of the 1964 Civil Rights Act if the examination is job related, consistent with business necessity, and there is no other available method of evaluation that is equally valid and less discriminatory. First, Rule 407 was not a valid basis for excluding the evidence of the process for making the 1998 promotions. The purpose of Rule 407 is to promote safety by removing the disincentive to take post-accident safety measures. Disparate-impact claims are not naturally described as an injury or harm allegedly caused by an event. Because an analysis of the disparate-impact claim requires the court to address the availability of an alternative promotional method, this situation falls within the scope of the exception contained in Rule 407, which explicitly does not require the exclusion of evidence of subsequent remedial measures when offered for another purpose, such as proving feasibility of precautionary measures. But despite the lower court's error in excluding that evidence, summary judgment for the City (D) is nevertheless affirmed. Even after considering the evidence of the 1998 promotional process, the minority officers (P) failed to show that Chicago (D) had an opportunity to adopt an alternative available method for evaluating the merit of officers seeking promotion to sergeants. The minority officers (P) argued that the City could have implemented merit promotions by using the process already used for selecting officers for D-2 positions. However, the D-2 selection process did not evaluate supervisory attributes that would be needed for the sergeant positions. The officers (P) also pointed out that certain promotions to lieutenant began taking merit into account 1995. But the merit evaluations took into account the sergeants' actual performance as supervisors and did not require evaluating potential ability as a supervisor. In addition, the pool of sergeants seeking promotion to lieutenant is significantly smaller than the pool of officers seeking promotion to sergeant.

DISSENT: (Williams, J.) The evidence regarding the 1998 promotions shows the existence of a valid alternative. There is at least a question of material fact as to whether the City (D) could have quickly implemented a task force's January 1997 recommendation to use 30 percent merit

Continued on next page.

promotions. A reasonable alternative is not unavailable simply because the employer has not completed its own inquiry into the validity of the alternative.

▶ *ANALYSIS*

This case stands for the simple notion that the existence of disparate impact does not necessarily constitute a violation of Title VII. Disparate impact is merely an element of the case.

■═■

Quicknotes

DISPARATE IMPACT Effect of a practice that appears neutral but, in fact, falls more harshly on one group of people because of the group's race, sex, national origin, age, or disability and that cannot be justified by business necessity.

■═■

Albemarle Paper Co. v. Moody

Company employer (D) v. Black employee (P)

422 U.S. 405 (1975).

NATURE OF CASE: Appeal from grant of equitable relief in Title VII discrimination case.

FACT SUMMARY: A class of black employees (P) challenged Albemarle Paper's (D) policy of requiring applicants for promotion to pass two general-ability tests.

RULE OF LAW
Discriminatory employment tests are impermissible unless they are predictive of or correlated with behavior relevant to the job.

FACTS: A class of present and former black employees (P) challenged Albemarle Paper's (D) policy of requiring applicants for promotions to pass two general-ability tests. At trial, Albemarle Paper (D) presented the testimony of an industrial psychologist who had studied the job relatedness of the two tests. He found a statistically significant correlation between individuals rated by their supervisors and their scores on the tests in some job groupings. On the basis of this study, the trial court held that Albemarle Paper (D) had carried its burden of proving the tests were job related. The appellate court reversed, and Albemarle Paper (D) appealed.

ISSUE: Are discriminatory employment tests impermissible unless they are predictive of or correlated with behavior relevant to the job?

HOLDING AND DECISION: (Stewart, J.) Yes. Discriminatory employment tests are impermissible unless they are predictive of or correlated with behavior relevant to the job. The Equal Employment Opportunity Commission (EEOC) has issued guidelines for determining whether employment tests are job related. Measured against these guidelines, Albemarle Paper's (D) study was materially defective because it failed to distinguish or compare the studied job groupings. Also, it compared test scores with subjective supervisorial rankings, using criteria that were extremely vague. Furthermore, it focused only on job groups near the top of the job ladder, leaving doubt as to whether the tests were a good measure of qualifications of new workers entering lower-level jobs. Finally, the study dealt only with experienced white workers, in contrast to the applicants themselves, who were young and black. Therefore, Albemarle Paper (D) has not proved the job relatedness of its testing program. Reversed.

ANALYSIS

Some employers have attempted to preserve otherwise discriminatory tests by setting lower pass rates or cutoff points for minorities. "Norming," as this practice is called, was specifically prohibited by § 106 when Congress passed the Civil Rights Act of 1991. When a cutoff is utilized—that is, passing all who are eligible, regardless of actual score—the passing score must be set at a level of normal work expectations.

■=■

Bryant v. City of Chicago

Minority promotion candidates (P) v. City (D)

200 F.3d 1092 (7th Cir. 2000).

NATURE OF CASE: Appeal from trial court ruling in favor of the employer.

FACT SUMMARY: Forty-four African American or Latino police sergeants (P) in the Chicago Police Department (D) who failed to be promoted to lieutenant after taking the 1994 police lieutenant examination sued the city on the basis of the test's disparate impact on minorities.

🏛 RULE OF LAW
The use of a test to determine promotions within a city police department does not violate Title VII if, despite its adverse impact on African-American and Latino applicants, the test is a reasonable measure of job performance.

FACTS: The city of Chicago (D) administered a written test for candidates for promotion to lieutenant. The test questions test-takers on their knowledge of the job and measures their skills as leaders. The test was developed and administered by a psychologist and lawyer who had developed many tests for police departments. Forty-four African American or Latino police sergeants (P) in the department (D) failed to be promoted to lieutenant after taking the 1994 police lieutenant examination. Minority promotions after the examination consisted of slightly less than 6 percent of the total promotions granted. The sergeants (P) sued under Title VII disparate-impact theory, and the district court ruled in favor of the City (D).

ISSUE: Does use of a test to determine promotions within a city police department violate Title VII if, despite its adverse impact on African-American and Latino applicants, the test is a reasonable measure of job performance?

HOLDING AND DECISION: (Wood, J.) No. The use of a test to determine promotions within a city police department does not violate Title VII if, despite its adverse impact on African-American and Latino applicants, the test is a reasonable measure of job performance. The Sergeants (P) bore the initial burden of establishing a prima facie case in a Title VII disparate-impact case by showing that the promotional method in question had an adverse impact on minorities. The burden then shifted to the City (D), which had to prove that the evaluation method was valid by showing that it is "job related" and "consistent with business necessity." The evaluation method can be shown to be job related through three tests: criterion related, content validity, or construct validity. If the City (D) succeeds in validating the evaluation method, the burden shifts back to the Sergeants (P) to prove that there was another available method of evaluation that was equally valid and less discriminatory. Here, the parties agreed that the evaluation method had a disparate impact.

The City (D) chose to prove that the evaluation method was job related through the content-validity test. An expert, the psychologist and lawyer who prepared and administered the examination, testified that the examination was content valid. The testimony of a scientific expert is admissible only if it is both relevant and reliable, and the district court had wide latitude in determining wither the City's (D) expert was reliable. The City's (D) expert has extensive academic and practical experience in developing evaluations, and he had conducted studies to substantiate his opinion that the evaluation was content valid. Therefore, the trial court did not commit error in admitting his testimony. In addition, his testimony was sufficient to support a finding that the examination was job related. Since there is no claim of employer pretext in this case, the only question is whether the evaluation test is a demonstrably reasonable measure of job performance. The examination measured a significant portion of the knowledge, skills, and abilities necessary for a police lieutenant, and, therefore, was content valid. Not only was the test developed and administered by an expert, but the peer review of the test was conducted and included police of various ranks, including minority officers. Because the district court did not commit clear error in so finding, its conclusion on this point is affirmed.

▶ ANALYSIS

In October 2000, the Supreme Court denied the sergeants' petition for review. Tests that are tailored to measure applicants' abilities, the content of which is developed by an expert in the field, generally will not violate Title VII, despite disparate impact.

Quicknotes

DISPARATE IMPACT Effect of a practice that appears neutral but, in fact, falls more harshly on one group of people because of the group's race, sex, national origin, age, or disability and that cannot be justified by business necessity.

CHAPTER 4

The Interrelation of the Three Theories of Discrimination

Quick Reference Rules of Law

PAGE

1. **The Interrelation of Individual and Systemic Disparate Treatment.**   A statistical conclusion that minorities are less likely to be promoted by an employer is not sufficient evidence to support a claim under Title VII of the 1964 Civil Rights Act and the Age Discrimination in Employment Act, where there is no other evidence of discrimination. (Baylie v. FRB)   *42*

2. **Applying the Two Systemic Theories in One Case.**   Strength-testing requirements for entry-level jobs, which have a disparate impact on women, violate Title VII of the 1964 Civil Rights Act if the tests are not justified as business necessity. (EEOC v. Dial Corporation)   *43*

Baylie v. FRB

Employees (P) v. Employer (D)

476 F.3d 522 (7th Cir. 2007).

NATURE OF CASE: Appeal of summary judgment in favor of employer.

FACT SUMMARY: Two employees (P) from a disbanded class action against the Federal Reserve Bank (D) in Chicago appealed a summary judgment ruling in favor of the bank (D).

RULE OF LAW

A statistical conclusion that minorities are less likely to be promoted by an employer is not sufficient evidence to support a claim under Title VII of the 1964 Civil Rights Act and the Age Discrimination in Employment Act, where there is no other evidence of discrimination.

FACTS: Two employees (P) from a disbanded class action against the Federal Reserve Bank (D) in Chicago appealed a summary judgment ruling in favor of the bank (D). The class action originally accused the bank (D) of race, sex, and age discrimination, and the class was decertified four years ago, allowing the class members to pursue individual claims. The two remaining employees (P) presented no evidence of discrimination at trial except the statistical analysis showing that black employees were less likely to be promoted than white. The statistics were part of a report by an expert.

ISSUE: Is a statistical conclusion that minorities are less likely to be promoted by an employer sufficient evidence to support a claim under Title VII of the 1964 Civil Rights Act and the Age Discrimination in Employment Act where there is no other evidence of discrimination?

HOLDING AND DECISION: (Easterbrook, J.) No. A statistical conclusion that minorities are less likely to be promoted by an employer is not sufficient evidence to support a claim under Title VII of the 1964 Civil Rights Act and the Age Discrimination in Employment Act, where there is no other evidence of discrimination. If the employees (P) had evidence suggesting that the probability that race accounted for a given rejection was, for example, 49.8 percent, then the addition of the statistical analysis would push the probability past 50 percent. In other words, the expert's conclusion could serve as a tiebreaker. But first there would have to be a tie, and plaintiffs' evidence does not come close to making this case a tossup that statistics might decide in their favor. But the bank's (D) suggestion that statistical evidence is never relevant outside a class action or a suit by a public agency on behalf of employees is also incorrect. Professional statistics is a rigorous means to analyze large numbers of events and inquire whether what appear to be patterns really are the result of chance. A statistical analysis is more helpful in a pattern-or practice case, where a judge will be asked to direct the employer to change how it makes hiring or promotion decisions. In individual cases, studies of probabilities are less helpful.

ANALYSIS

This case represents a straightforward discussion of the role and usefulness of statistical evidence in disparate-impact cases. Statistical evidence is not evidence of bias, but may bolster an employee's case where he or she can show through additional evidence that bias exists.

Quicknotes

DISPARATE IMPACT Effect of a practice that appears neutral but, in fact, falls more harshly on one group of people because of the group's race, sex, national origin, age, or disability, and that cannot be justified by business necessity.

EEOC v. Dial Corporation

Federal agency (P) v. Corporate employer (D)

469 F.3d 735 (8th Cir. 2006).

NATURE OF CASE: Appeal by employer of jury verdict for job applicants.

FACT SUMMARY: Dial Corporation (D) implemented a strength-testing test for job applicants working at its sausage plant, which had a disparate impact on women. The Equal Employment Opportunity Commission (P) sued on behalf of the women.

🏛 RULE OF LAW

Strength-testing requirements for entry-level jobs, which have a disparate impact on women, violate Title VII of the 1964 Civil Rights Act if the tests are not justified as business necessity.

FACTS: Dial Corporation (D) implemented a test for entry-level jobs in the sausage-making department of its Iowa plant in 2000. The jobs required the repetitive lifting of a 35-pound rod of sausages to a height of approximately 65 inches above floor level. Before the test was adopted, 46 percent of the individuals hired for the job had been women. After the test was implemented, 97 percent of male applicants, but only 38 percent of female applicants, passed. The Equal Employment Opportunity Commission (P) sued on behalf of the charging party [not identified in casebook excerpt] and 53 other women who were rejected for the entry-level jobs, arguing that the test had an illegal disparate impact on women. Dial (D) responded that the test was job related and necessary to reduce the number of on-the-job injuries at the plant. The plant's job-injury rate was reduced after the test was required.

[A jury found that Dial had engaged in a pattern or practice of intentional discrimination. The judge awarded backpay and health benefits.] Dial appealed, arguing there was insufficient evidence for a jury to find intentional discrimination. It also contested the court's finding of disparate impact, and claimed that the strength test, called the Work Tolerance Screen, was a business necessity because it reduced the number of injuries in the sausage-production area of the plant.

ISSUE: Do strength-testing requirements for entry-level jobs, which have a disparate impact on women, violate Title VII of the 1964 Civil Rights Act if the tests are not justified as business necessity?

HOLDING AND DECISION: (Murphy, J.) Yes. Strength-testing requirements for entry-level jobs, which have a disparate impact on women, violate Title VII of the 1964 Civil Rights Act if the tests are not justified as business necessity. EEOC (P) successfully showed that there was a dramatic difference between the number of men and women

hired at the plant after the introduction of the strength testing, and therefore both intentional discrimination and disparate impact bias was occurring. Dial's (D) claim that the testing lowered the number of on-the-job injuries made it a business necessity was rejected. Dial's (D) physiology expert testified that the strength test was highly representative of the actions required by the job and that EEOC (P) provided no conflicting evidence, but the injury rate for women employees was lower than that for men in two of the three years before Dial (D) implemented the test. The evidence did not require the district court to find that the decrease in injuries resulted from the implementation of the test instead of the other safety mechanisms Dial (D) started to put in place in 1996. Because Dial (D) failed to show that there was a business necessity, it was Dial's (D), and not EEOC's (P), burden to establish that there was not a less discriminatory alternative to the testing, and it failed to do so.

▶ ANALYSIS

Dial is known as a case representing the overlap of systemic disparate treatment theory and disparate impact theory. What links the theories is the existence of discrimination from the effects of an employer's decisions. Discriminatory effect implies intentional bias in disparate-treatment cases, and by themselves are unlawful without a business necessity in disparate impact cases.

◼▬◼

Quicknotes

DISPARATE IMPACT Effect of a practice that appears neutral but, in fact, falls more harshly on one group of people because of the group's race, sex, national origin, age, or disability and that cannot be justified by business necessity.

DISPARATE TREATMENT Unequal treatment of employees or of applicants for employment without justification.

◼▬◼

Special Problems in Applying Title VII, Section 1981, and the ADEA

Quick Reference Rules of Law

PAGE

1. **Coverage of Title VII, Section 1981, and the ADEA.** Independent contractors cannot sue hiring parties under the Americans with Disabilities Act and Title VII of the 1964 Civil Rights Act. (Lerohl v. Friends of Minnesota Sinfonia) 47

2. **Discrimination "Because of Sex."** Workplace harassment can violate Title VII even if the harasser and harassed employee are of the same sex. (Oncale v. Sundowner Offshore Services, Inc.) 48

3. **Discrimination on the Basis of Sexual Orientation.** Title VII of the 1964 Civil Rights Act does not protect employees whose gender nonconformity is not based on workplace conduct. (Vickers v. Fairfield Medical Center) 49

4. **Grooming and Dress Codes.** Company dress codes that are not motivated by gender stereotypes, and that do not cause burdens to fall unequally on men or women, do not constitute sex discrimination, and therefore do not violate Title VII of the 1964 Civil Rights Act. (Jespersen v. Harrah's Operating Co., Inc.) 50

5. **Discrimination Because of Pregnancy.** In general, an employer cannot dismiss a pregnant employee simply because it believes her pregnancy might prevent the employee from doing her job. (Maldonado v. U.S. Bank and Manufacturers Bank) 51

6. **Discrimination Because of Pregnancy.** A state statute that requires employers to provide leave and reinstatement to employees disabled by pregnancy is not preempted by Title VII of the Civil Rights Act of 1964, as amended by the Pregnancy Discrimination Act of 1978. (California Federal Savings & Loan Association v. Guerra) 52

7. **Sexual and Other Discriminatory Harassment.** For sexual harassment to be actionable, it must be sufficiently severe or pervasive to alter the conditions of the victim's employment and create an abusive working environment. (Meritor Savings Bank v. Vinson) 54

8. **Severe or Pervasive Harassment.** Sexual harassment is not required to be psychologically injurious in order to constitute an abusive work environment. (Harris v. Forklift Systems, Inc.) 55

9. **Vicarious Liability.** Employers are subject to vicarious liability for a hostile working environment created by a supervisor with authority over a victimized employee. (Burlington Industries, Inc. v. Ellerth) 56

10. **Vicarious Liability.** Title VII of the 1964 Civil Rights Act encompasses employer liability for a constructive discharge where a plaintiff can show it was reasonable to resign because of unendurable working conditions. (Pennsylvania State Police v. Suders) 57

11. **Vicarious Liability.** An employer is not strictly liable for a supervisor's sexual harassment of an employee where the employee receives a raise and a promotion, the employer has in place a sexual harassment policy and enforces it upon learning of the sexual harassment, and the employee fails to report the misconduct promptly. (Matvia v. Bald Head Island Management, Inc.) 59

12. **Discrimination on Account of Religion.** Summary judgment in favor of an employer is proper where an employee alleging religious discrimination and failure-to-accommodate claims fails to identify his religion or otherwise provide any guidance for determining what accommodation might be necessary. (Reed v. The Great Lakes Cos., Inc.) 61

CHAPTER 5

13. Discrimination on Account of Religion.   An employer is required to "reasonably accommodate" an employee's religious beliefs or practices unless doing so would cause the employer undue hardship. (Wilson v. U.S. West Communications) — *62*

14. National Origin and Alienage Discrimination.   (1) An employer that suspends a legal immigrant employee whose documentation has raised questions, until the employee is able to produce documentation establishing his right to work in the United States, does not violate Title VII of the 1964 Civil Rights Act's ban against discrimination based on race and national origin. (2) An employer that terminates a legal immigrant employee in response to a demand by the employee for an apology after the company suspended him for failing to provide documentation indicating his right to work in the United States does not violate Title VII of the 1964 Civil Rights Act's ban against discrimination based on race and national origin. (Zamora v. Elite Logistics, Inc.) — *63*

15. Retaliation.   Summary judgment for the employer defendant in a Title VII retaliation action is appropriate where no reasonable person would believe that the action complained of violated Title VII and where the employee plaintiff fails to show the requisite causal connection between protected activities and the alleged retaliation. (Clark County School District v. Breeden) — *65*

16. Protected Conduct.   Removing documents from a boss's desk in order to send them to a former co-worker who has a potential retaliation claim against the employer is not protected activity under Title VII of the 1964 Civil Rights Act. (Laughlin v. Metropolitan Washington Airports Authority) — *66*

17. Adverse Action.   The definition of retaliation under Title VII of the 1964 Civil Rights Act includes acts that are "materially adverse" to a reasonable employee, including transfers or suspensions that do not result in a loss of pay, benefits, or privileges. (Burlington Northern & Santa Fe Railway Co. v. White) — *67*

Lerohl v. Friends of Minnesota Sinfonia

Independent contractors (P) v. Hiring party (D)

322 F.3d 486 (8th Cir. 2003).

NATURE OF CASE: Appeal of summary judgment for the hiring party.

FACT SUMMARY: Two musicians brought suit against the symphony orchestra that hired them, under the Americans with Disabilities Act (ADA) and Title VII of the 1964 Act. The symphony claimed they could seek the protection of those laws in the employment context, because they are independent contractors.

🏛 RULE OF LAW
Independent contractors cannot sue hiring parties under the Americans with Disabilities Act and Title VII of the 1964 Civil Rights Act.

FACTS: Shelley Hanson (P) and Tricia Lerohl (P) sued the Friends of the Minnesota Sinfonia (D), a nonprofit corporation that governs the Minneapolis-based symphony. Hanson (P) alleged that the Sinfonia and its conductor violated the Americans with Disabilities Act by refusing to allow her to resume playing for the group after several months' absence due to injuries she sustained during a Sinfonia rehearsal. Lerohl (P) claimed that the Sinfonia (D) and the conductor violated Title VII of the 1964 Civil Rights Act by firing her in retaliation for complaining about the conductor's sexually harassing behavior. The district court granted summary judgment against Hanson (P), on the grounds that the ADA does not apply to her dispute with the Sinfonia (D) because she was an independent contractor rather than an employee. Subsequently, a different judge of the same court granted summary judgment against Lerohl (P), concluding that she too was an independent contractor and therefore outside the scope of Title VII protection.

ISSUE: Can independent contractors sue hiring parties under the Americans with Disabilities Act and Title VII of the 1964 Civil Rights Act?

HOLDING AND DECISION: No. Independent contractors cannot sue hiring parties under the Americans with Disabilities Act and Title VII of the 1964 Civil Rights Act. Hanson (P), Lerohl (P), and EEOC (P) argued that because the conductor controlled all rehearsals and concerts, he effectively controlled all Sinfonia musicians, making them employees entitled to the protections of Title VII and the ADA. Such an approach is contrary to the Supreme Court's repeated admonition to weigh all factors and aspects of the parties' relationship. In addition, the notion that musicians are always employees when they perform in an orchestra or band is problematic on a more practical level, since work by independent contractors is often, if not typically, performed to the exacting specifications of the hiring

party. The conductor's undisputed control in selecting music to be played, scheduling Sinfonia rehearsals and concerts, and determining the manner in which the concert music was collectively played was only one factor to be considered. Whether a skilled professional in a particular case was an employee or an independent contractor ultimately depends on the freedom-of-choice principle. Here, although the Sinfonia offered inducements to preferred performers, the musicians retained control over the extent to which they committed their available professional time to the Sinfonia. Moreover, it is highly significant that the Sinfonia did not withhold income or FICA taxes, that it documented payments to the musicians on 1099s, and that it provided no employee benefits other than contributions to the union pension fund.

▶ ANALYSIS

Remember to consider the totality of the circumstances when determining whether a person qualifies as an employee for purposes of ADA, Age Discrimination in Employment Act (ADEA), or Title VII. "Freedom of choice" seems to be the main consideration, but the existence of other characteristics, such as the absence of benefits, and the use of 1099s, also play into the analysis, and can determine the outcome.

■=■

Quicknotes

AGE DISCRIMINATION IN EMPLOYMENT ACT (ADEA) (29 U.S.C. § 621) 1967 act prohibiting age discrimination and retaliation in employment.

AMERICANS WITH DISABILITIES ACT (42 U.S.C. §§ 12101-12213) Enacted in 1990, this federal law prohibits discrimination in employment against Americans with physical or mental disabilities.

INDEPENDENT CONTRACTOR A party undertaking a particular assignment for another who retains control over the manner in which it is executed.

TITLE VII OF THE CIVIL RIGHTS ACT OF 1964 Law prohibiting discrimination in employment on the basis of race, color, religion, sex, and national origin.

■=■

Oncale v. Sundowner Offshore Services, Inc.

Sexually harassed male employee (P) v. Employer (D)

523 U.S. 75 (1998).

NATURE OF CASE: Appeal from summary judgment in a sexual discrimination suit.

FACT SUMMARY: Oncale (P), a man working on an oil platform, was sexually harassed by his male co-workers.

🏛 RULE OF LAW
Workplace harassment can violate Title VII even if the harasser and harassed employee are of the same sex.

FACTS: Joseph Oncale (P) worked for Sundowner (D) on an oil platform in 1991. Three other men working with Oncale (P), including his supervisor, subjected him to sex-related, humiliating actions. Oncale (P) claimed that he was physically assaulted and threatened with rape by the other men. When his complaints were ignored, Oncale (P) quit and filed suit for sexual harassment under Title VII. The district court granted summary judgment to Sundowner (D), holding that Title VII's prohibition against discrimination based on sex did not include situations in which both the harasser and harassed employee are of the same sex. The circuit court affirmed.

ISSUE: Can workplace harassment violate Title VII if the harasser and harassed employee are of the same sex?

HOLDING AND DECISION: (Scalia, J.) Yes. Workplace harassment can violate Title VII even if the harasser and harassed employee are of the same sex. Title VII evinces a congressional intent to stop the disparate treatment of men and women in employment. Thus, when the workplace is permeated with discriminatory intimidation and ridicule based on sex, the resulting abusive working environment is illegal. Nothing in Title VII indicates that the sex of the harasser or the harassed is relevant to the determination of whether there is an abusive work environment. Same-sex harassment may not have been the principal evil that Congress was concerned with stopping with Title VII, but its language suggests that it is still covered. The Court also rejects the view of other circuits that same-sex harassment claims are actionable only when plaintiff proves the harasser was motivated by sexual desire. The only relevant issue is whether the plaintiff can show that the behavior was based on sex and was so objectively offensive that it altered the conditions of his employment. Reversed.

▶ ANALYSIS

This decision clearly allows for sexual harassment claims in which the harasser is homosexual. However, it also goes further, removing the necessity for proving that the

harassment was based upon some sort of physical attraction. Still, cases of same-sex harassment in which the plaintiff is offended by the overt sexual conduct of a heterosexual harasser remain a gray area of the law.

■═■

Quicknotes

DISCRIMINATION Unequal treatment of a class of persons.

HARASSMENT Conduct directed at a particular person with the intent to inflict emotional distress and with no justification therefor; a criminal prosecution commenced without a reasonable expectation of its resulting in a conviction.

TITLE VII OF THE CIVIL RIGHTS ACT OF 1964 Law prohibiting discrimination in employment on the basis of race, color, religion, sex, and national origin.

■═■

Vickers v. Fairfield Medical Center

Employee (P) v. Employer (D)

453 F.3d 757 (6th Cir. 2006).

NATURE OF CASE: Appeal from summary judgment for employer.

FACT SUMMARY: Christopher Vickers (P), a private police officer, brought a claim against his employer, Fairfield Medical Center, alleging sex discrimination, sexual harassment, and retaliation under Title VII of the 1964 Civil Rights Act when he was taunted and harassed because co-workers believed he was gay.

🏛 RULE OF LAW
Title VII of the 1964 Civil Rights Act does not protect employees whose gender nonconformity is not based on workplace conduct.

FACTS: Vickers (P) was a private police officer for Fairfield Medical Center (D). While working at the hospital (D), he befriended a male doctor who was gay and assisted the doctor in an investigation. Vickers (P) claimed that when co-workers learned about his friendship with the doctor, they began making sexually based slurs, questioned his masculinity, and alleged he was gay. After Vickers (P) returned from a vacation with a male friend, the taunts allegedly escalated. Despite the alleged taunting, Vickers (P) claimed that the hospital's (D) police chief did not attempt to stop the behavior but instead frequently joined in the alleged harassment. Vickers (P) claimed that he considered reporting the harassment, but his supervisor told him reporting it would be futile. Ultimately, he contacted an attorney who initiated conversations with the hospital. After an investigation, the hospital (D) found there was no claim, although the officers involved did receive some suspensions. Vickers (P) attempted to change shifts, but his request was denied. He resigned after facing disciplinary action he believed was initiated in retaliation for the complaint. The U.S. District Court for the Southern District of Ohio granted summary judgment for the hospital (D), finding there was no Title VII claim.

ISSUE: Does Title VII of the 1964 Civil Rights Act protect employees whose gender nonconformity is not based on workplace conduct?

HOLDING AND DECISION: (Gibbons, J.) No. Title VII of the 1964 Civil Rights Act does not protect employees whose gender nonconformity is not based on workplace conduct. Vickers (P) failed to claim that he did not conform to traditional gender stereotypes in any observable way at work, and therefore did not allege a claim of sex stereotyping. Sexual orientation is not a prohibited basis for discriminatory acts under Title VII, and sexual orientation is irrelevant for purposes of Title VII, neither providing nor precluding a cause of action for sexual harassment, sex discrimination, or sex stereotyping. But Vickers (P) tries to argue that his sex stereotyping theory is supported a perception of homosexuality, an argument that is rejected because the theory of sex stereotyping is not broad enough to encompass such a claim. The harassment Vickers (P) complains of is more properly viewed as harassment based on Vickers's (P) perceived homosexuality, rather than on gender nonconformity. Vickers's claim does not fail merely because he was classified by his co-workers as a homosexual, but because he failed to allege that he did not conform to traditional gender stereotypes in any observable way at work.

DISSENT: (Lawson, J.) More thorough examination of the allegations by the court or a jury was necessary, given the complicated distinctions between gender conformity and sex discrimination. Drawing a line at the pleading stage of the lawsuit is inappropriate. According to the allegations, there was a basis for inferring that Vickers (P) was perceived as effeminate, and therefore could not be considered worthy of being thought of as a "real officer." That could lead to the conclusion that he was not tolerated because the job required only "manly men." Because he was perceived as gay, Vickers (P) failed to live up to these expectations. Thus the sex stereotyping theory should go forward.

▶ ANALYSIS

This decision was a two-to-one decision by the Sixth Circuit, and in the opinion, the majority grappled with another Sixth Circuit decision, *Smith v. City of Salem*, 378 F.3d 566 (6th Cir. 2004), which permitted a transgender firefighter to bring a claim under Title VII because transgenders challenge gender conformity. An en banc review of Vickers's case may be sought, given a split decision in the case and conflicting rulings in other Title VII cases within the Sixth Circuit.

▬▬◼

Quicknotes

DISCRIMINATION Unequal treatment of a class of persons.

HARASSMENT Conduct directed at a particular person with the intent to inflict emotional distress and with no justification therefor; a criminal prosecution commenced without a reasonable expectation of its resulting in a conviction.

TITLE VII OF THE CIVIL RIGHTS ACT OF 1964 Law prohibiting discrimination in employment on the basis of race, color, religion, sex, and national origin.

▬▬◼

Jespersen v. Harrah's Operating Co., Inc.

Employee (P) v. Employer (D)

444 F.3d 1104 (9th Cir. 2006) (en banc).

NATURE OF CASE: Appeal of dismissal of employee's sex-discrimination claim.

FACT SUMMARY: Darlene Jespersen (P) argued that the new makeup policy at the Harrah's Casino (D) in Reno, Nev., where she worked for 20 years, discriminates against women by subjecting them to job terms to which men are not subjected and requiring them to conform to gender stereotypes as a condition of employment. She brought suit against Harrah's (D) charging unequal burdens and sex stereotyping.

🏛 RULE OF LAW
Company dress codes that are not motivated by gender stereotypes, and that do not cause burdens to fall unequally on men or women, do not constitute sex discrimination, and therefore do not violate Title VII of the 1964 Civil Rights Act.

FACTS: Harrah's (D) had maintained a company policy that encouraged female bartenders to wear makeup throughout Darlene Jespersen's (P) 20-year tenure with the company. But it did not enforce the rule until 2000. That year, as a part of a new "Beverage Department Image Transformation" program implemented at 20 of its locations, including Reno, Harrah's (D) adopted a "Personal Best" program, which set new grooming and appearance standards. Under the program, male and female servers are required to wear black pants, a white shirt, a black vest, and a black bow tie. In addition, male servers are prohibited from wearing makeup, and must wear their hair above the collar, while female servers are required to wear makeup, and must "tease, curl, or style" their hair. The program's stated purpose is to ensure that beverage servers are "appealing to the eye," "firm and body toned," and "comfortable with maintaining this look while wearing the specified uniform." Jespersen (P) had no problem with the gender-neutral uniform requirements, but she did have a problem with the makeup rule. She did not wear it on or off the job, she said, and wearing it would conflict with her self-image. The trial court granted summary judgment to Harrah's (D). A split panel of the U.S. Court of Appeals affirmed on slightly different grounds (392 F.3d 1076 (9th Cir. 2004)).

ISSUE: Do company dress codes that are not motivated by gender stereotypes, and that do not cause burdens to fall unequally on men or women, constitute sex discrimination, and therefore violate Title VII of the 1964 Civil Rights Act?

HOLDING AND DECISION: (Schroeder, C.J.) No. Company dress codes that are not motivated by gender stereotypes, and that do not cause burdens to fall unequally

on men or women, do not constitute sex discrimination, and therefore do not violate Title VII of the 1964 Civil Rights Act. In this case, there was no evidence showing that complying with the "Personal Best" standards caused burdens to fall unequally on men or women, and there was no evidence to suggest Harrah's (D) motivation was to stereotype the women bartenders. Jespersen (P) relied solely on evidence that she had been a good bartender, and that she had personal objections to complying with the policy, in order to support her argument that Harrah's (D) "sells" and "exploits" its women employees. That is insufficient to survive summary judgment under Title VII of the 1964 Civil Rights Act. But the panel majority's holding that *Price Waterhouse v. Hopkins*, 490 U.S. 228 (1989) excluded grooming and appearance standards from the reach of the sex-stereotyping theory except where they amount to sexual harassment for failure to conform to commonly-held gender stereotypes is incorrect. Such a claim is viable outside of the harassment context, but Jespersen (P) did not come forward with enough proof to allow a jury to find in her favor. Affirmed.

▶ ANALYSIS

The court leaves open the possibility of a successful sex-stereotyping claim. The opinion states that had she put forth sufficient evidence, Jespersen might succeed on such a claim, since the *Price Waterhouse* precedent did not exclude grooming and appearance standards, as the panel majority held.

■=■

Quicknotes

DISCRIMINATION Unequal treatment of a class of persons.

TITLE VII OF THE CIVIL RIGHTS ACT OF 1964 Law prohibiting discrimination in employment on the basis of race, color, religion, sex, and national origin.

■=■

Maldonado v. U.S. Bank and Manufacturers Bank

Discharged pregnant employee (P) v. Employer (D)

186 F.3d 759 (7th Cir. 1999).

NATURE OF CASE: Appeal of summary judgment for the employer.

FACT SUMMARY: Jessica Maldonado (P) was fired the day after she told her supervisor that she was pregnant. Maldonado (P) sued, alleging sex discrimination in violation of the Pregnancy Discrimination Act. The district court granted U.S. Bank's (D) motion for summary judgment. Maldonado (P) appealed.

RULE OF LAW
In general, an employer cannot dismiss a pregnant employee simply because it believes her pregnancy might prevent the employee from doing her job.

FACTS: Jessica Maldonado (P) applied for a position as a part-time teller with U.S. Bank (D). She understood that the hiring supervisor had a particular need for part-timers during the peak summer months. Three days after she was interviewed, she learned she was pregnant and that the baby was due in July. She was offered the job, and while still in training, she told her supervisor that she was pregnant. The next day, she was fired. Maldonado (P) sued, alleging sex discrimination in violation of the Pregnancy Discrimination Act. The district court granted U.S. Bank's (D) motion for summary judgment. Maldonado (P) appealed.

ISSUE: In general, can an employer dismiss a pregnant employee simply because it believes her pregnancy might prevent the employee from doing her job?

HOLDING AND DECISION: (Cudahy, J.) No. In general, an employer cannot dismiss a pregnant employee simply because it believes her pregnancy might prevent the employee from doing her job. Title VII makes it unlawful to discriminate against any individual because of the individual's sex, and in 1978, Congress amended Title VII to extend protection to pregnant women. The PDA specifically addresses the stereotype that women are less desirable employees because they are liable to become pregnant. An unlawful employment practice occurs whenever pregnancy is a motivating factor for an adverse employment decision. The Bank (D) probably did not have a good faith basis in the spring to believe that Maldonado's (P) pregnancy would result in her unavailability during the summer. Maldonado (P) did not ask for leave or request other kind of special treatment. If the Bank (D) did have a good faith basis in the spring to believe that her pregnancy would result in a need for special treatment, its actions may have fallen under a narrow exception in the PDA that allows the employer to take adverse action against a pregnant employee. But given that the evidence must be viewed in light most favorable to Maldonado (P) on U.S. Bank's (D) motion for summary judgment, the district court's ruling must be reversed.

ANALYSIS

This case makes clear that there are circumstances under which it is permissible for an employer to consider an employee's pregnancy when making employment decisions. The employer need not have an actual request for special treatment by the pregnant employee, but may take adverse employment action on the basis of a good faith belief, based on sufficient evidence, that special treatment will be required.

Quicknotes

PREGNANCY DISCRIMINATION ACT Provides that discrimination "on the basis of sex" includes discrimination "because of or on the basis of pregnancy, childbirth or related conditions."

TITLE VII OF THE CIVIL RIGHTS ACT OF 1964 Law prohibiting discrimination in employment on the basis of race, color, religion, sex, and national origin.

California Federal Savings & Loan Association v. Guerra

Employer (P) v. Government commission (D)

479 U.S. 272 (1987).

NATURE OF CASE: Appeal from reversal of grant of plaintiff's summary judgment to enjoin enforcement of a state pregnancy-leave statute.

FACT SUMMARY: After one of its employees filed a complaint upon being told that neither her job nor any similar job was available at the end of her pregnancy leave, California Federal (Cal Fed) (P) brought this action, seeking a declaration that California law requiring reinstatement was inconsistent with and preempted by Title VII and an order enjoining enforcement of the statute.

RULE OF LAW

A state statute that requires employers to provide leave and reinstatement to employees disabled by pregnancy is not preempted by Title VII of the Civil Rights Act of 1964, as amended by the Pregnancy Discrimination Act of 1978.

FACTS: Section 12945(b)(2) of California's Fair Employment and Housing Act (FEHA) required employers subject to Title VII to provide female employees an unpaid pregnancy disability leave of up to four months. The Fair Employment and Housing Commission (FEHC) (D) construed that section to require California employers to reinstate an employee returning from such pregnancy leave to the job she previously held, unless it was no longer available due to business necessity. In *General Electric Co. v. Gilbert*, 429 U.S. 125 (1976), the Supreme Court ruled that discrimination on the basis of pregnancy was not sex discrimination under Title VII. In response to that decision, Congress passed the Pregnancy Discrimination Act of 1978 (PDA), which specified that sex discrimination included discrimination on the basis of pregnancy. Cal Fed (P) had a policy of allowing employees to take unpaid leaves for pregnancy, but expressly reserved the right to terminate an employee who had taken a leave of absence if a similar position was not available. When Lillian Garland notified her employer, Cal Fed (P), that she was able to return to work after having taken a pregnancy disability leave, she was informed that her job had been filled and that there were no receptionist or similar positions available. She then filed a complaint with Guerra (D), the FEHC (D) head. Prior to a scheduled hearing before the FEHC (D), Cal Fed (P) brought this action, seeking a declaration that § 12945(b)(2) was inconsistent with and preempted by Title VII and an injunction against enforcement of the section. The district court granted Cal Fed's (P) motion for summary judgment, holding that the state law was preempted by Title VII and was null, void, invalid, and inoperative under the Supremacy Clause of the Constitution. The court of appeals reversed. Cal Fed (P) appealed.

ISSUE: Is a state statute that requires employers to provide leave and reinstatement to employees disabled by pregnancy preempted by Title VII of the Civil Rights Act of 1964, as amended by the Pregnancy Discrimination Act of 1978?

HOLDING AND DECISION: (Marshall, J.) No. A state statute that requires employers to provide leave and reinstatement to employees disabled by pregnancy is not preempted by Title VII of the Civil Rights Act of 1964, as amended by the Pregnancy Discrimination Act of 1978. Congress has explicitly disclaimed any intent categorically to preempt state law or to "occupy the field" of employment discrimination law. Federal law may nonetheless preempt state law to the extent it actually conflicts with federal law. Such is the basis for the preemption at issue here. The narrow scope of preemption available under two sections of the 1964 Civil Rights Act reflects the importance Congress attached to state antidiscrimination laws in achieving Title VII's goal of equal employment opportunity. The legislative history of the Pregnancy Discrimination Act also supports a narrow interpretation of these provisions. Title VII, as amended by the Pregnancy Discrimination Act, and California's pregnancy disability leave statute share a common goal. Rather than limiting existing Title VII principles and objectives, the Pregnancy Discrimination Act extends them to cover pregnancy. By taking pregnancy into account, California's pregnancy disability leave statute allows women, as well as men, to have families without losing their jobs. The statute is narrowly drawn to cover only the period of actual physical disability on account of pregnancy, childbirth, and related medical conditions. Employers are free to give comparable benefits to other disabled employees, thereby treating women affected by pregnancy no better than other persons not so affected but similar in their ability or inability to work. Indeed, at oral argument, Cal Fed (P) conceded that compliance with both statutes is theoretically possible. Affirmed.

ANALYSIS

The Court noted that Senator Williams, a sponsor of the PDA, stated that the entire thrust behind that legislation was to guarantee women the basic right to participate fully and equally in the workforce, without denying them the fundamental right to full participation in family life. Congress had before it extensive evidence of discrimination against pregnancy, particularly in disability and health-insurance programs. In contrast to the thorough account of discrimination against pregnant workers, the legislative

Continued on next page.

history contained no discussion of preferential treatment of pregnancy, beyond acknowledgments of the existence of state statutes providing for such preferential treatment. It would thus seem fair to conclude that Congress did not intend this area to be preempted.

■═■

Quicknotes

PREEMPTION Doctrine holding that matters of national interest take precedence over matters of local interest; the federal law takes precedence over state law.

PREGNANCY DISCRIMINATION ACT Provides that discrimination "on the basis of sex" includes discrimination "because of or on the basis of pregnancy, childbirth or related conditions."

TITLE VII OF THE CIVIL RIGHTS ACT OF 1964 Law prohibiting discrimination in employment on the basis of race, color, religion, sex, and national origin.

■═■

Meritor Savings Bank v. Vinson

Employer (D) v. Discharged employee (P)

477 U.S. 57 (1986).

NATURE OF CASE: Appeal from reversal of the denial of relief in an action for sexual harassment.

FACT SUMMARY: After Vinson (P) was discharged by Meritor Bank (D) for taking excessive sick leave, she filed suit alleging that Taylor (D), manager of the branch where Vinson (P) was employed, had subjected her to sexual harassment during the entire four years of her employment.

🏛 RULE OF LAW
For sexual harassment to be actionable, it must be sufficiently severe or pervasive to alter the conditions of the victim's employment and create an abusive working environment.

FACTS: Vinson (P), hired as a trainee for Meritor Savings Bank (D), later became an assistant branch manager. Her advancement was based on merit alone. After Vinson (P) was discharged for excessive use of sick leave, she filed suit alleging that Taylor (D), manager of her branch, had sexually harassed her during the four years of her employment. Vinson (P) testified that out of fear of losing her job she eventually agreed to Taylor's (D) suggestion that they have sexual relations. She also testified that Taylor (D) fondled her in front of other employees and even forcibly raped her on several occasions. Taylor (D) denied the allegations. The district court denied relief, holding that any sexual relationship was voluntary. The court of appeals reversed and remanded, finding that unwelcome sexual advances violated Title VII. The Bank (D) appealed.

ISSUE: For sexual harassment to be actionable, must it be sufficiently severe or pervasive to alter the conditions of the victim's employment and create an abusive working environment?

HOLDING AND DECISION: (Rehnquist, J.) Yes. For sexual harassment to be actionable, it must be sufficiently severe or pervasive to alter the conditions of the victim's employment and create an abusive working environment. Vinson's (P) allegations in this case, which include not only pervasive harassment but also criminal conduct of the most serious nature, sufficiently state a claim for hostile environment sexual harassment. The fact that sex-related conduct was voluntary is not a defense to a sexual harassment suit brought under Title VII since the gravamen of such a claim is that the alleged sexual advances were unwelcome. Moreover, the prohibition against sexual harassment is not limited to discrimination that causes economic or tangible injury. Equal Employment Opportunity Commission (EEOC) guidelines fully support the view that harassment leading to non-economic injury can violate Title VII. Reversed and remanded.

▶ ANALYSIS

The court of appeals had stated that testimony about Vinson's (P) dress and personal fantasies, which the district court had admitted into evidence, had no place in this litigation. To the contrary, declared the Supreme Court, such evidence is obviously relevant, and the district court must determine the existence of sexual harassment in light of the record as a whole. While the district court must carefully weigh the applicable considerations in deciding whether to admit such evidence, there is no per se rule against its admissibility.

■═■

Quicknotes

HARASSMENT Conduct directed at a particular person with the intent to inflict emotional distress and with no justification therefor; a criminal prosecution commenced without a reasonable expectation of its resulting in a conviction.

TITLE VII OF THE CIVIL RIGHTS ACT OF 1964 Law prohibiting discrimination in employment on the basis of race, color, religion, sex, and national origin.

■═■

Harris v. Forklift Systems, Inc.

Sexually harassed employee (P) v. Employer (D)

510 U.S. 17 (1993).

NATURE OF CASE: Appeal from defense judgment in a Title VII action for sex discrimination.

FACT SUMMARY: Harris (P), a female employee of Forklift (D), brought a Title VII sex discrimination action based upon the offensive comments made by Hardy, Forklift's (D) president.

🏛 RULE OF LAW
Sexual harassment is not required to be psychologically injurious in order to constitute an abusive work environment.

FACTS: Teresa Harris (P) worked as a manager at Forklift (D) from 1985 until 1987. Throughout her employment, Hardy, the president of Forklift (D), insulted Harris (P) because of her sex and made her the target of unwanted sexual innuendos. In 1987, Harris (P) complained to Hardy about his conduct, and Hardy promised to stop. However, a short time later Hardy made another offensive comment to Harris (P) in front of other employees, and Harris (P) quit. Harris (P) then brought a Title VII action claiming that Hardy's conduct had created an abusive work environment because of her sex. The trial court held that Hardy's conduct did not create an abusive environment since it was not so severe as to be expected to seriously affect Harris's (P) psychological well-being. The court of appeals affirmed, and Harris (P) appealed.

ISSUE: Does sexual harassment have to be psychologically injurious in order to constitute an abusive work environment?

HOLDING AND DECISION: (O'Connor, J.) No. Sexual harassment is not required to be psychologically injurious in order to constitute an abusive work environment. Title VII makes it unlawful to discriminate against an employee on the basis of sex. Congress intended to prohibit all disparate treatment of men and women in employment practices, including the work environment. Thus, Title VII is violated when a workplace is permeated with discriminatory intimidation and ridicule that is sufficiently pervasive so as to alter the condition of the victim's working environment. Mere offensive comments are not sufficient to affect the conditions of employment. Harassing conduct, which both objectively and subjectively is so severe and pervasive as to create an abusive environment, is required to implicate Title VII protections. This level of harassment may be determined by looking at all the circumstances, including the frequency of the conduct, its severity, and whether it interferes with an employee's work performance. Psychological injury to the employee is not required. The district court erred in concluding that Harris's (P) working environment was not abusive because she did not suffer any psychological injury. Reversed.

▶ ANALYSIS

Justice Ginsburg concurred in the decision, writing separately to make clear that an employee should not be required to prove that her productivity declined as a result of the harassment. Prior to this decision, other courts had been urged to adopt a reasonable woman standard as opposed to a reasonable person standard for sexual harassment cases. This decision states that the harassment must be objectively abusive to a reasonable person and also subjectively abusive to the victim.

Quicknotes

HARASSMENT Conduct directed at a particular person with the intent to inflict emotional distress and with no justification therefor; a criminal prosecution commenced without a reasonable expectation of its resulting in a conviction.

REASONABLE PERSON STANDARD The standard of case exercised by one who possesses the intelligence, education, knowledge, attention, and judgment required by society of its members when governing behavior; the standard applies to a person's judgment when determining breach of a duty under the theory of negligence.

TITLE VII OF THE CIVIL RIGHTS ACT OF 1964 Law prohibiting discrimination in employment on the basis of race, color, religion, sex, and national origin.

Burlington Industries, Inc. v. Ellerth

Employer (D) v. Sexually harassed employee (P)

524 U.S. 742 (1998).

NATURE OF CASE: Appeal from summary judgment in a sexual harassment suit.

FACT SUMMARY: Ellerth (P) claimed that she was subjected to unwanted sexual advances by her supervisor but Burlington (D) claimed that she suffered no consequences for declining.

🏛 RULE OF LAW
Employers are subject to vicarious liability for a hostile working environment created by a supervisor with authority over a victimized employee.

FACTS: Kimberly Ellerth (P) worked as a salesperson for Burlington (D) in Chicago. She claimed that Ted Slowik, her supervisor, made many offensive comments to her during her employment and after making remarks about her breasts said that he could help or hurt her at the company. She did not inform any other Burlington (D) managers about Slowik's behavior. When the harassment continued, Ellerth (P) quit and filed suit. The district court granted summary judgment to Burlington (D), holding that there was a hostile work environment but Burlington (D) did not know of it. The court of appeals reversed, but there were eight separate opinions and no consensus for a rationale.

ISSUE: Are employers subject to vicarious liability for a hostile working environment created by a supervisor with authority over a victimized employee?

HOLDING AND DECISION: (Kennedy, J.) Yes. Employers are subject to vicarious liability for a hostile working environment created by a supervisor with authority over a victimized employee. Title VII harassment claims may include allegations that employment threats were carried out for declining sexual advances, or if there are no employment consequences, if the work environment becomes hostile and abusive. In the present case, it appears that there were no threats carried out against Ellerth (P) so the liability of Burlington (D) must be analyzed under the hostile-work-environment scheme. Under general agency principles, a master is subject to liability for the torts of the servant committed while acting in the scope of their employment. However, sexual harassment by a supervisor can not be considered conduct within the scope of employment. Additional agency principles allow for vicarious liability of employers for acts committed outside the scope of employment. These include apparent authority and the misuse of delegated authority. Thus, when a supervisor takes an employment action, the employer is subject to vicarious liability for these actions. However, as in the instant case, where no tangible employment action has been taken against a harassed

employee, the employer may raise an affirmative defense showing that reasonable care was taken to prevent and correct harassing behavior and that the employee failed to take any preventive or corrective opportunities provided. Since Ellerth (P) was relying on past case law suggesting that vicarious liability was only available for quid pro quo claims, she should have an opportunity to amend her claim and Burlington (D) should have the chance to prove its affirmative defense. Reversed and remanded.

▶ ANALYSIS

The Court here attempted to clarify the increasingly confusing law surrounding employer liability for harassment. Until 1991, damages were not available to victims of hostile work environment. Only injunctive relief was an option before Title VII was amended.

■━■

Quicknotes

HARASSMENT Conduct directed at a particular person with the intent to inflict emotional distress and with no justification therefor; a criminal prosecution commenced without a reasonable expectation of its resulting in a conviction.

■━■

Pennsylvania State Police v. Suders

Public employer (D) v. Employee (P)

542 U.S. 129 (2004).

NATURE OF CASE: Appeal of appeals court judgment in favor of employee.

FACT SUMMARY: Nancy Drew Suders (P) was a communications officer at a state police barracks. She filed a sexual harassment and constructive discharge lawsuit under Title VII of the 1964 Civil Rights Act against three supervisors and the barracks. The district court ruled in favor of the police (D), and the U.S. Court of Appeals for the Third Circuit reversed and remanded.

🏛 RULE OF LAW
Title VII of the 1964 Civil Rights Act encompasses employer liability for a constructive discharge where a plaintiff can show it was reasonable to resign because of unendurable working conditions.

FACTS: Nancy Drew Suders (P) worked as a communications officer at a Pennsylvania police barracks (D). She claimed that three supervisors (D) subjected her to continuous sexual harassment by repeatedly talking about sex with animals, grabbing their genitals, and making other comments and gestures. In June 1998, one of the supervisors (D) accused her of taking a missing accident file home with her. After the incident, Suders (P) said she approached an equal employment opportunity officer and told her she "might need some help." The officer gave Suders (P) her telephone number, but neither woman followed up on the conversation. In August 1998, Suders (P) again contacted the EEO officer, saying that she was being harassed and was afraid. The officer told Suders (P) to file a complaint but did not tell her how to obtain the necessary form. Two days later, Suders's (P) supervisors (D) arrested her for theft and she resigned from the force. The arrest came about after Suders (P) discovered hidden in the women's locker room exams she had taken to satisfy a state police job requirement. Her supervisors (D) had told her she failed the exams, but when she found them in the drawer, she concluded that the exams had never been graded. She took them because she considered the tests to be her property. When the supervisors (D) discovered the tests were missing, they dusted the drawer with a theft-detection powder that turns hands blue when touched. When Suders (P) attempted to return the tests, her hands turned blue. The supervisors (D) apprehended her, handcuffed her, photographed her, and brought her to an interrogation room and gave her her Miranda rights. Suders (P) resigned, and the theft charges were never brought against her. Suders (P) sued, arguing that she was subjected to sexual harassment and constructively discharged in violation of Title VII. The district court granted the state's (D) motion for summary judgment, finding that although Suders (P) established an actionable hostile environment, the employer (D)

effectively defended itself by asserting the *Ellerth/Faragher* defense and showing that Suders (P) never gave the employer (D) the chance to respond to her complaints. The Court of Appeals for the Third Circuit reversed and remanded the case, finding that Suders (P) demonstrated that the supervisors (D) had engaged in a pervasive pattern of sexual harassment. It also held that a constructive discharge, when proved, constitutes a tangible job action that precludes the employer from asserting the *Ellerth/Faragher* defense.

ISSUE: Does Title VII of the 1964 Civil Rights Act encompass employer liability for a constructive discharge where a plaintiff can show it was reasonable to resign because of unendurable working conditions?

HOLDING AND DECISION: (Ginsberg, J.) Yes. Title VII of the 1964 Civil Rights Act encompasses employer liability for a constructive discharge where a plaintiff can show it was reasonable to resign because of unendurable working conditions. The result for plaintiffs asserting constructive discharge is that a prevailing plaintiff is entitled to all the remedies available for a formal discharge. The plaintiff may recover post-resignation damages, including both backpay and, in fitting circumstances, front-pay, as well as the compensatory and punitive damages now provided for Title VII claims generally. To establish constructive discharge, the plaintiff would have to show that the abusive working environment became so intolerable that her resignation qualified as a fitting response. However, under the *Ellerth/Faragher* defense, when no tangible job action has been taken against a plaintiff, an employer can escape liability for a supervisor's sexual harassment by showing that it exercised reasonable care to prevent and promptly correct sexually harassing behavior, and that the plaintiff unreasonably failed to take advantage of any preventive or corrective opportunities to avoid harm. Therefore, unless Suders (P) can show the resignation was prompted by an official adverse job action, the employer (D) can avoid vicarious liability for the supervisors' acts by showing that it had in place a complaint system that Suders (P) unreasonably failed to use before quitting. The constructive discharge in and of itself does not count as an official adverse act. Reversed and remanded.

▶ ANALYSIS

By sending Suders's (P) case against the state police back to the Court of Appeals for the Third Circuit, the Supreme Court recognized for the first time that a constructive discharge claim could give rise to Title VII liability. The ruling overturns the Third Circuit's decision that a constructive

Continued on next page.

discharge, if proven, could establish a tangible job action, thus preventing the employer from asserting the *Ellerth/ Faragher* defense.

■■■

Quicknotes

HARASSMENT Conduct directed at a particular person with the intent to inflict emotional distress and with no justification therefor; a criminal prosecution commenced without a reasonable expectation of its resulting in a conviction.

TITLE VII OF THE CIVIL RIGHTS ACT OF 1964 Law prohibiting discrimination in employment on the basis of race, color, religion, sex, and national origin.

■■■

Matvia v. Bald Head Island Management, Inc.

Female employee (P) v. Employer (D)

259 F.3d 261 (4th Cir. 2001).

NATURE OF CASE: Appeal from summary judgment for employer in sexual harassment/hostile work environment action.

FACT SUMMARY: Matvia's (P) supervisor was terminated for making unwanted sexual advances toward her. Afterward, co-workers and managers ostracized her.

RULE OF LAW
An employer is not strictly liable for a supervisor's sexual harassment of an employee where the employee receives a raise and a promotion, the employer has in place a sexual harassment policy and enforces it upon learning of the sexual harassment, and the employee fails to report the misconduct promptly.

FACTS: Matvia's (P) supervisor, Terbush, at Bald Head Island Management, Inc. (BHIM) (D) made unwanted advances toward her and was terminated for sexual harassment after he forcibly attempted to kiss her. BHIM (D) had in place a policy against sexual harassment that encouraged employees to report improper behavior to their supervisor, personnel department, or the chief operating officer. According to Matvia (P), after Terbush's termination, co-workers and managers ostracized her. Matvia (P) brought a Title VII hostile environment claim, and the district court granted summary judgment to BHIM (D) in light of the affirmative defense that allows an employer to avoid strict liability for a supervisor's sexual harassment if no tangible action was taken against the employee and the employer can show that the employer exercised reasonable care to prevent and correct promptly any harassing behavior and that the employee unreasonably failed to take advantage of any preventative or corrective opportunities provided by the employer or to otherwise avoid harm. The circuit court granted review.

ISSUE: Is an employer strictly liable for a supervisor's sexual harassment of an employee where the employee receives a raise and a promotion, the employer has in place a sexual harassment policy and enforces it upon learning of the sexual harassment, and the employee fails to report the misconduct promptly?

HOLDING AND DECISION: (Traxler, J.) No. An employer is not strictly liable for a supervisor's sexual harassment of an employee where the employee receives a raise and a promotion, the employer has in place a sexual harassment policy and enforces it upon learning of the sexual harassment, and the employee fails to report the misconduct promptly. To prevail on a Title VII hostile work environment claim, Matvia (P) must establish as one of its elements some basis for imputing liability to BHIM (D). It was on this element that the district court granted summary judgment in light of

the affirmative defense available to BHIM (D). Reviewing the elements of the affirmative defense leads to the conclusion that there was no "tangible employment action" against Matvia (P) such as being discharged, demoted, or reassigned. In fact, during her tenure at BHIM (D), she received a raise, a promotion, and good evaluations. There was no evidence that she received these benefits in exchange for acquiescing in Terbush's advances through "silent suffering." These were the result of her taking on more responsibilities. Accordingly, the raise and promotion did not amount to tangible employment action, nor did the satisfactory evaluations, which were not given in exchange for sexual favors. Accordingly, BHIM (D) was entitled to raise its affirmative defense. As to the first prong of the affirmative defense (reasonable care to prevent and correct sexual harassment), the evidence does not show that BHIM's (D) prevention program was ineffective. The only evidence adduced by Matvia (P) that the program was deficient was that some employees had difficulty recalling the details of their orientation briefings. This alone does not mean that the policy was unclear or that the employees did not understand it, and the evidence showed that the employees were aware of the policy and knew to which company official to report harassment. As for correcting sexually harassing behavior, BHIM (D) first suspended Terbush upon learning of his misconduct, and twelve days later, after a complete investigation, fired him. This was prompt action. Matvia's (P) focus on the ostracism and uncivility exhibited toward her by her co-workers after Terbush's termination is misplaced, because after his attempted kiss, she suffered no more sexual harassment. Therefore, BHIM's (D) response to the ostracism is irrelevant to this prong of the affirmative defense. As to the second prong of the affirmative defense (unreasonable failure by the employee to take advantage of preventative or corrective opportunities), the evidence indicates that Matvia's (P) response was unreasonable. Matvia's (P) claim that she needed time to collect evidence against Terbush so company officials would believe her is rejected because case law makes clear that a victim of sexual harassment must report the misconduct, not investigate and gather evidence. In addition, Matvia's (P) refraining from reporting Terbush so she could determine whether Terbush was a "predator" or just an "interested man" is unavailing because the law does not make a distinction based on these categories. So long as the conduct is unwelcome, based on the employee's gender, and sufficiently pervasive or severe, the employee must report it. Here, Terbush's conduct fit these conditions, so Matvia (P) cannot be excused from failing to report this conduct. Fearing retaliation from co-workers, as Matvia (P) claimed she did, also does not excuse her duty to report sexual

Continued on next page.

harassment, especially because the reporting requirement is essential to sexual harassment law. Finally, because Terbush's advances began in September 1997 and ended on December 15, 1997, and because BHIM (D) did not learn about them until December 16, 1997, the only way to assess whether Matvia (P) failed to take advantage of preventative or corrective opportunities is to examine her actions from the time the unwelcome conduct began. Letting a plaintiff pick the time the harassment began for purposes of the affirmative defense only, would "make a mockery of this inquiry" and would violate the basic tenets of fairness. Accordingly, BHIM (D) also established the second prong of its affirmative defense. Affirmed.

▶ *ANALYSIS*

Matvia's (P) theory of "silent suffering" would transform any ordinary employment action into tangible employment action and would render summary judgment for an employer an impossibility. Under this theory, any non-adverse, mundane employment action, such as granting sick leave or upgrading an employee's equipment, would constitute tangible employment action and deprive the employer of the affirmative defense. Of course, when a supervisor guilty of sexual harassment does bestow benefits in exchange for an employee's silence, denial of summary judgment for the employer is the desired outcome.

■═■

Quicknotes

AFFIRMATIVE DEFENSE A manner of defending oneself against a claim not by denying the truth of the charge, but by the introduction of some evidence challenging the plaintiff's right to bring the claim.

HARASSMENT Conduct directed at a particular person with the intent to inflict emotional distress and with no justification therefor; a criminal prosecution commenced without a reasonable expectation of its resulting in a conviction.

TITLE VII OF THE CIVIL RIGHTS ACT OF 1964 Law prohibiting discrimination in employment on the basis of race, color, religion, sex, and national origin.

■═■

Reed v. The Great Lakes Cos., Inc.

Employee (P) v. Employer (D)

330 F.3d 931 (7th Cir. 2003).

NATURE OF CASE: Appeal of summary judgment in favor of employer.

FACT SUMMARY: Melvin Reed (P) sued his employer for religious discrimination and failure to accommodate his religion. The trial court granted summary judgment in favor of the employer.

🏛 RULE OF LAW
Summary judgment in favor of an employer is proper where an employee alleging religious discrimination and failure-to-accommodate claims fails to identify his religion or otherwise provide any guidance for determining what accommodation might be necessary.

FACTS: Melvin Reed (P) was the executive housekeeper of the newly opened Milwaukee Holiday Inn, which was operated by the Great Lakes Companies Inc. (D). The Gideons provided newly opened hotels owned by Great Lakes (D) with a free copy of the Bible for each of its hotel rooms, and customarily met with hotel representatives when supplying the bibles. Reed (P) and his manager attended a meeting with the Gideons, but Reed (P) walked out of the meeting when it unexpectedly included Bible reading and prayer. After a confrontation with his manager about his behavior, he was fired for insubordination. Reed (P) sued Great Lakes (D), alleging intentional religious bias and failure to accommodate his religion in violation of Title VII of the 1964 Civil Rights Act. The district court granted summary judgment to Great Lakes (D), finding that Reed (P) had failed to support his claims and imposed sanctions against Reed (P) and his lawyer because of Reed's (P) 15-year pattern of filing employment discrimination cases. Reed (P) appealed.

ISSUE: Is summary judgment in favor of an employer proper where an employee alleging religious discrimination and failure-to-accommodate claims fails to identify his religion or otherwise provide any guidance for determining what accommodation might be necessary?

HOLDING AND DECISION: (Posner, J.) Yes. Summary judgment in favor of an employer is proper where an employee alleging religious discrimination and failure-to-accommodate claims fails to identify his religion or otherwise provide any guidance for determining what accommodation might be necessary. Title VII prohibits discrimination against an employee based on the employee's religion, and even extends to an employee's "antipathy to religion." So, even if Reed (P) were an atheist, Title VII would provide protection if he in fact suffered discrimination as a result of his beliefs. In this case, however, Reed (P) never identified what his beliefs were, or what measures Great Lakes (D) should take to accommodate his beliefs, and there is therefore no indication that he was fired because of his religious beliefs. There is evidence, however, that he was fired because of his abrupt departure from the meeting with the Gideons, and for insubordination. But while the summary judgment is affirmed, the order of sanctions is reversed and remanded because Reed's (P) sanctions were appropriate only if his intentional discrimination claim could be characterized as frivolous, and it was unclear whether the trial judge had properly considered that question.

▶ ANALYSIS

This case illustrates the difficult task of distinguishing between asking for an accommodation to a religious belief and the right to disobey a superior's orders. As the court states: "There is a line, indistinct but important, between an employee who seeks an accommodation to his religious faith and an employee who asserts as Reed did an unqualified right to disobey orders that he deems inconsistent with his faith though he refuses to indicate at what points that faith intersects the requirements of his job."

■=■

Quicknotes

DISCRIMINATION Unequal treatment of a class of persons.

SUMMARY JUDGMENT Judgment rendered by a court in response to a motion made by one of the parties, claiming that the lack of a question of material fact in respect to an issue warrants disposition of the issue without consideration by the jury.

■=■

Wilson v. U.S. West Communications

Dismissed employee (P) v. Former employer (D)

58 F.3d 1337 (8th Cir. 1995).

NATURE OF CASE: Appeal in action claiming religious discrimination.

FACT SUMMARY: U.S. West Communications (D) fired Wilson (P) after Wilson refused to cover an antiabortion button that she wore to work every day depicting a fetus.

🏛 RULE OF LAW
An employer is required to "reasonably accommodate" an employee's religious beliefs or practices unless doing so would cause the employer undue hardship.

FACTS: In July 1990, Wilson (P) made a religious vow that she would wear an antiabortion button at all times. The button showed a color photograph of a fetus and the phrases "Stop Abortion" and "They're forgetting someone." The button caused disruptions among the other workers at U.S. West (D). In August 1990, Wilson's (P) supervisors at U.S. West (D) met with Wilson and asked her to either cover the button while at work, wear the button only in her cubicle, or wear a different button with the same message but without the photograph. Wilson (P) refused and proceeded to wear a T-shirt with similar depictions on it. U.S. West (D) told Wilson (P) not to report to work wearing anything depicting a fetus. U.S. West (D) sent Wilson (P) home for wearing the button and T-shirt, then fired Wilson (P) for missing work while unexcused for three consecutive days. Wilson (P) sued U.S. West alleging that her firing constituted religious discrimination. The lower court ruled that requiring Wilson (P) to cover up the button was a reasonable accommodation and entered judgment for U.S. West (D). Wilson (P) appealed.

ISSUE: Is an employer required to "reasonably accommodate" an employee's religious beliefs or practices unless doing so would cause the employer undue hardship?

HOLDING AND DECISION: (Gibson, J.) Yes. An employer is required to "reasonably accommodate" an employee's religious beliefs or practices unless doing so would cause the employer undue hardship. Here, Wilson (P) established a prima facie case of religious discrimination by informing her employer that her religious beliefs conflicted with an employment requirement, and then being reprimanded for failing to comply with the conflicting requirement. U.S. West (D), however, provided Wilson (P) a reasonable accommodation. Covering the button would cure the disruption in the workplace because Wilson's belief required her only to wear the button, but not to be a living witness. Forcing Wilson's (P) co-workers to accept Wilson's (P) insistence on wearing this particular depiction is antithetical to the concept of reasonable accommodation. Title VII does not require an employer to allow an employee to impose his religious views on others, but merely to accommodate an employee's religious views. Affirmed.

▶ ANALYSIS

In 1972, Congress amended Title VII to include a special theory of liability for religious discrimination. Section 701(j) states, "The term 'religion' includes all aspects of religious observance and practice, as well as belief, unless an employer demonstrates that he is unable to reasonably accommodate to an employee's or prospective employee's religious observance or practice without undue hardship on the conduct of the employer's business." The Supreme Court, however, construes this provision narrowly.

■=■

Quicknotes

DISCRIMINATION Unequal treatment of a class of persons.

TITLE VII OF THE CIVIL RIGHTS ACT OF 1964 Law prohibiting discrimination in employment on the basis of race, color, religion, sex, and national origin.

■=■

Zamora v. Elite Logistics, Inc.

Legal immigrant employee (P) v. Employer (D)

478 F.3d 1160 (10th Cir. 2007) (en banc).

NATURE OF CASE: Appeal of summary judgment in favor of employer.

FACT SUMMARY: An employer who had heard rumors that there was going to be a raid by federal immigration officials conducted a thorough review of the documentation of its workers, to ensure they were authorized to work in the United States. The investigation indicated that the social security number assigned to Ramon Zamora (P) was being used by someone else. The company therefore asked him, and 35-40 other workers with similar issues, to produce adequate documentation of right to work in the United States, and suspended them until they produced the documentation. Eventually, Zamora (P) did so, but after demanded an apology and explanation. The company refused his demands, and fired him.

RULE OF LAW

(1) An employer that suspends a legal immigrant employee whose documentation has raised questions, until the employee is able to produce documentation establishing his right to work in the United States, does not violate Title VII of the 1964 Civil Rights Act's ban against discrimination based on race and national origin.

(2) An employer that terminates a legal immigrant employee in response to a demand by the employee for an apology after the company suspended him for failing to provide documentation indicating his right to work in the United States does not violate Title VII of the 1964 Civil Rights Act's ban against discrimination based on race and national origin.

FACTS: Ramon Zamora (P) came to the United States from Mexico and received a social security number in the early 1980s. He became a legal permanent resident in 1987. When Elite (D) hired Zamora (P) in August 2001 to work at its food warehouse and distribution center, he presented his alien registration card and his social security card and signed an I-9 form. After receiving a tip that Immigration and Naturalization Service [now Immigration and Customs Enforcement] inspectors might be coming to the warehouse, Elite (D) took quick action to determine the employment status of its workers, fearing that it may have hired some illegal works during a mid-2000 hiring phase. The company hired contractors to check the social security numbers of approximately 650 employees and the contractors identified problems with 35 to 40 numbers. Zamora (P) was among those in which problems were discovered. Elite (D) gave

Zamora (P) a notice stating that he had ten days to provide documentation that he was permitted to work in the United States. Zamora (P) did not comply. The same notice was given to all the other workers identified by the contractors. The company (D) suspended Zamora (P), telling him that he could not work until he brought in appropriate documentation. Zamora (P) then presented an INS document showing he had applied for naturalization and an SSA earnings record, but there was still confusion about the number because it allegedly had been used by someone else. When the company (D) finally determined that the social security number belonged to Zamora (P), they contacted him and asked him to return to work. Zamora (P) presented a letter to the company demanding an apology and an explanation. The company (D) refused to apologize, gave Zamora (P) his last paycheck, and ordered him to leave. Zamora (P) filed a lawsuit in the U.S. District Court for the District of Kansas, which granted summary judgment for the company. A panel of the Tenth Circuit reversed and found there was evidence that Elite (D) Logistics was overly stringent when it suspended Zamora (P) in anticipation of a possible raid by the INS. The Tenth Circuit split, however, on whether Zamora's (P) demand for an apology, which was greeted with "just get the hell out of here," should also go to trial.

ISSUE:

(1) Does an employer that suspends a legal immigrant employee whose documentation has raised questions, until the employee is able to produce documentation establishing his right to work in the United States, violate Title VII of the 1964 Civil Rights Act's ban against discrimination based on race and national origin?

(2) Does an employer that terminates a legal immigrant employee in response to a demand by the employee for an apology after the company suspended him for failing to provide documentation indicating his right to work in the United States violate Title VII of the 1964 Civil Rights Act's ban against discrimination based on race and national origin?

HOLDING AND DECISION: (Ebel, J.)

(1) No. An employer that suspends a legal immigrant employee whose documentation has raised questions, until the employee is able to produce documentation establishing his right to work in the United States, does not violate Title VII of the 1964 Civil Rights Act's ban against discrimination based on race and national origin. [The en banc Tenth Circuit split seven to seven on the issue of Zamora's (P) suspension from his job with Elite (D) because of confusion over the authenticity of

Continued on next page.

Zamora's (P) social security number, leaving the trial court decision intact.]

(2) No. An employer that terminates a legal immigrant employee in response to a demand by the employee for an apology after the company suspended him for failing to provide documentation indicating his right to work in the United States does not violate Title VII of the 1964 Civil Rights Act's ban against discrimination based on race and national origin. There was no evidence of bias. First, the alleged Title VII of the 1964 Civil Rights Act bias in the suspension, if it exists, cannot be linked as a motivating factor to the termination decision, even though they occurred within four days of each other, because there was an intervening event of reinstatement. The suspension and termination must be viewed as discrete, separate events. Elite (D) did not terminate Zamora (P) until Zamora (P) requested a written explanation and apology as a condition for his returning to work. Vigorous compliance with the Immigration Control and Reform Act should not be seen as evidence of Title VII discrimination. Second, if any action beyond facial examination of eligibility documents is discriminatory, then the entire Basic Pilot Program—which is designed to curb the growing problem of document fraud and identity theft—might be called into question, since it is premised on the examination of data discrepancies rather than documents.

CONCURRENCE: (McConnell, J.) Elite's (D) suspension of Zamora (P) and the rigid questioning of documents was not discrimination, but instead an attempt to determine whether document fraud was taking place. Although IRCA compliance may only require a social security number check, the lead concurrence said it was not unreasonable to ask for further proof that identity fraud was not taking place. This reasoning was based on the "context" of the company's comments and that they were asking for rigid enforcement based on the context of avoiding an INS raid. It may have been wrong, but it was not unreasonable for Elite (D) to believe that examination of the naturalization certificate would fail to bring Elite (D) into compliance with IRCA, which makes it unlawful for an employer to continue to employ an alien in the United States knowing the alien to be unauthorized. Elite (D) may have reasonably believed that while examination of a facially valid naturalization certificate would satisfy Elite's (D) statutory duties at the hiring stage, specific questions about a worker's documentation created a duty on the part of the employer to investigate and resolve the specific concerns.

DISSENT: (Lucero, J.) The same decision-maker suspended, reinstated, and terminated Zamora (P) over a four-day period of time, and therefore it was reasonable to assume that discrimination that inspired one act infected all three acts. Notwithstanding the grant of permission to return to work, there is no principled reason to view the suspension and termination as discrete, separate events. A "virtual safe-harbor against Title VII claims" is created by

suggesting that an employer who is conducting an IRCA investigation should be immune from the allegation that the investigation is discriminatory. Justice McConnell's use of "context" in understanding Elite's (D) behavior failed to acknowledge that Zamora's (P) entire case hinged on the IRCA compliance as a pretext for discrimination.

▶ ANALYSIS

This is not likely the last we'll hear from the Tenth Circuit on this issue, given the deep division among members of the court. The en banc court split 7-7 on the issue of Zamora's (P) suspension and 9-5 in backing the trial court's finding that there was no evidence of bias. The majority opinion was brief, and much of the legal analysis appearing in a series of concurrences and a dissent from the majority decision. And as to the issues, in the lead concurrence authored by McConnell, 6 judges argued that vigorous compliance with the Immigration Control and Reform Act should not be seen as evidence of Title VII discrimination.

■=■

Quicknotes

DISCRIMINATION Unequal treatment of a class of persons.

PRETEXT Ostensible reason or motive assigned or assumed as a color or cover for the real reason or motive.

■=■

Clark County School District v. Breeden

Employer (D) v. Employee claiming retaliation (P)

532 U.S. 268 (2001).

NATURE OF CASE: Appeal from reversal of summary judgment for employer in Title VII retaliation action.

FACT SUMMARY: Breeden (P) claimed her employer, Clark County School District (D), retaliated against her for complaining about, and for filing charges and bringing suit for, an allegedly discriminatory comment made by her male supervisor.

🏛 RULE OF LAW
Summary judgment for the employer defendant in a Title VII retaliation action is appropriate where no reasonable person would believe that the action complained of violated Title VII and where the employee plaintiff fails to show the requisite causal connection between protected activities and the alleged retaliation.

FACTS: At a meeting with Breeden (P) and a male employee to review job applicant's psychological evaluation reports, Breeden's (P) male supervisor read aloud a sexually explicit remark that one applicant had made to a co-worker, looked at Breeden (P), and stated, "I don't know what that means." The other employee replied, "Well, I'll tell you later," and both men chuckled. Breeden (P) complained about the comment to the offending supervisor, to Assistant Superintendent Rice, and other officials of their employer, Clark County School District (School District) (D). Pursuant to Title VII, she subsequently filed a 42 U.S.C. § 2000e-3(a) retaliation claim against the School District (D), asserting that she was punished for these complaints and also for filing charges against the School District (D) with the Nevada Equal Rights Commission and the Equal Employment Opportunity Commission (EEOC) and for filing the Title VII suit itself. Almost three years after the date of the offending statement (April 10, 1997), Breeden's (P) union was informed that she would be transferred, and she was, in May 1997. Although Breeden (P) filed her suit on April 1, 1997, she did not serve the School District (D) until April 11, 1997—one day after her (P) transfer was announced. The district court granted the School District (D) summary judgment, but the circuit court reversed. The Supreme Court granted review.

ISSUE: Is summary judgment for the employer defendant in a Title VII retaliation action appropriate where no reasonable person would believe that the action complained of violated Title VII and where the employee plaintiff fails to show the requisite causal connection between protected activities and the alleged retaliation?

HOLDING AND DECISION: (Per curiam) Yes. Summary judgment for the employer defendant in a Title VII retaliation action is appropriate where no reasonable person would believe that the action complained of violated Title VII and where the employee plaintiff fails to show the requisite causal connection between protected activities and the alleged retaliation. Breeden's (P) claims are insufficient to withstand a summary judgment motion. No one could reasonably believe that the incident of which Breeden (P) complained violated Title VII. Sexual harassment is actionable under Title VII only if it is so severe or pervasive as to alter the conditions of the victim's employment and create an abusive working environment. Simple teasing, offhand comments, and isolated incidents (unless extremely serious) will not amount to discriminatory changes in employment terms and conditions. The action of Breeden's (P) supervisor and co-worker are at worst an isolated incident that cannot remotely be considered "extremely serious." Regarding Breeden's (P) claim that she was punitively transferred for filing charges and the present suit, she failed to show the requisite causal connection between her protected activities and the transfer. The School District (D) did not implement the transfer until twenty months after Breeden (P) filed her charges, and it was clear from the record that it had been contemplating the transfer before it learned of her suit. Reversed.

▶ ANALYSIS

Breeden (P) presented two distinct claims of retaliation. The first was for "opposition" conduct (her internal complaints) and the second was for "participation" conduct (the filing of charges with the Nevada Equal Rights Commission and the EEOC). Participation conduct has received greater protection than opposition conduct. Whereas opposition conduct must be supported by a reasonable, good-faith belief that the employer acted unlawfully or a finding that the employer's action was in fact unlawful, no such determination appears to be necessary for participation conduct.

▬▬■

Quicknotes

DISCRIMINATION Unequal treatment of a class of persons.

RETALIATION The infliction of injury or penalty upon another in return for an injury or harm caused by that party.

TITLE VII OF THE CIVIL RIGHTS ACT OF 1964 Law prohibiting discrimination in employment on the basis of race, color, religion, sex, and national origin.

▬▬■

Laughlin v. Metropolitan Washington Airports Authority

Employee (P) v. Employer (D)

149 F.3d 253 (4th Cir. 1998).

NATURE OF CASE: Appeal of summary judgment in favor of employer.

FACT SUMMARY: Karen Laughlin (P) sued for retaliation under Title VII of the 1964 Civil Rights Act after she was fired for removing documents from her boss's desk in order to send them to a co-worker who might have had a retaliation claim against the employer.

🏛 RULE OF LAW
Removing documents from a boss's desk in order to send them to a former co-worker who has a potential retaliation claim against the employer is not protected activity under Title VII of the 1964 Civil Rights Act.

FACTS: Karen Laughlin (P) worked as a secretary for Augustus Melton, a manager at Washington National Airport. After Kathy LaSauce, one of Laughlin's co-workers, complained that her supervisor had retaliated against her for providing testimony regarding a third co-worker's EEO claim, Melton wrote a warning to the supervisor. The supervisor left for another job before Melton's warning was signed or delivered. When Laughlin (P) saw the letter to the supervisor on Melton's desk, she concluded that her boss was trying to prevent LaSauce from having adequate access to relevant documents for a future lawsuit. Laughlin (P) copied the documents and sent them to LaSauce. Laughlin (P) was fired for releasing the draft letter of reprimand. When she sued under Title VII, claiming unlawful retaliation for protected activity, the District Court for the Eastern District of Virginia granted the airport's motion for summary judgment. Laughlin (P) appealed to the Fourth Circuit.

ISSUE: Is removing documents from a boss's desk in order to send them to a former co-worker who has a potential retaliation claim against the employer-protected activity under Title VII of the 1964 Civil Rights Act?

HOLDING AND DECISION: (Williams, J.) No. Removing documents from a boss's desk in order to send them to a former co-worker who has a potential retaliation claim against the employer is not protected activity under Title VII of the 1964 Civil Rights Act. Protected activities under Title VII fall into two distinct categories: participation in proceedings arising from a discrimination charge and opposition to unlawful practices. Laughlin (P) failed to prove that she engaged in either form of activity protected under Title VII. When Laughlin (P) removed and copied the documents, LaSauce was not involved in any Title VII investigation, and Laughlin (P) therefore was not assisting LaSauce's discrimination claim, as she claimed. LaSauce had

recently resigned, but had not yet filed suit. In addition, LaSauce testified that she was surprised to receive the documents in the mail, indicating that there was no pending investigation, proceeding, or hearing when Laughlin (P) took and copied the material. Therefore, Laughlin's (P) actions do not fall into the participation category of activity. Laughlin's (P) actions also did not constitute opposition, which includes the use of informal grievance procedures as well as staging informal protests and voicing one's opinion in order to bring attention to an employer's discriminatory activities, the court said. To determine whether an employee is engaged in legitimate opposition activity, the purpose of Title VII—to protect persons engaging in reasonable activities opposing discrimination—must be balanced against Congress's equally manifest desire not to tie the hands of employers in selecting and controlling their personnel. Applying that balancing test to Laughlin's (P) case, the employer's interest in maintaining security and confidentiality of sensitive personnel documents outweighs Laughlin's (P) interests in providing those documents to LaSauce. Laughlin's (P) reaction to the situation was disproportionate and unreasonable.

▶ ANALYSIS

The ruling in this case does not stand for the notion that employees are entitled to rifle through the desks of their employers under the guise of assisting a Title VII investigation. On the facts of this case, Laughlin may have had a case if LaSauce had begun proceedings against the employer, but as Melton's secretary, she already had access to his files. Another employee may not have been justified in entering Melton's office, without knowing about the existence of the memo, and retrieving it from his desk.

■=■

Quicknotes

DISCRIMINATION Unequal treatment of a class of persons.

TITLE VII OF THE CIVIL RIGHTS ACT OF 1964 Law prohibiting discrimination in employment on the basis of race, color, religion, sex, and national origin.

■=■

Burlington Northern & Santa Fe Railway Co. v. White

Employer (D) v. Employee (P)

126 S. Ct. 2405 (2006).

NATURE OF CASE: Appeal of judgment for employee in retaliation case.

FACT SUMMARY: Sheila White (P) was transferred and suspended, but then awarded backpay by her employer to cover the suspension period. A jury awarded her damages in her employment discrimination trial. On appeal, Burlington Northern (D) argued that she did not suffer an adverse employment action, so she did not have the right to sue under Title VII.

RULE OF LAW
The definition of retaliation under Title VII of the 1964 Civil Rights Act includes acts that are "materially adverse" to a reasonable employee, including transfers or suspensions that do not result in a loss of pay, benefits, or privileges.

FACTS: Sheila White (P) was the only woman working in the Maintenance of Way Department of the Burlington Northern Santa Fe Railroad's (D) Tennessee facility. After she complained of harassment by her supervisor, White was transferred from her position as a forklift operator to less desirable duties as a track laborer, though her job classification remained the same. She was subsequently suspended for 37 days without pay, but was eventually reinstated and given full backpay. White (P) filed suit in federal court. A jury rejected her claims of sex discrimination but found that she had been retaliated against for complaining about sex discrimination, in violation of Title VII of the 1964 Civil Rights Act. The jury awarded her $43,000 in damages. On appeal, Burlington Northern (D) argued that White (P) had not suffered "adverse employment action," and therefore could not bring the suit, because she had not been fired, demoted, denied a promotion, or denied wages. The Sixth Circuit Court of Appeals disagreed, finding that the suspension without pay—even if backpay was eventually awarded—was an adverse employment action, as was the change of responsibilities within the same job category.

ISSUE: Does the definition of retaliation under Title VII of the 1964 Civil Rights Act include acts that are "materially adverse" to a reasonable employee, including transfers or suspensions that do not result in a loss of pay, benefits, or privileges?

HOLDING AND DECISION: (Breyer, J.) Yes. The definition of retaliation under Title VII of the 1964 Civil Rights Act includes acts that are "materially adverse" to a reasonable employee, including transfers or suspensions that do not result in a loss of pay, benefits, or privileges. Congressional intent and the language of the statutes indicate that while the substantive discrimination provision of Title VII is designed to prevent injury to individuals based on status, such as gender, the anti-retaliation provision seeks to prevent harm based on conduct, such as the reporting by an employee that he or she has been harassed. The retaliation provision of Title VII covers those, and only those, employer actions that would be "materially adverse" to a reasonable employee or job applicant. In other words, the employer's actions must be harmful to the point that they could dissuade a reasonable worker from making, or supporting, a charge of discrimination. In this case, White's (P) suspension and transfer were "materially adverse," in that it could dissuade a reasonable worker from making or supporting a charge of discrimination, and therefore constitute retaliatory discrimination that violates Title VII. Affirmed.

▶ ANALYSIS

The holding in this case resolved a circuit split. Pay special attention to the Court's distinction between substantive discrimination and retaliatory discrimination. Under the Court's ruling, discrimination has to occur in the workplace in order to be actionable under Title VII, but retaliation doesn't. That is, Title VII proscribes retaliatory actions that occur outside the workplace. The justices wrote that the retaliation provision is not limited just to the "terms, conditions, and benefits" of employment because employers can chill dissent and the reporting of discrimination in other ways. Although preventing discrimination can be achieved by prohibiting employment-related discrimination, it is not as simple to discourage retaliation, according to the justices. The Court wrote that a provision limited to employment-related actions would not "deter the many forms that effective retaliation can take." Thus, "such a limited construction would fail to fully achieve the anti-retaliation provision's 'primary purpose,' namely, '[m]aintaining unfettered access to statutory remedial mechanisms.'"

■══■

Quicknotes

RETALIATION The infliction of injury or penalty upon another in return for an injury or harm caused by that party.

TITLE VII OF THE CIVIL RIGHTS ACT OF 1964 Law prohibiting discrimination in employment on the basis of race, color, religion, sex, and national origin.

■══■

Quick Reference Rules of Law

PAGE

1. **The Meaning of "Disability": Actual Disability.** Persons infected with the human immunodeficiency virus (HIV) are covered under the Americans with Disabilities Act (ADA). (Bragdon v. Abbott) — *71*

2. **The Meaning of "Disability": Actual Disability.** To demonstrate a substantial limitation in the major life activity of performing manual tasks and, therefore, whether a person with carpal tunnel syndrome is "disabled" under the Americans with Disabilities Act (ADA), an individual must show that the impairment prevents or restricts him or her from performing tasks that are of central importance to most people's daily lives. (Toyota Motor Manufacturing, Kentucky, Inc. v. Williams) — *72*

3. **The Meaning of "Disability": Actual Disability.** In determining whether an individual is substantially limited with respect to a major life activity under the disabled definition of the Americans with Disabilities Act (ADA), such disability must be determined taking into consideration any corrective measures. (Sutton v. United Air Lines, Inc.) — *74*

4. **The Meaning of "Disability": Regarded as Having Such an Impairment.** Where a plaintiff seeks to show that an employer's requirement substantially limits the major life activity of working, the plaintiff must allege he is unable to work in a broad class of jobs, and not a single job, as compared with the average person having comparable training, skills and abilities. (Sutton v. United Air Lines, Inc.) — *76*

5. **The Meaning of "Disability": Regarded as Having Such an Impairment.** An employer does not violate the Americans with Disabilities Act (ADA) if it fires an employee because of a physical condition, but does not regard him as disabled within the meaning of the ADA. (EEOC v. Schneider National, Inc.) — *77*

6. **The Meaning of "Qualified Individual with a Disability": Essential Job Functions.** Shift rotation can be considered a nondiscriminatory essential function of a position for purposes of the Americans with Disabilities Act. (Rehrs v. The Iams Company) — *79*

7. **The Meaning of "Qualified Individual with a Disability": The Duty of Reasonable Accommodation.** An employer's showing that a requested accommodation conflicts with seniority rules is ordinarily sufficient to show, as a matter of law, that an "accommodation" is not "reasonable" unless the employee presents evidence of special circumstances that makes a seniority-rule exception reasonable in the particular case. (US Airways, Inc. v. Barnett) — *80*

8. **The Meaning of "Qualified Individual with a Disability": The Duty of Reasonable Accommodation.** An employer who has an established policy to fill vacant job positions with the most qualified applicant is not required to assign a qualified disabled employee to a vacant position if the disabled employee is not the most qualified applicant for the position. (Huber v. Wal-Mart) — *82*

9. **The Meaning of "Qualified Individual with a Disability": The Duty of Reasonable Accommodation.** The duty of reasonable accommodation is satisfied when the employer does what is necessary to enable the disabled worker to work in reasonable comfort. (Vande Zande v. State of Wisconsin Department of Administration) — *83*

10. **The Meaning of "Qualified Individual with a Disability": The Duty of Reasonable Accommodation.** Under Washington law, conduct resulting from a disability is part of the disability, rather than a separate basis for termination. (Gambini v. Total Renal Care, Inc.) — *84*

CHAPTER 6

11. Discriminatory Qualification Standards: Direct Threat.   The Americans with Disabilities   *85*
Act (ADA) permits an Equal Employment Opportunity Commission (EEOC) regulation that
authorizes an employer to refuse to hire an individual because his performance on the job
would endanger his own health, owing to a disability. (Chevron U.S.A. Inc. v. Echazabal)

12. Discriminatory Qualification Standards: Job-Related and Consistent with Business   *87*
Necessity.   Under the Americans with Disabilities Act (ADA), an employer who requires as a
job qualification that an employee meet an otherwise applicable federal safety regulation need
not justify enforcing the regulation solely because its standard may be waived in an individual
case. (Albertson's, Inc. v. Kirkingburg)

Bragdon v. Abbott

Dentist (D) v. HIV-infected patient (P)

524 U.S. 624 (1998).

NATURE OF CASE: Appeal from summary judgment in a discrimination action.

FACT SUMMARY: Bragdon (D), a dentist, refused to treat Abbott (P), infected with HIV, anywhere other than a hospital.

🏛 RULE OF LAW
Persons infected with the human immunodeficiency virus (HIV) are covered under the Americans with Disabilities Act (ADA).

FACTS: Abbott (P), infected with HIV since 1986, visited Bragdon (D), a dentist, to have a cavity filled in 1994. Bragdon (D) refused to treat Abbott except in a hospital. Abbott (P) sued for illegal discrimination under the ADA. The district court granted summary judgment to Abbott (P) on the issue of whether HIV infection constituted a disability under the ADA and the court of appeals affirmed. Bragdon (D) appealed.

ISSUE: Are persons infected with the HIV virus covered under the ADA?

HOLDING AND DECISION: (Kennedy, J.) Yes. Persons infected with the HIV virus are covered under the ADA. The statute defines disability as a physical or mental impairment that substantially limits one of more of the major life activities of an individual. In order to analyze the present case, first we consider whether HIV infection is a physical impairment. Generally, impairment refers to any physiological disorder affecting the major body systems. The HIV virus invades various cells in the blood and tissues of a person. It kills white blood cells and affects the body's immune system. Although the effects aren't immediately apparent, even the initial stage of infection involves an assault on the immune system. Accordingly, it is clear that HIV infection is a physical impairment from the moment of infection. The second consideration under the ADA is whether the impairment affects a major life activity. In the present case, reproduction has been the activity at issue. Certainly, reproduction is a major life activity. Finally, courts must look to see if the impairment substantially limits the major life activity. In this case, it is clear that women infected with HIV are at risk of infecting their male partners and any children they give birth to. Although conception and childbirth are not impossible with HIV, they become more dangerous to the public health. Therefore, HIV infection is a disability under the ADA because it is a physical impairment that substantially limits reproduction. Affirmed.

▶ ANALYSIS

This decision conforms with administrative and agency interpretation of the scope of the ADA. In fact, it represents a bit of deference to this interpretation. Some commentators were critical of the Court's holding that reproduction was a major life activity under the ADA. Many fear that it will open up a wide range of litigation from individuals who suffer from infertility and other disorders of the reproductive system.

Quicknotes

AMERICANS WITH DISABILITIES ACT (42 U.S.C. §§ 12101-12213) Enacted in 1990, this federal law prohibits discrimination in employment against Americans with physical or mental disabilities.

Toyota Motor Manufacturing, Kentucky, Inc. v. Williams

Employer (D) v. Employee with carpal tunnel syndrome (P)

534 U.S. 184 (2002).

NATURE OF CASE: Appeal from grant of partial summary judgment for employee with carpal tunnel syndrome in suit alleging failure to accommodate in an Americans with Disabilities Act (ADA) action.

FACT SUMMARY: Williams (P) claimed she was unable to perform her automobile assembly-line job because she was disabled by carpal tunnel syndrome and sued Toyota Motor Manufacturing, Kentucky, Inc. (Toyota) (D) for failing to provide her with a reasonable accommodation as required by the ADA.

🏛 RULE OF LAW
To demonstrate a substantial limitation in the major life activity of performing manual tasks and, therefore, whether a person with carpal tunnel syndrome is "disabled" under the Americans with Disabilities Act, an individual must show that the impairment prevents or restricts him or her from performing tasks that are of central importance to most people's daily lives.

FACTS: Williams (P) worked with pneumatic tools at Toyota (D) and developed carpal tunnel syndrome. Williams's (P) physician placed her on permanent work restrictions, and Toyota (D) assigned Williams (P) to modified-duty jobs. When some of the job duties caused Williams (P) increased pain, she requested an accommodation, which allegedly was refused. Williams (P) was eventually placed under a no-work-of-any-kind restriction by her physicians. She stopped working, and Toyota (D) terminated her for poor attendance. She sued Toyota (D) for failing to provide her with a reasonable accommodation as required by the ADA. The district court granted Toyota (D) summary judgment, holding that Williams's (P) impairment did not qualify as a "disability" under the ADA because it had not "substantially limited" any "major life activity" and that there was no evidence that Williams (P) had had a record of a substantially limiting impairment or that Toyota (D) had regarded her as having such an impairment. The Sixth Circuit reversed, finding that the impairments substantially limited Williams (P) in the major life activity of performing manual tasks. The Supreme Court granted review.

ISSUE: To demonstrate a substantial limitation in the major life activity of performing manual tasks and, therefore, whether a person with carpal tunnel syndrome is "disabled" under the ADA, must an individual show that the impairment prevents or restricts him or her from performing tasks that are of central importance to most people's daily lives?

HOLDING AND DECISION: (O'Connor, J.) Yes. To demonstrate a substantial limitation in the major

life activity of performing manual tasks, and, therefore, whether a person with carpal tunnel syndrome is "disabled" under the ADA, an individual must show that the impairment prevents or restricts him or her from performing tasks that are of central importance to most people's daily lives. The Sixth Circuit did not apply the proper standard in determining that Williams (P) was disabled under the ADA, because it analyzed only a limited class of manual tasks and failed to ask whether Williams's (P) impairments prevented or restricted her from performing tasks that are of central importance to most people's daily lives. The Court's consideration of what an individual must prove to demonstrate a substantial limitation in the major life activity of performing manual tasks is guided by the ADA's disability definition. "Substantially" in the phrase "substantially limits" suggests "considerable" or "to a large degree," and thus clearly precludes impairments that interfere in only a minor way with performing manual tasks. Moreover, because "major" means important, "major life activities" refers to those activities that are of central importance to daily life. In order for performing manual tasks to fit into this category, the tasks in question must be central to daily life. To be substantially limited in the specific major life activity of performing manual tasks, therefore, an individual must have an impairment that prevents or severely restricts the individual from doing activities that are of central importance to most people's daily lives. The impairment's impact must also be permanent or long term. It is insufficient for individuals attempting to prove disability status under this test to merely submit evidence of a medical diagnosis of an impairment. Instead, the ADA requires them to offer evidence that the extent of the limitation caused by their impairment in terms of their own experience is substantial. That the ADA defines "disability" with respect to an individual makes clear that Congress intended the existence of a disability to be determined in such a case-by-case manner. An individualized assessment of the effect of an impairment is particularly necessary when the impairment is one such as carpal tunnel syndrome, in which symptoms vary widely from person to person. The court of appeals erred in suggesting that, in order to prove a substantial limitation in the major life activity of performing manual tasks, a plaintiff must show that her manual disability involves a "class" of manual activities and that those activities affect the ability to perform tasks at work. Nothing in the ADA's text, the Court's opinions, or the regulations suggests that a class-based framework should apply outside the context of the major life activity of working. Although the court of appeals

Continued on next page.

addressed the different major life activity of performing manual tasks, its analysis erroneously focused on Williams's (P) inability to perform manual tasks associated only with her job. Rather, the central inquiry must be whether the claimant is unable to perform the variety of tasks central to most people's daily lives. Also without support is the court of appeals's assertion that the question of whether an impairment constitutes a disability is to be answered only by analyzing the impairment's effect in the workplace. That the ADA "disability" definition applies not only to the portion of the ADA dealing with employment but also to the other provisions dealing with public transportation and public accommodations demonstrates that the definition is intended to cover individuals with disabling impairments regardless of whether they have any connection to a workplace. Moreover, because the manual tasks unique to any particular job are not necessarily important parts of most people's lives, occupation-specific tasks may have only limited relevance to the manual-task inquiry. In this case, repetitive work with hands and arms extended at or above shoulder levels for extended periods, the manual task on which the court of appeals relied, is not an important part of most people's daily lives. Household chores, bathing, and brushing one's teeth, in contrast, are among the types of manual tasks of central importance to people's daily lives, so the court of appeals should not have disregarded Williams's (P) ability to do these activities. Reversed.

▌ANALYSIS

The unanimous decision in this case was a very narrow one—namely what constitutes a substantial limitation on the performance of manual tasks. The Court did not decide whether Williams's impairment actually substantially limited her ability to perform manual tasks or any other major life activities.

■══■

Quicknotes

AMERICANS WITH DISABILITIES ACT (42 U.S.C. §§ 12101-12213) Enacted in 1990, this federal law prohibits discrimination in employment against Americans with physical or mental disabilities.

■══■

Sutton v. United Air Lines, Inc.

Applicants (P) v. Prospective employer (D)

527 U.S. 471 (1999).

NATURE OF CASE: Suit alleging disability discrimination in violation of the Americans with Disabilities Act (ADA).

FACT SUMMARY: Petitioners, twin sisters who both suffered from severe myopia, brought suit against United Air Lines, Inc. (United) (D) alleging that United's (D) failure to offer them pilot positions constituted unlawful disability discrimination in violation of the ADA.

🏛 RULE OF LAW
In determining whether an individual is substantially limited with respect to a major life activity under the disabled definition of the ADA, such disability must be determined taking into consideration any corrective measures.

FACTS: Petitioners, twin sisters who both suffered from severe myopia, applied to United (D) for employment as commercial airline pilots. During their interviews they were told that a mistake had been made in inviting them to interview since they did not meet the minimum vision requirement. Their interviews were terminated and neither was offered a position. Petitioners filed suit alleging United (D) discriminated against them on account of their disability in violation of the ADA. The district court dismissed for failure to state a claim since they could fully correct their visual impairments, they were not actually substantially limited in any major life activity, and therefore they were not disabled under the ADA. The court of appeals affirmed.

ISSUE: In determining whether an individual is substantially limited with respect to a major life activity under the disabled definition of the ADA, must such disability be determined taking into consideration any corrective measures?

HOLDING AND DECISION: (O'Connor, J.) Yes. In determining whether an individual is substantially limited with respect to a major life activity under the disabled definition of the ADA, such disability must be determined taking into consideration any corrective measures. The ADA prohibits discrimination against qualified individuals with disabilities. "Disability" is defined as (1) a physical or mental impairment substantially limiting one or more major life activities; (2) a record of such impairment; or (3) being regarded as having such impairment. The first issue is whether the petitioners stated a claim under the definition of disability; that is, whether they have alleged that they possess a physical impairment that substantially limits them in one or more major life activities. Since petitioners claim that with corrective measures they are not actually disabled, it must be determined whether disability is to be determined

with reference to corrective measures. Petitioners argued that whether an impairment is substantially limiting should be determined without regard to corrective measures. United (D) argued that an impairment does not substantially limit a major life activity if it is corrected and that the EEOC guidelines conflict with the plain meaning of the ADA. United (D) is correct. Taking the ADA as a whole, corrective measures must be considered in determining whether a person is substantially limited with respect to a major life activity, and thus "disabled," under the ADA. Three provisions of the ADA support this conclusion. First the term "disability" is defined as a physical or mental impairment that substantially limits one or more major life activities of the individual. This requires that the person presently be substantially limited with respect to the activity, and not potentially or hypothetically limited. Where the person is able to take corrective measures to mitigate the impairment, it cannot be said to substantially limit a major life activity. Second, a determination of whether a person suffers from a disability must be made on an individual basis. The Equal Employment Opportunity Commission (EEOC) guidelines stating that the person be evaluated in his uncorrected state runs directly contrary to this individual inquiry. Last, findings enacted as part of the ADA indicate that Congress did not intend to include within the statute's scope all those persons whose uncorrected conditions would constitute disabilities. Since a disability must be determined with respect to corrective measures, the petitioners failed to state a claim that they are substantially limited in a major life activity. Affirmed.

DISSENT: (Stevens, J.) It is clear that the term disability under the ADA was meant to refer to the individual's past or present condition without regard to mitigation that has resulted from rehabilitation, self-improvement, corrective devices or medication.

DISSENT: (Breyer, J.) In addition to Justice Stevens's dissent, I would add that if the more liberal interpretation led to too many lawsuits that proved to be without merit, the EEOC could through regulation restrict that definition to exclude those who can correct their vision impairments with correct lenses. Such regulation would restrict the overly broad extension of the statute feared by the majority.

▌ *ANALYSIS*

The authority to promulgate rules under the ADA is divided among three different agencies: the EEOC, Attorney General, and the Secretary of Transportation. However, no agency was delegated the authority to promulgate regulations implementing the ADA's general provisions, including the definition of

Continued on next page.

the term "disability." The EEOC, however, did promulgate such regulation and thereby exceeded its authority.

■══■

Quicknotes

AMERICANS WITH DISABILITIES ACT (42 U.S.C. §§ 12101-12213) Enacted in 1990, this federal law prohibits discrimination in employment against Americans with physical or mental disabilities.

■══■

Sutton v. United Air Lines, Inc.

Vision-impaired pilot applicants (P) v. Prospective employer (D)

527 U.S. 471 (1999).

NATURE OF CASE: Suit alleging employment discrimination under the Americans with Disabilities Act (ADA).

FACT SUMMARY: Petitioners, persons seeking the position of global airline pilot, alleged that United Air Line's (United) (D) vision requirement violated the ADA since it substantially limited their major life activity of working.

RULE OF LAW
Where a plaintiff seeks to show that an employer's requirement substantially limits the major life activity of working, the plaintiff must allege he is unable to work in a broad class of jobs, and not a single job, as compared with the average person having comparable training, skills and abilities.

FACTS: Petitioners, twin sisters who both suffered from severe myopia, applied to United (D) for employment as commercial airline pilots. During their interviews they were told that a mistake had been made in inviting them to interview since they did not meet the minimum vision requirement. Their interviews were terminated and neither was offered a position. Petitioners filed suit alleging United (D) discriminated against them on account of their disability in violation of the ADA. The district court dismissed for failure to state a claim since they could fully correct their visual impairments, they were not actually substantially limited in any major life activity, and therefore they were not disabled under the ADA. The court of appeals affirmed.

ISSUE: Where a plaintiff seeks to show that an employer's requirement substantially limits the major life activity of working, must the plaintiff allege he is unable to work in a broad class of jobs, and not a single job, as compared with the average person having comparable training, skills and abilities?

HOLDING AND DECISION: (O'Connor, J.) Yes. Where a plaintiff seeks to show that an employer's requirement substantially limits the major life activity of working, the plaintiff must allege he is unable to work in a broad class of jobs, and not a single job, as compared with the average person having comparable training, skills and abilities. The plaintiff's inability to perform a single job is not a substantial limitation on the major life activity of working. Failure to state a claim that an individual has an actual disability under § 12102(2)(A) does not end the inquiry. Next it must be determined whether the individual may be regarded as having a disability under § 12102(2)(C). This requires a showing that the individual has "a physical or mental impairment that substantially limits one or more of the major life activities of such individual." This applies to situations in which the employer mistakenly believes the person has a physical impairment that substantially limits one or more

major life activities, or a that an actual, nonlimiting impairment substantially limits one or more major life activities. Both situations require the covered entity to have a mistaken belief either that one has a substantially limiting impairment that he either does not have or that is not so substantially limiting. The misperception generally is the result of stereotypic assumptions not indicative of the individual's ability. Here the petitioners are physically impaired; however, they argue that United (D) mistakenly believes such impairment substantially limits their ability to engage in the major life activity of working. The petitioners also argue that United's (D) vision requirement is based on stereotype and limits their ability to work by precluding their obtainment of the position of "global airline pilot." Without more, evidence of a vision requirement is not enough to violate the ADA. Employers may establish certain physical criteria necessary for employment. The ADA is violated, however, when an employer makes an employment decision based on a physical impairment, real or imagined, that is regarded as substantially limiting a major life activity. Petitioners have failed to state a claim that United (D) regarded their poor eyesight as substantially limiting them in their major life activity of working. Since the position of global airline pilot is only a single job, petitioners have not shown that United (D) regarded petitioners as having a substantially limiting impairment since there were several other positions for which the petitioners were qualified. Since petitioners failed to show United's (D) vision requirement showed United's (D) belief that they were substantially impaired, the court of appeals correctly dismissed their claim that they be regarded as disabled. Affirmed.

ANALYSIS

The court must consider several factors in determining whether a person is "substantially limited" in the major life activity of working. These include the number and types of jobs from which the plaintiff is denied, which require the same training and skills and fall within the geographic area to which the plaintiff has reasonable access. § 1630.2(j)(3)(ii). If other such positions exist for which the individual is not disqualified, then he is not substantially limited in the major life activity of working under the ADA.

▬▬■

Quicknotes

AMERICANS WITH DISABILITIES ACT (42 U.S.C. §§ 12101-12213) Enacted in 1990, this federal law prohibits discrimination in employment against Americans with physical or mental disabilities.

▬▬■

EEOC v. Schneider National, Inc.

EEOC (P) v. Employer (D)

481 F.3d 507 (7th Cir. 2007).

NATURE OF CASE: Appeal of summary judgment for the employer.

FACT SUMMARY: A truck driver with an excellent driving record was fired when his employer discovered he had a condition that causes his blood pressure to suddenly drop and cause fainting spells. The U.S. Equal Employment Opportunity Commission (P) filed a lawsuit on the driver's behalf. Even though the condition is treatable, and the risk of a fainting spell is small, the lower court granted summary judgment in favor of the employer, holding that the employer did not violate the Americans with Disabilities Act (ADA) by having standards for drivers that were higher than most other companies.

🏛 **RULE OF LAW**
An employer does not violate the ADA if it fires an employee because of a physical condition, but does not regard him as disabled within the meaning of the ADA.

FACTS: Jerome Hoefner was a valued employee of Schneider National, Inc. (Schneider) (D) with an excellent driving record. Schneider (D) nevertheless fired Hoefner from his truck-driving job after he experienced a fainting spell while off work and was diagnosed with neurocardiogenic syncope, a nervous system disorder that can cause a sudden drop in blood pressure. Department of Transportation standards do not bar individuals with neurocardiogenic syncope from driving on public highways a truck with a gross vehicular weight of more than 26,000 pounds or a vehicle used to transport hazardous materials or at least 16 passengers. Despite this, and despite the fact that the condition is treatable with medication, Schneider was skittish about allowing employees diagnosed with neurocardiogenic syncope to drive trucks, because two years earlier, a Schneider (D) driver who had recently been diagnosed with the condition drove his truck off a bridge and was killed. Even though investigators were unable to determine whether the condition caused the accident, the company (D) instituted a policy barring any driver with neurocardiogenic syncope. Schneider (D) encouraged Hoefner to apply for a nondriving job with the company, but he found another driving job with a different company. Since receiving his diagnosis, he repeatedly has been cleared to drive by doctors and has received a renewal of his DOT medical certificate. The U.S. District Court for the Eastern District of Wisconsin granted summary judgment to Schneider (D) on The U.S. Equal Employment Opportunity Commission's (P) claim that the company regarded Hoefner as having an impairment that substantially limits the major life activity of working. The district court found that Schneider (D) only viewed Hoefner as unable to work as a truck driver for that company, not that he was unable to drive trucks generally.

ISSUE: Does an employer violate the ADA if it fires an employee because of a physical condition, but does not regard him as disabled within the meaning of the ADA?

HOLDING AND DECISION: (Posner, J.) No. An employer does not violate the ADA if it fires an employee because of a physical condition, but does not regard him as disabled within the meaning of the ADA. Schneider (D) did not have a mistaken understanding of neurocardiogenic syncope. Rather, the company (D) was simply unwilling to risk a possible repetition of the accident that resulted in the death of another driver with the condition. The risk of that occurring is not zero, because Hoefner could forget to take his medication and the drug he takes is not totally efficacious. The risk of danger to the driver may be small, but Schneider (D) is entitled to determine how much risk is too great for it to be willing to take. In addition, the liability implications for Schneider (D) could be high, if there were an accident, as victims' lawyers would wave the previous accident in front of the jury, asking it to award punitive damages because the company had continued to employ drivers with neurocardiogenic syncope after having been warned by the earlier accident. The decision to avoid risk is a decision irrelevant to liability under the ADA, even if that company's degree of risk aversion was unique in its industry. Finally, there is no evidence that Schneider (D) considers neurocardiogenic syncope to impair any life activity other than driving a truck for Schneider, and perhaps for some other truck companies that like Schneider (D) have safety standards higher than the minimum required by the federal government.

▌ *ANALYSIS*

The court's holding seems to incorporate a fair reading of *Sutton v. United Air Lines, Inc.*, 527 U.S. 471 (1999), but the discussion of risk aversion seems to have undesirable repercussions. Judge Posner seems to be saying that an employer who inflicts an adverse employment action on an employee on the basis of an irrational fear does not run afoul of the ADA if the employer really believes it is acting irrationally. Taken to the extreme, that reasoning allows a school system to fire a kindergarten teacher with diabetes that is medically treated, on the small risk that she could have a seizure in class, if that small chance scares the employer. To conclude that the ADA has nothing to say about such a decision seems to undercut its purpose.

Continued on next page.

Quicknotes

AMERICANS WITH DISABILITIES ACT (42 U.S.C. §§ 12101-12213) Enacted in 1990, this federal law prohibits discrimination in employment against Americans with physical or mental disabilities.

■=■

Rehrs v. The Iams Company

Employee (P) v. Employer (D)

486 F.3d 353 (8th Cir. 2007).

NATURE OF CASE: Appeal of summary judgment in favor of the employer.

FACT SUMMARY: The employer refused to assign an employee to a fixed shift schedule, in accordance with the employee's doctor's wishes, because of his disability. The employee sued, arguing that the employer's actions violated the Americans with Disabilities Act (ADA).

🏛 RULE OF LAW
Shift rotation can be considered a nondiscriminatory essential function of a position for purposes of the ADA.

FACTS: Rehrs (P), who has Type 1 diabetes, was working at an Iams plant on a fixed 4 P.M. to midnight shift. After P&G (D) acquired Iams, P&G (D) instituted a rotating-shift schedule for all warehouse technicians, which consisted of two daily, 12-hour shifts, starting at 6:00 A.M. and 6:00 P.M., respectively. Rehrs (P) worked the new rotating shift until February 2002 when he had a heart attack, leading to bypass surgery and the implantation of a defibrillator and pacemaker. A month after his return to work, Rehrs (P) was temporarily placed on a fixed daytime schedule at the request of his doctor to more easily maintain his blood sugar level. He worked a straight eight-hour shift for the next 60 days. But P&G (D) refused to make the accommodation permanent, arguing that shift rotation was an essential part of his job. Rehrs (P) sued under the Americans with Disabilities Act. The trial court granted P&G's (D) summary judgment motion, finding that, even if his diabetes constituted a disability under the ADA, Rehrs (P) was not a qualified individual with a disability because he could not perform an essential job function—shift rotation.

ISSUE: Can shift rotation be considered a nondiscriminatory essential function of a position for purposes of the ADA?

HOLDING AND DECISION: (Riley, J.) Yes. Shift rotation can be considered a nondiscriminatory essential function of a position for purposes of the ADA. Under the ADA, an accommodation that would cause other employees to work harder, longer, or be deprived of opportunities is not mandated. According to P&G (D), shift rotation increases productivity. To not have shift rotation would hurt the company as far as production is concerned, and exempting only one employee from shift rotation would undermine the team concept, create inequities in the workforce, and place a heavier or unfavorable burden on other technicians at the facility. The fact that the plant could operate on a straight-shift schedule is irrelevant

to a determination of whether the shift schedule is an essential function of the job, because P&G (D) does not have to exercise the same business judgment as other employers who may believe a straight shift is more productive. The fact that the duties performed at the facility on the day shift are the same duties performed on the night shift is also of no moment. The term "essential function" encompasses more than core job requirements. Finally, an employer does not concede that a job function is nonessential simply by voluntarily assuming the limited burden associated with a temporary accommodation, and the fact that P&G (D) allowed him a temporary exemption from shift rotation therefore does not demonstrate that shift rotation is not essential.

▶ ANALYSIS

Essential functions are determined by reference to the employer's judgment as to what is essential, the written description for the position, advertising or applicant interviews, the time spent performing the function, the consequences of not requiring performance of the function, the terms of any relevant collective-bargaining agreement, the experience of past holders of the position, and the experience of employees who currently hold similar jobs. In essence, the employer determines the essential functions of a job.

■▬■

Quicknotes

AMERICANS WITH DISABILITIES ACT (42 U.S.C. §§ 12101-12213) Enacted in 1990, this federal law prohibits discrimination in employment against Americans with physical or mental disabilities.

■▬■

U.S. Airways, Inc. v. Barnett

Employer (D) v. Disabled employee (P)

535 U.S. 391 (2002).

NATURE OF CASE: Appeal from summary judgment for employee in reasonable-accommodation action under the Americans with Disabilities Act (ADA).

FACT SUMMARY: Barnett (P), who had an injured back, asked his employer, U.S. Airways, Inc. (U.S. Airways) (D), to make an exception to the company's seniority system that would enable him to keep his mailroom job. U.S. Airways (D) refused his requested accommodation.

🏛 RULE OF LAW
An employer's showing that a requested accommodation conflicts with seniority rules is ordinarily sufficient to show, as a matter of law, that an "accommodation" is not "reasonable" unless the employee presents evidence of special circumstances that makes a seniority-rule exception reasonable in the particular case.

FACTS: After Barnett (P) injured his back while a cargo handler for U.S. Airways (D), he transferred to a less physically demanding mailroom position, where he was for two years. His mailroom position later became open to seniority-based employee bidding under U.S. Airways's seniority system, and employees senior to him planned to bid on the job. U.S. Airways refused his request to accommodate his disability by allowing him to remain in the mailroom, and he lost his job. He then filed suit under the ADA. Finding that altering a seniority system would result in an "undue hardship" to both U.S. Airways (D) and its nondisabled employees, the district court granted the company summary judgment. The court of appeals reversed, holding that the seniority system was merely a factor in the undue-hardship analysis and that a case-by-case, fact-intensive analysis is required to determine whether any particular assignment would constitute an undue hardship. The Supreme Court granted review.

ISSUE: Is an employer's showing that a requested accommodation conflicts with seniority rules is ordinarily sufficient to show, as a matter of law, that an "accommodation" is not "reasonable" unless the employee presents evidence of special circumstances that makes a seniority-rule exception reasonable in the particular case?

HOLDING AND DECISION: (Breyer, J.) Yes. An employer's showing that a requested accommodation conflicts with seniority rules is ordinarily sufficient to show, as a matter of law, that an "accommodation" is not "reasonable" unless the employee presents evidence of special circumstances that makes a seniority-rule exception reasonable in the particular case. U.S. Airways (D) interprets the ADA as applied to seniority systems to mean that an accommodation that would violate the rules of a seniority system would always be "not reasonable." In Barnett's (P) view, such an accommodation is never "not reasonable." U.S. Airway's (D) claims that a seniority system virtually always trumps a conflicting accommodation demand, based on its view of how the ADA treats workplace "preferences." Given that the ADA specifies that sometimes preferences will be necessary to achieve its basic equal-opportunity goal, coupled with the ADA's silence about the exempting effect of neutral rules, the Court is convinced that the ADA does not create any automatic exemption. Simply because an accommodation would provide a preference, in the sense that it would permit the disabled worker to violate a rule that others must obey, does not, in and of itself, automatically show that the accommodation is "not reasonable." Barnett (P) argues that "reasonable accommodation" means only "effective accommodation" so that a court can consider only whether the requested accommodation meets an individual's disability-related needs and nothing more. Under this theory, a seniority-rule violation, which has nothing to do with an accommodation's effectiveness, has nothing to do with its reasonableness. However, Barnett's (P) interpretation of "reasonable" is incorrect, as it is the word "accommodation" that requires effectiveness, not "reasonable." An effective accommodation could still prove to be unreasonable because of its impact on the business or on other employees. As to Barnett's (P) contention that any other view would create a practical burden of proof problem, many lower courts have reconciled the phrases "reasonable accommodation" and "undue hardship" in a practical way, holding that a plaintiff/employee, in order to defeat a defendant/employer's summary judgment motion, need only show that an "accommodation" seems reasonable on its face, i.e., ordinarily or in the run of cases. The defendant/employer then must show special (typically case-specific) circumstances demonstrating undue hardship in the particular circumstances. Neither U.S. Airways's (D) position nor Barnett's (P) position is a proper interpretation of the ADA. Ordinarily or in the run of cases, a request for an accommodation that would violate a seniority system is not a reasonable one. The statute does not require proof on a case-by-case basis that a seniority system should prevail, because it would not be reasonable in the run of cases that the assignment trump such a system's rules. Analogous case law has recognized the importance of seniority to employee-management relations. A typical seniority system provides important employee benefits by creating, and fulfilling, employee expectations of fair, uniform treatment (e.g., job security and an opportunity for

Continued on next page.

steady and predictable advancement based on objective standards) that might be undermined if an employer were required to show more than the system's existence. Nothing in the statute suggests that Congress intended to undermine seniority systems in such a way. The plaintiff remains free to show that special circumstances warrant a finding that, despite the seniority system's presence, the requested accommodation is reasonable on the particular facts. Special circumstances might alter the important expectations created by a seniority system. The plaintiff might also show that the system already contains exceptions such that, in the circumstances, one further exception is unlikely to matter. The plaintiff has the burden of showing special circumstances and must explain why, in the particular case, an exception to the seniority system can constitute a reasonable accommodation, even though in the ordinary case it cannot. Vacated and remanded.

DISSENT: (Scalia, J.) The majority is mistaken that a seniority system can ever be overridden by an accommodation. This mistake stems from an interpretation of the ADA that makes all employment rules and practices subject to suspension when a court finds that doing so is a reasonable means of enabling a disabled person to keep his job. The language of the ADA requires employers to modify or remove policies and practices that burden a disabled person "because of [his] disability"; to eliminate barriers that would not be barriers but for the employee's disability. This does not include rules and practices that bear no more heavily on the disabled employee than upon others. This is true also of seniority systems, which burden the disabled and nondisabled alike. Even if imposing the seniority system has the harsh effect of leaving the disabled employee without a job, that does not make the seniority system a disability-related obstacle. The practical effect of the majority's decision, through the rebuttable presumption it creates, is to give disabled employees the power, whenever they can show "special circumstances," to undercut bona fide seniority systems by subjecting them to constant litigation.

DISSENT: (Souter, J.) Nothing in the ADA insulates seniority rules from the "reasonable accommodation" requirement. Because seniority systems do not enjoy special protection under the ADA, a consideration of facts peculiar to this case is necessary to determine if Barnett (P) carried his burden of showing that his requested accommodation was reasonable. Here, Barnett (P) held the mailroom job for two years before requesting the accommodation, thus not asking for a change, but to continue the status quo. All he asked was that the airline not declare the position "vacant." He did not ask to bump any other employees and no one would have lost a job on his account. There was no evidence presented that there would have been any ripple effects from his request, especially since U.S. Airways (D) took pains to ensure that its seniority rules were noncontractual and modifiable at will. Therefore, Barnett (P) has shown that his requested accommodation was

reasonable, and the burden ought to shift to U.S. Airways (D) to prove undue hardship.

▶ *ANALYSIS*

As Justice Souter points out in his dissent, the seniority system at issue in this case was noncontractual. A seniority system contained in a collective-bargaining agreement is contractually enforceable. The lower courts, including the court of appeals, had agreed that a collectively-bargained-for seniority system would trump a disabled employee's request for reassignment to a vacant position under the ADA, but refused to extend such deference to a seniority system that was not the product of collective bargaining. Here, the majority assumes that a unilaterally imposed seniority system confers the same advantages on workers as does one that is the result of collective bargaining. Justice O'Connor would agree with the majority only in the case where the unilaterally imposed system was legally enforceable.

■■■

Quicknotes

AMERICANS WITH DISABILITIES ACT (42 U.S.C. §§ 12101-12213) Enacted in 1990, this federal law prohibits discrimination in employment against Americans with physical or mental disabilities.

COLLECTIVE BARGAINING Negotiations between an employer and employee that are mediated by a specified third party.

■■■

Huber v. Wal-Mart

Employee (P) v. Employer (D)

486 F.3d 480 (8th Cir.), *cert. dismissed*, 2008 U.S. LEXIS 1095 (2008).

NATURE OF CASE: Appeal by employer of summary judgment for employee.

FACT SUMMARY: A disabled employee was denied a request for reassignment, and sued, arguing she was entitled to the reassignment as reasonable accommodation for her disability.

🏛 RULE OF LAW
An employer who has an established policy to fill vacant job positions with the most qualified applicant is not required to assign a qualified disabled employee to a vacant position if the disabled employee is not the most qualified applicant for the position.

FACTS: Huber (P) worked for Wal-Mart (D) as a filler of grocery orders. After sustaining a permanent injury to her right arm and hand, she sought, as a reasonable accommodation, reassignment to a router position, which was vacant and equivalent under the Americans with Disabilities Act (ADA). Wal-Mart (D) denied her request and required her to apply and compete for the position with other applicants, pursuant to its policy of hiring the most qualified applicant. Wal-Mart (D) hired a non-disabled applicant, and claimed that although Huber (P) was qualified with or without an accommodation to perform the duties of the router position, she was not the most qualified candidate. Huber (P) was placed at another facility in a janitorial position.

ISSUE: Is an employer who has an established policy to fill vacant job positions with the most qualified applicant required to assign a qualified disabled employee to a vacant position if the disabled employee is not the most qualified applicant for the position?

HOLDING AND DECISION: (Riley, J.) No. An employer who has an established policy to fill vacant job positions with the most qualified applicant is not required to assign a qualified disabled employee to a vacant position if the disabled employee is not the most qualified applicant for the position. The ADA is not an affirmative-action statute and does not require an employer to reassign a qualified disabled employee to a vacant position when such a reassignment would violate a legitimate nondiscriminatory policy of the employer to hire the most qualified candidate. Giving Huber (P) the maintenance job was a reasonable accommodation of her disability. The maintenance position may not have been a perfect substitute job, or the employee's most preferred alternative job, but an employer is not required to provide a disabled employee with an accommodation that is ideal from the employee's perspective, only an accommodation that was reasonable. Wal-Mart (D) did not discriminate against Huber (P), and treated her no better or worse than all other candidates for the position.

▶ ANALYSIS

The Supreme Court agreed to consider whether Wal-Mart (D) was required under the ADA to reassign Huber (P) to the vacant position she sought in December 2007. In January 2008, the parties entered a confidential settlement, and Huber (P) then withdrew her appeal. The Supreme Court then dismissed the case.

■▬■

Quicknotes

AFFIRMATIVE ACTION A form of benign discrimination designed to remedy existing discrimination by favoring one group over another.

AMERICANS WITH DISABILITIES ACT (42 U.S.C. §§ 12101-12213) Enacted in 1990, this federal law prohibits discrimination in employment against Americans with physical or mental disabilities.

■▬■

Vande Zande v. State of Wisconsin Department of Administration

Disabled employee (P) v. State employer (D)

44 F.3d 538 (7th Cir. 1995).

NATURE OF CASE: Appeal following summary judgment in a disability discrimination case.

FACT SUMMARY: State of Wisconsin Department of Administration (D) refused to allow Lori Vande Zande (P) to work full time at home and did not lower the height of a kitchen sink in the office provided for employees during coffee breaks and lunch.

🏛 RULE OF LAW
The duty of reasonable accommodation is satisfied when the employer does what is necessary to enable the disabled worker to work in reasonable comfort.

FACTS: Vande Zande (P), a paraplegic who worked for Wisconsin (D), occasionally developed pressure ulcers as a result of her disability, which required her to stay at home. While in the office, Vande Zande (P) had access to a nearby sink in the bathroom, which was lowered to accommodate her handicap. The sink in the nearby kitchenette was not lowered. Wisconsin (D) made numerous accommodations for her, including buying special, adjustable furniture, adjusting Vande Zande's (P) schedule to accommodate her numerous medical appointments, and making changes to the plans for a locker room in the new state office building. However, Vande Zande (P) claimed that Wisconsin (P) was required: (1) to allow Vande Zande (P) to work full time at home and provide her with a computer when she had a serious bout of pressure ulcers and (2) to lower the kitchenette sink. Vande Zande (P) changed jobs and sued Wisconsin (D). The trial court granted Wisconsin's (D) motion for summary judgment, and Vande Zande (P) appealed.

ISSUE: Is the duty of reasonable accommodation satisfied when the employer does what is necessary to enable the disabled worker to work in reasonable comfort?

HOLDING AND DECISION: (Posner, C.J.) Yes. The duty of reasonable accommodation is satisfied when the employer does what is necessary to enable the disabled worker to work in reasonable comfort. Here, Wisconsin (D) reasonably accommodated Vande Zande (P). An employer, especially a government agency with a mandate to keep costs down, is not required to allow an employee to work at home, particularly where team work and efficiency will be compromised. Instead of requiring Wisconsin (D) to permit her to work from home, Vande Zande (P) was given a reduced work load and was able to utilize some of her accumulated sick time so that she incurred no loss of income. Because Vande Zande (P) had access to a lowered sink in the bathroom to wash out coffee cups and such, Wisconsin (D) was not required to spend the money to lower the kitchen sink. An employer does not have a duty to expend even modest amounts of money to bring about absolutely identical working conditions for disabled and nondisabled workers. Affirmed.

▶ ANALYSIS

Typically, questions arise as to the burden of proof required in disability-discrimination cases. Often, an employer must prove that its actions were based on legitimate, nondiscriminatory reasons. However, once the employer has admitted that its actions were based on the employee's disability, the burden of proof as to whether such actions were acceptable continues to be litigated.

■■■

Quicknotes

DISCRIMINATION Unequal treatment of a class of persons.

■■■

Gambini v. Total Renal Care, Inc.

Employee (P) v. Employer (D)

486 F.3d 1087 (9th Cir. 2007).

NATURE OF CASE: Appeal of trial judgment for the employer.

FACT SUMMARY: Gambini (P), who was under treatment for a bipolar disorder, burst into profanities at a meeting and was fired. She asked her employer, DaVita (D), to reconsider because her behavior was a consequence of her bipolar condition. DaVita (D) refused. A jury found in favor of the employer.

🏛 RULE OF LAW
Under Washington law, conduct resulting from a disability is part of the disability, rather than a separate basis for termination.

FACTS: Gambini (P), who was under treatment for a bipolar disorder, burst into profanities at a meeting in which she was criticized for her attitude and disposition and assigned an improvement plan. Gambini (P) had informed her supervisors about her condition, and she kept them aware of her medication problems. During the meeting when her temper erupted, she was undergoing a medication change, heightening the volatility of her mood swings. Her outburst resulted in her termination shortly afterward. Gambini (P) argued her behavior was a consequence of her bipolar condition and urged DaVita (D) to reconsider, but the company refused. She sued in the U.S. District Court for the Western District of Washington, claiming violations of the Washington Law Against Discrimination and the Family and Medical Leave Act. A jury found for DaVita and she appealed.

ISSUE: Under Washington law, is conduct resulting from a disability part of the disability, rather than a separate basis for termination?

HOLDING AND DECISION: (Shadur, J.) Yes. Under Washington law, conduct resulting from a disability is part of the disability, rather than a separate basis for termination. The trial court should have instructed the jury that conduct resulting from a disability is part of the disability under Washington law rather than a separate basis for termination. The district court abused its discretion when it declined to give that instruction and such an exclusion was not harmless error, but a failure to fairly and adequately cover the issues presented and state the law correctly. A properly instructed jury might have concluded that it was her personality and not her work product that motivated DaVita (D).

▶ ANALYSIS

The court's analysis of the issue was based on the Americans with Disabilities Act (ADA), despite the fact that the case involved Washington law. Many state laws providing victims of discrimination with causes of action in state court emulate the ADA, Title VII, and the Age Discrimination in Employment Act (ADEA), but when reading a federal court opinion dealing with a state law, be sure to identify language by the court indicating that the court's analysis is based on a comparable federal law. Do not simply make that assumption.

■=■

Quicknotes

AGE DISCRIMINATION IN EMPLOYMENT ACT (ADEA) (29 U.S.C. § 621) 1967 act prohibiting age discrimination and retaliation in employment.

AMERICANS WITH DISABILITIES ACT (42 U.S.C. §§ 12101-12213) Enacted in 1990, this federal law prohibits discrimination in employment against Americans with physical or mental disabilities.

HARMLESS ERROR An error taking place during trial that does not require the reviewing court to overturn or modify the trial court's judgment in that it did not affect the appellant's substantial rights or the disposition of the action.

TITLE VII OF THE CIVIL RIGHTS ACT OF 1964 Law prohibiting discrimination in employment on the basis of race, color, religion, sex, and national origin.

■=■

Chevron U.S.A. Inc. v. Echazabal

Employer (D) v. Disabled employee (P)

536 U.S. 73 (2002).

NATURE OF CASE: Appeal from reversal of summary judgment for employer in an Americans with Disabilities Act (ADA) discrimination action.

FACT SUMMARY: Echazabal (P) was laid off because his liver condition would be exacerbated by continuing to work at Chevron U.S.A. Inc.'s (Chevron) (D) oil refineries. Echazabal (P) sued under the ADA, and Chevron (D) defended under an Equal Employment Opportunity Commission (EEOC) regulation that authorizes an employer to refuse to hire an individual because his performance on the job would endanger his own health, owing to a disability.

🏛 **RULE OF LAW**
The ADA permits an EEOC regulation that authorizes an employer to refuse to hire an individual because his performance on the job would endanger his own health, owing to a disability.

FACTS: Echazabal (P) worked for independent contractors at one of Chevron's (D) oil refineries until Chevron (D) refused to hire him because of a liver condition, which its doctors said would be exacerbated by continued exposure to toxins at the refinery. The contractor employing him laid him off in response to Chevron's (D) request that it reassign him to a job without exposure to toxins or remove him from the refinery. Echazabal (P) filed suit, claiming, among other things, that Chevron's (D) actions violated the ADA. Chevron (D) defended under an EEOC regulation permitting the defense that a worker's disability on the job would pose a direct threat to his health. The district court granted Chevron (D) summary judgment, but the court of appeals reversed, finding that the regulation exceeded the scope of permissible rulemaking under the ADA. The Supreme Court granted review.

ISSUE: Does the ADA permit an EEOC regulation that authorizes an employer to refuse to hire an individual because his performance on the job would endanger his own health, owing to a disability?

HOLDING AND DECISION: (Souter, J.) Yes. The ADA permits an EEOC regulation that authorizes an employer to refuse to hire an individual because his performance on the job would endanger his own health, owing to a disability. The ADA's discrimination definition covers a number of things an employer might do to block a disabled person from advancing in the workplace, such as "using qualification standards . . . that screen out or tend to screen out an individual with a disability." The Act uses the definition to create an affirmative defense for action under a qualification standard "shown to be job-related for the position in question and ... consistent with business necessi-

ty," which "may include a requirement that an individual shall not pose a direct threat to the health or safety of other individuals in the workplace." The EEOC's regulation carries the defense one step further, allowing an employer to screen out a potential worker with a disability for risks on the job to his own health or safety. Echazabal (P) relies on the canon expressio unius exclusio alterius—expressing one item of an associated group excludes another left unmentioned—for his argument that the ADA, by recognizing only threats to others, precludes the regulation, which relates to threats to self, as a matter of law. The first strike against the expression-exclusion rule here is in the statute, which includes the threat-to-others provision as an example of legitimate qualifications that are "job-related and consistent with business necessity." These spacious defensive categories seem to give an agency a good deal of discretion in setting the limits of permissible qualification standards. Additionally, the expansive "may include" phrase points directly away from the sort of exclusive specifications that Echazabal (P) claims. Strike two is the failure to identify any series of terms or things that should be understood to go hand in hand, which are abridged in circumstances supporting a sensible inference that the term left out must have been meant to be excluded. Echazabal (P) claims that Congress's adoption only of the threat-to-others exception in the ADA was a deliberate omission of the threat-to-self exception included in the EEOC's regulation implementing the precursor Rehabilitation Act of 1973, which has language identical to that in the ADA. But this is not an unequivocal implication of congressional intent. Because the EEOC was not the only agency interpreting the Rehabilitation Act of 1973, its regulation did not establish a clear, standard pairing of threats to self and others. And, it is likely that Congress used such language in the ADA knowing what the EEOC had made of that language under the earlier statute. The third strike is simply that there is no apparent stopping point to the argument that, by specifying a threat-to-others defense, Congress intended a negative implication about those whose safety could be considered. For example, could Congress have meant that an employer could not defend a refusal to hire when a worker's disability would threaten others outside the workplace? Because Congress has not spoken exhaustively on threats to a worker's own health, the regulation can claim adherence under the rule in *Chevron U.S.A. Inc. v. Natural Resources Defense Council, Inc.*, 467 U.S. 837 (1984), so long as it makes sense of the statutory defense for qualification standards that are "job-related and consistent with business necessity." Chevron's (D) reasons for claiming that the regulation is reasonable include, inter alia, that it allows Chevron (D) to avoid the risk of

Continued on next page.

violating the Occupational Safety and Health Act of 1970 (OSHA). Whether an employer would be liable under OSHA for hiring an individual who consents to a job's particular dangers is an open question, but the employer would be courting trouble under OSHA. The EEOC's resolution exemplifies the substantive choices that agencies are expected to make when Congress leaves the intersection of competing objectives both imprecisely marked and subject to administrative leeway. Nor can the EEOC's resolution be called unreasonable as allowing the kind of workplace paternalism the ADA was meant to outlaw. The ADA was trying to get at refusals to give an even break to classes of disabled people, while claiming to act for their own good in reliance on untested and pretextual stereotypes. This sort of sham protection is just what the regulation disallows by demanding a particularized enquiry into the harms an employee would probably face. Finally, that the threat-to-self defense reasonably falls within the general "job related" and "business necessity" standard does not reduce the "direct threat" language to surplusage; the provision made a conclusion clear that might otherwise have been fought over in litigation or administrative rulemaking. Reversed.

▶ ANALYSIS

In this case, the EEOC was interpreting a provision of Title I, the chapter on which the EEOC has been expressly delegated rulemaking authority, and the EEOC's definition was found in the regulation itself, not in an Interpretive Guidance. These factors undoubtedly explain the Court's decision to defer to the EEOC.

■══■

Quicknotes

AGENCY REGULATIONS Rules promulgated by a government agency pursuant to its equitable authority.

■══■

Albertson's, Inc. v. Kirkingburg

Employer (D) v. Visually impaired employee (P)

527 U.S. 555 (1999).

NATURE OF CASE: Suit alleging disability discrimination under the Americans with Disabilities Act (ADA).

FACT SUMMARY: Kirkingburg (P), a truck driver for Albertson's (D), alleged that his amblyopia, a condition rendering him effectively blind in one eye, constituted a disability under the ADA.

RULE OF LAW
Under the ADA, an employer who requires as a job qualification that an employee meet an otherwise applicable federal safety regulation need not justify enforcing the regulation solely because its standard may be waived in an individual case.

FACTS: Kirkingburg (P), a truck driver, suffered from amblyopia, an uncorrectable eye condition that caused 20/200 vision in his left eye. Although his vision did not meet the Department of Transportation standards for commercial truck drivers, he was erroneously certified and hired by Albertson's (D). The district court granted Albertson's (D) motion for summary judgment on the ground that Kirkingburg (P) was not "qualified." The court of appeals reversed. Albertson's (D) appealed.

ISSUE: Under the ADA, must an employer who requires as a job qualification that an employee meet an otherwise applicable federal safety regulation justify enforcing the regulation solely because its standard may be waived in an individual case?

HOLDING AND DECISION: (Souter, J.) No. Under the ADA, an employer who requires as a job qualification that an employee meet an otherwise applicable federal safety regulation need not justify enforcing the regulation solely because its standard may be waived in an individual case. An employee can be a "qualified individual with a disability" when that employee is unable to perform the essential functions of his present job, regardless of the level of accommodation offered, but can perform the essential functions of other available jobs within the company with or without a reasonable accommodation. Albertson's (D) argued that even if Kirkingburg (P) was disabled, he was not a "qualified" individual with a disability because Albertson's (D) merely required the minimum level of visual acuity set forth in the federal regulations. Under the ADA, employers may justify their use of qualification standards that screen out or tend to screen out individuals with disabilities so long as such standards are job related and consistent with business necessity and if performance of the job cannot be otherwise accomplished by reasonable accommodation. Kirkingburg (P) argued that the ADA does not authorize an employer to follow a facially applicable regulatory standard subject to waiver without inquiring as to whether the employee meets that standard and that the employer must show the waivable regulatory standard is job related and consistent with business necessity. The waiver program was enacted primarily as an experiment with public safety. The employer need not bear the burden of justifying a job disqualification that would tend to exclude disabled persons when the employer chooses to abide by the regulatory standard, despite the government's willingness to waive it. Reversed.

CONCURRENCE: (Thomas, J.) I prefer to hold that Kirkingburg (P) was not qualified to perform the job he sought under the ADA. I concur in the Court's opinion subject to the understanding that federal standards may be critical in determining whether a plaintiff is a "qualified individual with a disability."

ANALYSIS

The Court here held that employers who hired employees subject to federal regulations are permitted to enforce absolute prohibitions on drivers who do not meet the federal standards. Moreover, the employer need not make an individual assessment nor demonstrate that the qualifications were justified as job related or a business necessity.

Quicknotes

AMERICANS WITH DISABILITIES ACT (42 U.S.C. §§ 12101-12213) Enacted in 1990, this federal law prohibits discrimination in employment against Americans with physical or mental disabilities.

CHAPTER 7

Enforcing Antidiscrimination Laws

Quick Reference Rules of Law

PAGE

1. **Filing a Timely Charge.**   A plaintiff cannot bring a salary discrimination suit under Title VII of the 1964 Civil Rights Act when the disparate pay is received during the 180-day statutory limitations period, but is the result of discriminatory pay decisions that occurred outside the limitations period. (Ledbetter v. the Goodyear Tire & Rubber Company, Inc.)   *90*

2. **Class Actions: Requirements of Rule 23(a).**   A class of 1.5 million members, consisting of female employees of one company, can be certified under Federal Rule of Civil Procedure 23(a). (Dukes v. Wal-Mart, Inc.)   *91*

Ledbetter v. the Goodyear Tire & Rubber Company, Inc.

Employer (D) v. Employee (P)

127 S. Ct. 2162 (2007).

NATURE OF CASE: Appeal of the Eleventh Circuit's reversal of judgment for the employee.

FACT SUMMARY: Lilly Ledbetter (P) brought an action for discrimination against her employer, Goodyear Tire & Rubber Company, Inc. (Goodyear Tire) (D). A jury found in her favor, and Goodyear Tire (D) appealed, arguing that she brought her claim after the expiration of the limitations period that applies to Title VII of the 1964 Civil Rights Act. Ledbetter (P) argued that discrimination in pay is different from other types of employment discrimination and therefore should be governed by a different rule.

🏛 RULE OF LAW
A plaintiff cannot bring a salary discrimination suit under Title VII of the 1964 Civil Rights Act when the disparate pay is received during the 180-day statutory limitations period, but is the result of discriminatory pay decisions that occurred outside the limitations period.

FACTS: Lilly Ledbetter (P) sued Goodyear Tire (D) for gender discrimination, claiming that the company (D) had given her a low salary because of her gender. A jury found for Ledbetter (P) and awarded her over $3.5 million, which the district judge later reduced to $360,000. Goodyear Tire (D) appealed, citing a Title VII provision that requires that discrimination complaints be made within 180 days of the employer's discriminatory conduct. The jury was allowed to examine Ledbetter's (P) entire career for evidence of discrimination, and Goodyear Tire (D) argued that the jury should only have considered the one annual salary review that had occurred within the 180-day limitations period before Ledbetter's (P) complaint. The U.S. Court of Appeals for the Eleventh Circuit reversed the lower court, but ruled that the jury could examine Ledbetter's (P) career for evidence of discrimination as far back as the last annual salary review before the start of the 180-day limitations period. Only those annual reviews that could have affected Ledbetter's (P) payment during the 180 days could be evaluated. The circuit court found no evidence of discrimination in those reviews, so it reversed the district court and dismissed Ledbetter's (P) complaint.

ISSUE: Can a plaintiff bring a salary discrimination suit under Title VII of the 1964 Civil Rights Act when the disparate pay is received during the 180-day statutory limitations period, but is the result of discriminatory pay decisions that occurred outside the limitations period?

HOLDING AND DECISION: (Alito, J.) No. A plaintiff cannot bring a salary discrimination suit under Title VII of the 1964 Civil Rights Act when the disparate

pay is received during the 180-day statutory limitations period, but is the result of discriminatory pay decisions that occurred outside the limitations period. Ledbetter's (P) claim was time-barred by Title VII's limitations period. Discriminatory conduct that was not charged within the statutory time limits cannot be resurrected simply because the effects of it are still felt. For a timely claim, Ledbetter (P) would have needed to file within 180 days of a discriminatory salary decision. It is not significant that paychecks she received during the 180 days prior to her claim were affected by the past discrimination. Discriminatory intent is a crucial element of a Title VII disparate-treatment claim, but each instance of Goodyear Tire's (D) discriminatory intent fell outside the limitations period. The short time limit was enacted to ensure quick resolution of pay discrimination disputes, which can become more difficult to defend against as time passes. To adopt Ledbetter's (P) argument would be to allow even discriminatory pay decisions made 20 years ago to be the subject of Title VII claims.

DISSENT: (Ginsburg, J.) The majority's ruling is out of tune with the realities of wage discrimination and constitutes a cramped interpretation of Title VII, incompatible with the statute's broad remedial purpose. The legislature may act to correct this Court's "parsimonious" reading of Title VII.

▶ ANALYSIS

The Equal Employment Opportunity Commission (EOC) charging period for a discriminatory claim is triggered when a discrete unlawful, discriminatory practice takes place. The adverse effects that result from that past discrimination do not constitute a new violation. Therefore, a new charging period does not begin when the effects alone occur.

■══■

Quicknotes

DISPARATE TREATMENT Unequal treatment of employees or of applicants for employment without justification.

TITLE VII OF THE CIVIL RIGHTS ACT OF 1964 Law prohibiting discrimination in employment on the basis of race, color, religion, sex, and national origin.

■══■

Dukes v. Wal–Mart, Inc.

Class of female employees (P) v. Employer (D)

2007 U.S. App. LEXIS 28558 (9th Cir. 2007).

NATURE OF CASE: Petition for class certification.

FACT SUMMARY: Six female employees (P) sought certification of a class of similarly situated employees in a discrimination claim against Wal-Mart (D).

> ## 🏛 RULE OF LAW
> A class of 1.5 million members, consisting of female employees of one company, can be certified under Federal Rule of Civil Procedure 23(a).

FACTS: Six female employees (P) sued Wal-Mart (D) on behalf of all similarly situated employees, alleging that the company's (D) subjective promotion system prevented women from applying for or being considered for management-track positions. The district court certified the class of over 1.5 million current and former female Wal-Mart employees (P) in June 2004, finding that plaintiffs (P) showed that Wal-Mart's (D) pay policies were significantly uniform across stores and that the policies contain a common feature of subjectivity relevant to plaintiffs' claims of class-wide sex discrimination. Plaintiffs (P) sought back and front pay, punitive damages, and injunctive relief. Under the district court's ruling, class members for whom there is no objective data documenting an interest in challenged promotions would be limited to injunctive and declaratory relief with respect to promotion claims.

ISSUE: Can a class of 1.5 million members, consisting of female employees of one company, be certified under Federal Rule of Civil Procedure 23(a)?

HOLDING AND DECISION: (Pregerson, J.) Yes. A class of 1.5 million members, consisting of female employees of one company, can be certified under Federal Rule of Civil Procedure 23(a). The anecdotal and statistical evidence supported a finding that Wal-Mart (D) had a uniform personnel and management structure that created commonality across the country. The plaintiffs' (P) expert opinions, factual evidence, statistical evidence, and anecdotal evidence present significant proof of a corporate policy of discrimination and support the plaintiffs' contention that female employees (P) nationwide were subjected to a common pattern and practice of discrimination. Evidence of Wal-Mart's (D) subjective decision-making policy raises an inference of discrimination and provides further evidence of a common practice. The trial court properly found that Wal-Mart's (D) corporate policies and subjective decision-making supported the contention that there was a common nationwide practice of discrimination and therefore the large number of hourly and management employees (P)—both current and former—had a common experience of alleged discrimination. In addition, the trial court was correct in finding the class was proper under

Rule 23(b)(2), even in light of the presence of a request for punitive damages and backpay, which are not a bar to a class action in the Ninth Circuit. Plaintiffs (P) stated that their primary intention in bringing this case was to obtain injunctive and declaratory relief—not money damages—and Wal-Mart (D) failed to effectively rebut plaintiffs' (P) statements or cast doubt on their reliability.

DISSENT: (Kleinfeld, J.) Certification threatens the rights of the women involved in the lawsuit, and deprives Wal-Mart (D) of the chance to mount an appropriate defense. The class does not represent the interests of all the class members because undeserving class members could be awarded damages while more deserving potential victims would be denied larger awards if the class is thrown out because of weak claims. Whether there is commonality in the class, and specifically whether the seven named plaintiffs were typical of the class that could grow to be as large as two million members, is also questionable. Finally, the request for back pay and punitive damages may undermine the request for injunctive and declaratory relief, especially given the presence of former employees who may be uninterested in effecting change inside their former employer's organization.

▶ ANALYSIS

This is widely touted as the largest employment discrimination class action in history. While the size of the class remains unclear, it could reach 2 million by the time it is tried. Wal-Mart has said that the company would seek a rehearing of the case or en banc review, because the decision strayed from Supreme Court and Ninth Circuit precedent.

▰▰▰

Quicknotes

CLASS ACTION A suit commenced by a representative on behalf of an ascertainable group that is too large to appear in court, who shares a commonality of interests and who will benefit from a successful result.

CLASS CERTIFICATION Certification by a court's granting of a motion to allow individual litigants to join as one plaintiff in a class action against the defendant.

DECLARATORY JUDGMENT A judgment of the court establishing the rights of the parties.

INJUNCTION A court order requiring a person to do, or prohibiting that person from doing, a specific act.

PUNITIVE DAMAGES Damages exceeding the actual injury suffered for the purposes of punishment of the defendant, deterrence of the wrongful behavior or comfort to the plaintiff.

▰▰▰

Judicial Relief

Quick Reference Rules of Law

PAGE

1. **Introduction.** Backpay as a remedy should be denied only for reasons that would not frustrate Title VII purposes of eradicating discrimination and making persons whole for injuries suffered through past discrimination. (Albemarle Paper Co. v. Moody) 94

2. **Reinstatement, Retroactive Seniority, and Injunctive Relief.** As a matter of law, § 706(g) of Title VII does not bar the award of lost seniority to a class-action plaintiff. (Franks v. Bowman Transportation Co.) 95

3. **Who Gets Retroactive Seniority and Backpay?** An incumbent employee's failure to apply for a job is not an inexorable bar to an award of retroactive seniority. (Teamsters v. United States) 96

4. **The Backpay Period.** Employers may toll the continuing accrual of backpay liability under Title VII by offering the claimant the job previously denied, without including retroactive seniority. (Ford Motor Co. v. EEOC) 97

5. **The Backpay Period.** After-acquired evidence of misconduct that would have resulted in discharge does not preclude employees from relief under the Age Discrimination in Employment Act (ADEA). (McKennon v. Nashville Banner Publishing Co.) 98

6. **Front Pay.** The decision whether to order the equitable remedy of reinstatement or, in the alternative, to award front pay is a decision for the trial judge, whereas the amount of the front-pay award is left to the jury's discretion. (Cassino v. Reichhold Chemicals, Inc.) 99

7. **Compensatory Damages.** In order to recover compensatory damages for emotional distress, a plaintiff must show that the defendant's unlawful conduct caused the emotional distress. (Turic v. Holland Hospitality, Inc.) 100

8. **Compensatory Damages.** A front-pay award is not an element of compensatory damages under Title VII. (Pollard v. E.I. du Pont de Nemours & Co.) 101

9. **Punitive Damages.** For purposes of punitive damages, an employer may not be held vicariously liable for the discriminatory employment decisions of managerial agents if the decisions are contrary to the employer's good faith efforts to comply with Title VII. (Kolstad v. American Dental Association) 102

10. **Liquidated Damages.** Where an employer willfully discriminates against an employee due to age, then liquidated damages can be imposed even if the Age Discrimination in Employment Act (ADEA) violation is not a formal, facially discriminatory policy. (Hazen Paper Co. v. Biggins) 103

11. **Attorneys' Fees.** Prevailing defendants are entitled to attorney-fee awards only when the plaintiff brings a frivolous action without foundation. (Christiansburg Garment Co. v. EEOC) 104

12. **Attorneys' Fees.** The "catalyst theory" is not a permissible basis for the award of attorneys' fees under the Fair Housing Amendments Act of 1988 and the Americans with Disabilities Act of 1990. (Buckhannon Board & Care Home, Inc. v. West Virginia Department of Health and Human Resources) 105

13. **Attorneys' Fees.** The critical factor in calculating attorneys' fees in civil rights cases, including employment discrimination cases, is the amount the reasonable client would pay. (Arbor Hill Concerned Citizens Neighborhood Association v. County of Albany) 107

Albemarle Paper Co. v. Moody

Employer (D) v. Class of former employees (P)

422 U.S. 405 (1975).

NATURE OF CASE: Review of an award of back-pay to employees in a class-action discrimination suit.

FACT SUMMARY: Albemarle Paper Co. (D) contended that the court of appeal abused its discretion in awarding former employee Moody (P) backpay as a result of its unlawful discriminatory system of job seniority.

🏛 RULE OF LAW
Backpay as a remedy should be denied only for reasons that would not frustrate Title VII purposes of eradicating discrimination and making persons whole for injuries suffered through past discrimination.

FACTS: Moody (P) brought a class-action against Albemarle Paper Co. (Albemarle) (D) for injunctive relief against Albemarle's (D) unlawful discriminatory system of job seniority. The district court found that Albemarle's (D) organization was racially segregated and left black employees in lower paying jobs. The trial court ordered Albemarle (D) to implement a "plant-wide" system of seniority, but the court refused to award backpay to the Moody (P) class. The court of appeal reversed, holding that backpay can only be denied in "special circumstances." The Supreme Court granted review.

ISSUE: Should backpay be denied only for reasons that would not frustrate Title VII purposes of eradicating discrimination and making persons whole for injuries suffered through past discrimination?

HOLDING AND DECISION: (Stewart, J.) Yes. Backpay as a remedy should be denied only for reasons that would not frustrate Title VII purposes of eradicating discrimination and making persons whole for injuries suffered through past discrimination. It is the purpose of Title VII to make persons whole for injuries suffered due to unlawful employment discrimination. Furthermore, Title VII deals with legal injuries of an economic nature that occur due to racial or antiminority discrimination. Thus, the court not only has the power but the duty to render a decree that will eliminate, as much as possible, the discriminatory effect of the past discrimination, as well as bar any discrimination in the future. Therefore, the award for backpay is measured by the principle that the persons aggrieved by the unlawful discrimination be, as much as possible, restored to a position where they would have been were it not for the unlawful discrimination. Affirmed.

CONCURRENCE: (Rehnquist, J.) To the extent that the district court retains substantial discretion as to whether or not to award backpay, the award is properly considered equitable, and neither party may demand a jury trial.

▶ ANALYSIS

The right to a jury trial guaranteed by the Seventh Amendment attaches only to legal, not equitable, civil claims. The award for backpay under Title VII is an equitable remedy and thus completely discretionary under the holding of this case. Justice Rehnquist's concurrence emphasized that the right to a jury trial is dependent on how such relief is characterized. Contrary to Title VII actions, the award of backpay is considered a legal remedy in other types of actions, such as ADEA actions, which do give the petitioner a right to a jury trial.

Quicknotes

EQUITABLE REMEDY A remedy that is based upon principles of fairness as opposed to rules of law; a remedy involving specific performance rather than money damages.

Franks v. Bowman Transportation Co.

Black applicants (P) v. Prospective employer (D)

424 U.S. 747 (1976).

NATURE OF CASE: Review of a judgment denying seniority relief in a Title VII class-action alleging racially discriminatory employment practices.

FACT SUMMARY: Franks (P), a black applicant who was refused employment by Bowman Transportation Co. (Bowman) (D), contended that an award of seniority relief was appropriate under the remedial provisions of § 706(g) of Title VII.

🏛 RULE OF LAW
As a matter of law, § 706(g) of Title VII does not bar the award of lost seniority to a class-action plaintiff.

FACTS: Franks (P), along with other black applicants (P) who had sought to be hired at Bowman (D) for driving positions, filed a class-action suit under Title VII for racially discriminatory hiring and discharge practices. The court found a Title VII violation. The court enjoined Bowman (D) from continued discriminatory practices and ordered that Franks (P) and other members (P) of the class be given priority in hiring for the driving positions. However, the court denied an award of seniority relief. Franks (P) appealed, but the court of appeals affirmed by holding that § 703(h), which permits bona fide seniority systems, barred seniority relief. The Supreme Court granted certiorari.

ISSUE: Is an award of seniority relief appropriate under the remedial provisions of § 706(g) of Title VII?

HOLDING AND DECISION: (Brennan, J.) Yes. As a matter of law, § 706(g) of Title VII does not bar the award of seniority relief to a class-action plaintiff. There is nothing in Title VII or in the legislative history that shows Congress's intent to bar seniority relief to victims of illegal discrimination. The central purpose of Title VII is to make persons whole for injuries suffered by unlawful employment discrimination. However, seniority relief may not be required in all circumstances, and the court must use sound equitable discretion in awarding relief. Reversed.

CONCURRENCE AND DISSENT: (Powell, J.) The majority holding does not recognize a difference between "benefit" and "competitive" types of seniority.

▶ ANALYSIS

In this case, the Court ordered Bowman (D) to give Franks (P) priority when filling its driving positions. The general rule is that the court may grant such relief unless special circumstances exist. One example of a "special circumstance" is where the discriminated employee fails to qualify for the job.

See *Kamberos v. GTE Automatic Electric*, 603 F.2d 598 (7th Cir. 1979). Another is where an effective relationship between the employee and employer has been rendered impossible. See *Ellis v. Ringgold School District*, 832 F.2d 27 (3d Cir. 1987).

Quicknotes

CLASS ACTION A suit commenced by a representative on behalf of an ascertainable group that is too large to appear in court, who shares a commonality of interests and who will benefit from a successful result.

TITLE VII OF THE CIVIL RIGHTS ACT OF 1964 Law prohibiting discrimination in employment on the basis of race, color, religion, sex, and national origin.

Teamsters v. United States

Employer (D) v. Federal government (P)

431 U.S. 324 (1977).

NATURE OF CASE: Review of judgment ordering seniority relief in an employment discrimination case.

FACT SUMMARY: T.I.M.E.-D.C. (D), a transportation company, claimed that retroactive seniority relief was too broad a remedy to grant to persons who the federal government (P) had not shown to be actual victims of unlawful discrimination.

🏛 RULE OF LAW
An incumbent employee's failure to apply for a job is not an inexorable bar to an award of retroactive seniority.

FACTS: The United States (P) brought a civil rights action against T.I.M.E.-D.C. (D) for engaging in a pattern and practice of discrimination against minorities in the hiring of line drivers. Both lower courts concluded that T.I.M.E.-D.C. (D) violated the statute by engaging in a pattern or practice of discrimination. The court of appeals awarded incumbent employees retroactive seniority whether or not they had in fact applied for line-driver jobs. T.I.M.E.-D.C. (D) appealed.

ISSUE: Is an incumbent employee's failure to apply for a job an inexorable bar to an award of retroactive seniority?

HOLDING AND DECISION: (Stewart, J.) No. An incumbent employee's failure to apply for a job is not an inexorable bar to an award of retroactive seniority. Instead, a nonapplicant must be given an opportunity to prove that he was deterred from applying for the job by the employer's discriminatory practices. The purpose of Title VII is to achieve equal employment and to remove the barriers that operate in favor of white males over minority employees. The Court has interpreted Congress's vesting of broad equitable power in the courts under Title VII a desire to make possible "the most complete relief possible." As a result, courts have a duty to award a remedy that eliminates past and future discrimination. A court must award a seniority remedy in order to make whole persons who suffered unlawful discrimination unless there is some reason for denying it. Thus, the remedy of seniority may appropriately be awarded to incumbent, nonapplicants who are able to prove that they would have applied for positions but for T.I.M.E.-D.C.'s (D) practice of discriminatory rejection. The federal government (P) must carry its burden of proof with regard to each individual. Reversed and remanded.

▶ ANALYSIS

This case illustrates the distinction employers would like to make between those minority employees who have actually applied for a position within the company and were then turned down and those employees who did not apply. As to the former group, proof of a pattern or practice of discrimination supports an inference that any particular employment decision was made in pursuit of that policy. The federal government (P) then need only show that an alleged discriminatee unsuccessfully applied for a position. The burden then shifts to the employer to demonstrate that the individual applicant was denied an employment opportunity for lawful reasons. The above decision holds that nonapplicants should be given an opportunity to show they should likewise be presumptively entitled to relief.

■=■

Quicknotes

BURDEN OF PROOF The duty of a party to introduce evidence to support a fact that is in dispute in an action.

TITLE VII OF THE CIVIL RIGHTS ACT OF 1964 Law prohibiting discrimination in employment on the basis of race, color, religion, sex, and national origin.

■=■

Ford Motor Co. v. EEOC

Employer (D) v. Government agency (P)

458 U.S. 219 (1982).

NATURE OF CASE: Appeal of an award of back-pay damages for employment discrimination.

FACT SUMMARY: Two women applicants (P) discriminated against by Ford Motor Co. (Ford) (D) were awarded backpay although they had rejected job offers from Ford (D) that didn't include retroactive seniority.

🏛 RULE OF LAW
Employers may toll the continuing accrual of backpay liability under Title VII by offering the claimant the job previously denied, without including retroactive seniority.

FACTS: In 1971, Gaddis (P) and Starr (P) applied for jobs as picker-packers at Ford (D) and were rejected. After Gaddis (P) and Starr (P) filed charges with the Equal Employment Opportunity Commission (EEOC) (P), the Commission (P) sued under Title VII on their behalf for sex discrimination. In 1973, Gaddis (P) and Starr (P) were recalled for one year by a former employer. Later that year, Ford (D) offered Gaddis (P) and Starr (P) jobs but without any seniority rights, which they rejected. In 1975, Gaddis (P) and Starr (P) entered a CETA nurses training program. The trial court subsequently awarded backpay to Gaddis (P) and Starr (P) from 1971 until the trial date in 1977, reducing the award by the amount of wages they earned during the period, but refused to order the additional relief of seniority rights sought by the EEOC. Ford (D) appealed, contending that the backpay should have been cut off completely at three different junctures: at the time of the recall, on the date Gaddis (P) and Starr (P) rejected Ford's job offer, and again when they entered the CETA training program. The court of appeals affirmed, and the Supreme Court granted review.

ISSUE: May employers toll the continuing accrual of backpay liability under Title VII by offering the claimant the job previously denied, without including retroactive seniority?

HOLDING AND DECISION: (O'Connor, J.) Yes. Employers may toll the continuing accrual of backpay liability under Title VII by offering the claimant the job previously denied, without including retroactive seniority. The primary objective of Title VII is to bring employment discrimination to an end. The rules implemented to achieve this objective encourage Title VII defendants to promptly make curative job offers, thereby bringing about voluntary compliance. If an employer must offer costly retroactive seniority to a claimant who has not yet proved discrimination in order to toll backpay liability, there is less

incentive to hire the claimant. Therefore, absent special circumstances, Title VII claimants have an obligation to accept an unconditional offer of the job originally sought to preserve the right to backpay. Since Ford (D) offered Gaddis (P) and Starr (P) in 1973 the job they originally sought in 1971, their backpay liability is cut off as of 1973. Reversed.

DISSENT: (Blackmun, J.) The majority's rule violates the clear dictates of Title VII, which allow the trial court discretion to fashion remedies that will provide complete relief. It is also flatly inconsistent with the policy that backpay should only be denied for reasons that would frustrate the purpose of Title VII. Furthermore, Ford's (D) extremely ambiguous job offer, without any job security for Gaddis (P) and Starr (P), satisfies the majority's own "special circumstances" exception.

▶ ANALYSIS

The decision leaves open the question of whether an employer can toll its backpay liability by offering the Title VII claimant a similar, but not identical, job to the one originally sought. Lower courts have generally settled on a "substantial equivalence" standard. In *Ford*, the majority and the dissent bitterly accused each other of being indifferent to the concerns of claimants. Justice Blackmun was certainly correct in pointing out the irony of the majority's decision in significantly reducing Gaddis (P) and Starr's (P) damages award in order to address these concerns.

■■■

Quicknotes

TITLE VII OF THE CIVIL RIGHTS ACT OF 1964 Law prohibiting discrimination in employment on the basis of race, color, religion, sex, and national origin.

TOLL To bar, suspend or stop, such as a statute of limitations period.

■■■

McKennon v. Nashville Banner Publishing Co.

Long-term employee (P) v. Employer (D)

513 U.S. 352 (1995).

NATURE OF CASE: Appeal from summary judgment for defendant in action for legal and equitable relief for wrongful termination.

FACT SUMMARY: Sixty-two-year-old McKennon (P) was dismissed by Nashville Banner Publishing Co. (Banner) (D), but after-acquired evidence of misconduct precluded relief in her age-discrimination suit.

🏛 **RULE OF LAW**
After-acquired evidence of misconduct that would have resulted in discharge does not preclude employees from relief under the Age Discrimination in Employment Act (ADEA).

FACTS: McKennon (P) had worked for the Nashville Banner Publishing Co. (D) for 30 years before being terminated at the age of 62. McKennon (P) claimed that her age was the reason for dismissal. She sued under the Age Discrimination in Employment Act of 1967 (ADEA). McKennon (P) sought both legal and equitable remedies, including backpay. In discovery, McKennon (P) admitted that she had copied several confidential documents about Banner's (D) financial condition. Banner (D) claimed that removing confidential documents was grounds for dismissal and precluded relief under the ADEA. The district court granted summary judgment in favor of Banner (D). The district court held that McKennon's (P) misconduct was grounds for termination. The Sixth Circuit affirmed on the same grounds. The Supreme Court granted certiorari.

ISSUE: Does after-acquired evidence of wrongdoing that would have resulted in discharge preclude employees from any relief under the ADEA?

HOLDING AND DECISION: (Kennedy, J.) No. After-acquired evidence of wrongdoing that would have resulted in discharge does not preclude employees from relief under the ADEA. The ADEA reflects a societal condemnation of invidious bias in employment decisions. The objective of the ADEA and similar statutes is to eliminate discrimination in the workplace. Included in that objective are deterrence and compensation for injuries. The ADEA allows an injured employee a right of action to obtain the authorized relief. When an injured employee seeks redress, that employee vindicates both the deterrence and compensation objectives of the ADEA. To allow after-acquired evidence of wrongdoing to be a total bar to relief would not be in accord with the statutory goals of the ADEA. While the "unclean hands" defense may bar some forms of equitable relief, that defense does not bar relief when a private suit serves an important public purpose. In this case, the awarding of backpay is the appropriate remedy. The calculating of backpay shall commence from the date of wrongful termination to the date the new information was discovered. Reversed.

▶ **ANALYSIS**

An employer may not use after-acquired evidence unless it can establish that the wrongdoing was of such severity that the employee in fact would have been terminated on those grounds alone. Similarly, in cases of "resume fraud," the employer probably must show that the false information on which the employee was hired would be grounds for dismissal in and of itself. In other words, whether an employee would have been hired on the correct qualifications rather than on the fraudulent ones is irrelevant. The inquiry is whether, upon discovery of the resume fraud, the employee would have been terminated because of it.

■=■

Quicknotes

DISCRIMINATION Unequal treatment of a class of persons.

UNCLEAN HANDS Equitable doctrine denying relief to a party who seeks a remedy in relation to an action in which he did not act fairly.

■=■

Cassino v. Reichhold Chemicals, Inc.

Fired employee (P) v. Employer (D)

817 F.2d 1338 (9th Cir. 1987).

NATURE OF CASE: Review of a jury verdict awarding $492,000 in damages under the Age Discrimination in Employment Act (ADEA).

FACT SUMMARY: Reichhold Chemicals (D) contended that the court erred by failing to instruct the jury that a finding of hostility is required for a front-pay award and that former employee Cassino (P) failed to establish future damages.

RULE OF LAW
The decision whether to order the equitable remedy of reinstatement or, in the alternative, to award front pay is a decision for the trial judge, whereas the amount of the front-pay award is left to the jury's discretion.

FACTS: Cassino (P) was fired from Reichhold Chemicals (D) at the age of 52. Cassino (P) filed a suit against Reichhold Chemicals (D) based on a violation of the Age Discrimination in Employment Act (ADEA) and state anti-discrimination laws. The jury awarded Cassino (P) $81,000 in backpay, $150,000 in front pay, $246,000 in liquidated damages, and $15,000 in damages on the state-law claims. The trial court left the jury to its own discretion as to the amount of front pay. Reichhold Chemicals (D) appealed the jury award.

ISSUE: Is the decision to order the equitable remedy of reinstatement or, in the alternative, to award front pay a decision for the trial judge?

HOLDING AND DECISION: (Schroeder, J.) Yes. The decision whether to order the equitable remedy of reinstatement or, in the alternative, to award front pay is a decision for the trial judge, whereas the amount of the front-pay award is left to the jury's discretion. In discriminatory discharge cases, the ADEA provides the remedy of front pay when reinstatement is not feasible due to hostility in the employment relationship. Here, the district court did not abuse its authority to award front pay because the record showed that some hostility developed between Cassino (P) and Reichhold Chemicals (D) during the litigation. Furthermore, expert testimony is not required to prove future earnings or the effect of inflation and interest rates on that value. However, this award must be reduced by the amount Cassino (P) could earn using reasonable mitigation efforts. Reversed.

▶ ANALYSIS

Front pay is an award of future wages the plaintiff would have earned had he not been fired. Once it is determined that reinstatement is not possible due to employer-employee hostility, the trial court may use its discretion to award front pay as a lump-sum award as a substitute for reinstatement. However, a few courts may deny front pay where the plaintiff has received a liquidated damages award.

Quicknotes

DAMAGES Monetary compensation that may be awarded by the court to a party who has sustained injury or loss to his person, property or rights due to another party's unlawful act, omission or negligence.

EQUITABLE REMEDY A remedy that is based upon principles of fairness as opposed to rules of law; a remedy involving specific performance rather than money damages.

LIQUIDATED DAMAGES An amount of money specified in a contract representing the damages owed in the event of breach.

Turic v. Holland Hospitality, Inc.

Terminated pregnant employee (P) v. Employer (D)

85 F.3d 1211 (6th Cir. 1996).

NATURE OF CASE: Suit alleging employment discrimination under Title VII.

FACT SUMMARY: Holland Hospitality (D) violated Title VII by terminating Turic's (P) employment on the basis that Turic (P), who was pregnant, contemplated an abortion. The court granted her various relief, including $50,000 for emotional distress.

RULE OF LAW
In order to recover compensatory damages for emotional distress, a plaintiff must show that the defendant's unlawful conduct caused the emotional distress.

FACTS: [Facts not stated in casebook excerpt.]

ISSUE: In order to recover compensatory damages for emotional distress, must a plaintiff show that the defendant's unlawful conduct caused the emotional distress?

HOLDING AND DECISION: (Krupansky, J.) Yes. In order to recover compensatory damages for emotional distress, a plaintiff must show that the defendant's unlawful conduct caused the emotional distress. The plaintiff's testimony and the circumstances in the particular case are sufficient to make that showing. Here the court determined that Turic (P), a young, single mother who found herself pregnant for the second time, was vulnerable and dependent upon her employment. Vulnerability is relevant in this case since her supervisors had knowledge of her vulnerable condition upon terminating her employment. Moreover, a tortfeasor takes its victims as he finds them. Thus the trial court did not err in considering Turic's (P) economic and emotional state. Under Title VII a plaintiff may demonstrate emotional injury by giving testimony without medical support. Damages for mental and emotional distress, however, must be shown by "competent evidence." This includes the testimony of others. Here witnesses testified that after her discharge, Turic (P) was extremely upset. Turic (P) also testified that she suffered from nightmares, weight loss, and extreme nervousness. The trial court's award of compensatory damages was not grossly excessive. Affirmed.

ANALYSIS

Actual injury must be demonstrated in order for a plaintiff to recover damages for emotional distress. Here the court distinguished the present case from cases denying an award of compensatory damages for emotional distress, in which the plaintiffs failed to demonstrate physical symptoms of their distress.

Quicknotes

COMPENSATORY DAMAGES Measure of damages necessary to compensate victim for actual injuries suffered.

EMOTIONAL DISTRESS Extreme personal suffering that results from another's conduct and for which damages may be sought.

TORTFEASOR Party that commits a tort or wrongful act.

POLLARD v. E.I. du PONT de NEMOURS & CO.

Sexually harassed employee (P) v. Employer (D)

532 U.S. 843 (2001).

NATURE OF CASE: Appeal from decision that front pay is an element of compensatory damages.

FACT SUMMARY: Pollard (P) prevailed on her claim of sexual harassment against her employer, E.I. du Pont de Nemours & Co. (D), and was awarded $300,000 in compensatory damages, the maximum permitted under the statutory cap for such damages. She claimed that front pay is not an element of compensatory damages, and therefore should not be subject to the statutory cap.

RULE OF LAW

A front-pay award is not an element of compensatory damages under Title VII.

FACTS: Pollard (P) sued E.I. du Pont de Nemours & Co. (D), her former employer, alleging that she had been subjected to a hostile work environment based on her sex, in violation of Title VII. Finding that the harassment resulted in a medical leave of absence for psychological assistance and her eventual dismissal for refusing to return to the same hostile work environment, the district court awarded her, among other damages, $300,000 in compensatory damages—the maximum permitted under 42 U.S.C. § 1981(b)(3). The district court held that front pay—money awarded for lost compensation during the period between judgment and reinstatement or in lieu of reinstatement—was subject to the damages cap of 42 U.S.C. § 1981a(b)(3). The court of appeals affirmed. The Supreme Court granted review.

ISSUE: Is a front-pay award an element of compensatory damages under Title VII?

HOLDING AND DECISION: (Thomas, J.) No. A front-pay award is not an element of compensatory damages under Title VII. Under § 706(g) in Title VII, as originally enacted in 1964, when a court found that an employer had intentionally engaged in an unlawful employment practice, the court was authorized to award such remedies as injunctions, reinstatement, backpay, and lost benefits. Because this provision closely tracked the language of § 10(c) of the National Labor Relations Act (NLRA), § 10(c)'s meaning before the Civil Rights Act of 1964 was enacted provides guidance as to § 706(g)'s proper meaning. In applying § 10(c), the National Labor Relations Board consistently had made "backpay" awards up to the date the employee was reinstated or returned to the position he should have been in had the NLRA violation not occurred, even if such event occurred after judgment. Consistent with that interpretation, courts finding unlawful intentional discrimination in Title VII actions awarded this same type of backpay (known today as "front pay" when it occurs after the judgment) under § 706(g). After

Congress expanded § 706(g)'s remedies in 1972 to include "any other equitable relief as the court deems appropriate," courts endorsed a broad view of front pay, which included front-pay awards made in lieu of reinstatement. In 1991, without amending § 706(g), Congress further expanded the available remedies to include compensatory and punitive damages, subject to § 1981a(b)(3)'s cap. The 1991 Act's plain language makes clear that the newly authorized § 1981a remedies were in addition to the relief authorized by § 706(g). Thus, if front pay was a type of relief authorized under § 706(g), it is excluded from the meaning of compensatory damages under § 1981a and it would not be subject to § 1981a(b)(3)'s cap. As the original language of § 706(g) authorizing backpay awards was modeled after the same language in the NLRA, backpay awards (now called front-pay awards under Title VII) made for the period between the judgment date and the reinstatement date were authorized under § 706(g). Because there is no logical difference between front-pay awards made when there eventually is reinstatement and those made when there is not, front-pay awards made in lieu of reinstatement are authorized under § 706(g) as well. To distinguish between the two cases would lead to the strange result that employees could receive front pay when reinstatement eventually is available but not when it is unavailable—whether because of continuing hostility between the plaintiff and the employer or its workers, or because of psychological injuries that the discrimination has caused the plaintiff. Thus, the most egregious offenders could be subject to the least sanctions. Front-pay awards made in lieu of reinstatement are authorized under § 706(g), and, therefore, are not limited by § 1981a. Reversed and remanded.

ANALYSIS

Despite the Court's extensive statutory analysis in this case, at the heart of the decision is the Court's consideration of front pay as an equitable remedy that serves as a replacement for the remedy of reinstatement in situations in which reinstatement would be inappropriate. This view was in contrast with the Sixth Circuit's view that front pay was a legal award for future pecuniary losses.

Quicknotes

COMPENSATORY DAMAGES Measure of damages necessary to compensate victim for actual injuries suffered.

EQUITABLE REMEDY A remedy that is based upon principles of fairness as opposed to rules of law; a remedy involving specific performance rather than money damages.

Kolstad v. American Dental Association

Employee (P) v. Employer (D)

527 U.S. 526 (1999).

NATURE OF CASE: Suit for punitive damages under Title VII.

FACT SUMMARY: Kolstad (P) brought suit against the American Dental Association (Association) (D) for failing to appoint her to position of director, alleging gender discrimination in violation of Title VII.

🏛 RULE OF LAW
For purposes of punitive damages, an employer may not be held vicariously liable for the discriminatory employment decisions of managerial agents if the decisions are contrary to the employer's good faith efforts to comply with Title VII.

FACTS: Kolstad (P) and Spangler both applied for the vacancy in the position of Director of Legislation and Legislative Policy for the American Dental Association (D). Spangler was selected and Kolstad (P) brought suit claiming that the stated reasons were a pretext for gender discrimination. The district court rejected Kolstad's (P) request for a jury instruction on punitive damages. The jury concluded that the Association (D) had discriminated against Kolstad (P) on the basis of sex and awarded her backpay. The court of appeals concluded that before the question of punitive damages goes to the jury the defendant must be shown to have engaged in egregious conduct. Kolstad (P) appealed.

ISSUE: For purposes of punitive damages, may an employer be held vicariously liable for the discriminatory employment decisions of managerial agents if the decisions are contrary to the employer's good faith efforts to comply with Title VII?

HOLDING AND DECISION: (O'Connor, J.) No. For purposes of punitive damages, an employer may not be held vicariously liable for the discriminatory employment decisions of managerial agents if the decisions are contrary to the employer's good faith efforts to comply with Title VII. Punitive damages may be recovered under Title VII only if the employer has engaged in intentional discrimination "with malice or with reckless indifference to the federally protected rights of the aggrieved individual." Under the Civil Rights Act of 1991 punitive damages are available in Title VII claims. The Act limits such awards only to cases of intentional discrimination. Thus it does not apply to cases relying in the disparate-impact theory of discrimination. The structure of § 1981a demonstrates Congress's intent to limit punitive damages recovery to cases of intentional discrimination. The terms "malice" and "reckless" ultimately focus on the employer's state of mind. The statute further narrows recovery to where the employer acted with "malice or with reckless indifference of the plaintiff's federally protected rights." This refers to the

employer's knowledge that he was engaging in illegal conduct, not knowledge he was acting discriminatorily. The plaintiff also must impute liability for punitive damages to the defendant. In the employer context, punitive damages may be imputed to an employer because of an act of an agent if: "(1) the principal authorized the act and the manner in which it was performed; (2) the agent was unfit and the principal was reckless in employing him; (3) the agent was employed in a managerial capacity and was acting in the scope of his employment; or (4) the principal or a managerial agent ratified or approved the act." Restatement (Second) of Torts § 909. Under the agency rules an employee may be acting within the scope of his employment even if he engages in acts expressly forbidden by the employer. Thus, even if the employer made efforts to comply with Title VII it would be held liable for the discriminatory acts of its agents while acting in a managerial capacity. The Restatement rules are in need of revision. For purposes of punitive damages, an employer may not be held vicariously liable for the discriminatory employment decisions of managerial agents if the decisions are contrary to the employer's good faith efforts to comply with Title VII. Remanded.

▌ ANALYSIS

In a similar way, compensatory damages in Title VII cases rely on a determination of intentional discrimination. However, plaintiffs must meet an even higher standard to recover punitive damages.

Quicknotes

COMPENSATORY DAMAGES Measure of damages necessary to compensate victim for actual injuries suffered.

GOOD FAITH An honest intention to abstain from taking advantage of another.

PUNITIVE DAMAGES Damages exceeding the actual injury suffered for the purposes of punishment of the defendant, deterrence of the wrongful behavior or comfort to the plaintiff.

RECKLESSNESS Conduct that is conscious and creates a substantial and unjustifiable risk of harm to others.

TITLE VII OF THE CIVIL RIGHTS ACT OF 1964 Law prohibiting discrimination in employment on the basis of race, color, religion, sex, and national origin.

VICARIOUS LIABILITY The imputed liability of one party for the unlawful acts of another.

Hazen Paper Co. v. Biggins

Employer (D) v. Fired older employee (P)

507 U.S. 604 (1993).

NATURE OF CASE: Review of a judgment notwithstanding the verdict on the issue of "willfulness" in an age discrimination suit.

FACT SUMMARY: After Biggins (P) received a jury verdict in his favor finding a "willful violation" of the Age Discrimination in Employment Act (ADEA), Hazen Paper Company (Hazen) (D) contended that the standard for liquidated damages only applied to cases where the alleged age discrimination is a formal, facially discriminatory policy.

RULE OF LAW
Where an employer willfully discriminates against an employee due to age, then liquidated damages can be imposed even if the ADEA violation is not a formal, facially discriminatory policy.

FACTS: When Biggins (P) was fired by Hazen Paper Co. (D), he brought a suit against Hazen (D) for a violation of the Age Discrimination in Employment Act (ADEA). The jury found Hazen (D) had "willfully" violated the Act, and, pursuant to § 7(b), the jury awarded liquidated damages. Hazen (D) moved for judgment notwithstanding the verdict. The court granted the motion only with respect to the jury's finding of "willfulness." Biggins (P) appealed, and the court of appeals reversed. Hazen (D) appealed, and the Supreme Court granted certiorari.

ISSUE: Can liquidated damages be imposed where an employer willfully discriminates against an employee due to age, even if the age discrimination is not a formal, facially discriminatory policy?

HOLDING AND DECISION: (O'Connor, J.) Yes. Where an employer willfully discriminates against an employee due to age, then liquidated damages can be imposed even if the age discrimination is not a formal, facially discriminatory policy. The ADEA provides for liquidated damages where the violation was "willful," which means that the employer either knew or showed reckless disregard as to whether its conduct was prohibited by the ADEA. The Act does not require a formal, publicized policy on the reliance of age in an employment decision. The fact that Hazen (D) relied on age in making its employment decision but left it as an undisclosed factor is irrelevant. Once a "willful" violation has been shown, Biggins (P) does not need to prove Hazen's (D) conduct was outrageous, demonstrate Hazen's (D) motivation, or prove that age was the predominant factor in making the employment decision. Affirmed.

ANALYSIS

As with punitive damages, liquidated damages serve to punish and deter the employer. As such, some courts have permitted discriminatees to recover both liquidated damages and prejudgment interest. See, e.g., *Kelly v. American Standard, Inc.*, 640 F.2d 974 (9th Cir. 1981). Other circuits hold contra, having concluded that liquidated damages are partially compensatory. Courts have also differed in their calculations of the liquidated damage awards themselves; although all include unpaid wages, there is a disagreement about the inclusion of lost fringe benefits, lost health insurance, and front-pay awards.

Quicknotes

COMPENSATORY DAMAGES Measure of damages necessary to compensate victim for actual injuries suffered.

JUDGMENT NOTWITHSTANDING THE VERDICT A judgment entered by the trial judge reversing a jury verdict if the jury's determination has no basis in law or fact.

LIQUIDATED DAMAGES An amount of money specified in a contract representing the damages owed in the event of breach.

PUNITIVE DAMAGES Damages exceeding the actual injury suffered for the purposes of punishment of the defendant, deterrence of the wrongful behavior or comfort to the plaintiff.

Christiansburg Garment Co. v. EEOC

Employer (D) v. Government agency (P)

434 U.S. 412 (1978).

NATURE OF CASE: Appeal of the denial of attorney fees in a Title VII action.

FACT SUMMARY: Christiansburg Garment Co. (D), having prevailed in a Title VII action brought by the Equal Employment Opportunity Commission (EEOC) (P), sought attorney fees.

🏛 RULE OF LAW
Prevailing defendants are entitled to attorney-fee awards only when the plaintiff brings a frivolous action without foundation.

FACTS: Helm filed charges of racial discrimination with the Equal Employment Opportunity Commission (EEOC) (P) in 1968 against Christiansburg Garment (D). Two years later, the Equal Employment Opportunity Commission (EEOC) (P) informed Helm that conciliation efforts had failed and issued him a right-to-sue letter. Helm did not file an individual action. In 1972, an amendment to Title VII allowed the EEOC (P) to prosecute charges pending with the EEOC (P). The EEOC (P) then instituted an action against Christiansburg Garment (D). The trial court ruled that the Helm charges had not been pending before the EEOC (P) at the time of the 1972 amendment and granted summary judgment against the EEOC (P). Christiansburg Garment (D) petitioned the court for attorney fees pursuant to § 706(k) of Title VII. The trial court denied the award, finding that the EEOC (P) action was not unreasonable or meritless. The appeals court affirmed, and Christiansburg Garment (D) appealed.

ISSUE: Are defendants entitled to attorney-fee awards when they prevail in Title VII actions?

HOLDING AND DECISION: (Stewart, J.) No. Prevailing defendants are entitled to attorney-fee awards only when the plaintiff brings a frivolous action without foundation. Section 706(k) of Title VII allows courts discretion to award attorney fees to the prevailing party. A prevailing plaintiff is ordinarily awarded these fees in all but special circumstances in order to advance the policies underlying Title VII. Plaintiffs are the instrument chosen by Congress to vindicate the high-priority policy of ending employment discrimination. Additionally, awards to prevailing plaintiffs come at the expense of violators of federal law. These equitable considerations are not present for prevailing defendants. Furthermore, the legislative history of the attorney-fee provision indicates that Congress sought only to discourage frivolous and unjustified lawsuits in allowing prevailing defendants to recover attorney fees. Therefore, prevailing defendants in Title VII actions may recover attorney fees only when the litigation had no legal or factual basis. The EEOC's (P) suit against Christiansburg Garment (D) was not frivolous because it was an issue of first impression requiring judicial resolution. Affirmed.

▶ ANALYSIS

Under this decision, the employer seeking a fee award does not have to prove that the plaintiff actually acted in bad faith in bringing suit. Some courts have ruled that an employee's private action after the EEOC has determined there is no probable cause for discrimination is not necessarily frivolous. See *Eichman v. Linden & Sons, Inc.*, 752 F.2d 1246 (7th Cir. 1985).

Quicknotes

LEGISLATIVE HISTORY The process by which a bill is enacted into law, which reflects the legislature's intention enacting that law.

TITLE VII OF THE CIVIL RIGHTS ACT OF 1964 Law prohibiting discrimination in employment on the basis of race, color, religion, sex, and national origin.

Buckhannon Board & Care Home, Inc. v. West Virginia Department of Health and Human Resources

Private litigant (P) v. State agency (D)

532 U.S. 598 (2001).

NATURE OF CASE: Appeal from denial of attorney's fees in action under the Fair Housing Amendments Act (FHAA) and the Americans with Disabilities Act (ADA).

FACT SUMMARY: Buckhannon Board and Care Home, Inc.'s (Buckhannon) (P) assisted-living residences were ordered closed by the state fire marshal because some residents were incapable of "self-preservation" as defined by state law. Buckhannon (P) brought suit seeking declaratory and injunctive relief that the "self-preservation" requirement violated the FHAA and the ADA. The state legislature then eliminated the "self-preservation" requirement, and Buckhannon (P) sought attorney's fees as a "prevailing party."

RULE OF LAW
The "catalyst theory" is not a permissible basis for the award of attorney's fees under the FHAA and ADA.

FACTS: Buckhannon Board and Care Home, Inc. (P), which operated assisted-living residences, failed an inspection by the West Virginia fire marshal's office because some residents were incapable of "self-preservation" as defined by state law. After receiving orders to close its facilities, Buckhannon (P) brought suit seeking declaratory and injunctive relief that the "self-preservation" requirement violated the FHAA and the ADA. The state legislature then eliminated the "self-preservation" requirement, and the district court granted the state's (D) motion to dismiss the case as moot. Buckhannon (P) requested attorney's fees as the "prevailing party" under the FHAA and ADA under the "catalyst theory," which posits that a plaintiff is a "prevailing party" if it achieves the desired result because the lawsuit brought about a voluntary change in the defendant's conduct. The district court denied the motion and the court of appeals affirmed. The Supreme Court granted review.

ISSUE: Is the "catalyst theory" a permissible basis for the award of attorney's fees under the FHAA and ADA?

HOLDING AND DECISION: (Rehnquist, C.J.) No. The "catalyst theory" is not a permissible basis for the award of attorney's fees under the FHAA and ADA. Under the "American Rule," parties are ordinarily required to bear their own attorney's fees, and courts follow a general practice of not awarding fees to a prevailing party absent explicit statutory authority. Congress has employed the legal term of art "prevailing party" in numerous statutes authorizing awards of attorney's fees. A "prevailing party" is one who has been awarded some relief by a court.

Both judgments on the merits and court-ordered consent decrees create a material alteration of the parties' legal relationship and thus permit an award. The "catalyst theory," however, allows an award where there is no judicially sanctioned change in the parties' legal relationship. Under this theory, a plaintiff could recover attorney's fees if it established that the complaint had sufficient merit to withstand a motion to dismiss for lack of jurisdiction or failure to state a claim. This is not the type of legal merit the Court has found necessary for an award of attorney's fees. A defendant's voluntary change in conduct, although perhaps accomplishing what the plaintiff sought to achieve by the lawsuit, lacks the necessary judicial imprimatur on the change. Although Buckhannon (P) asserts that the "catalyst theory" is necessary to prevent defendants from unilaterally mooting an action before judgment in an attempt to avoid an award of attorney's fees to the plaintiff, the legislative history cited by petitioners is at best ambiguous as to the availability of the "catalyst theory"; and, particularly in view of the "American Rule," such history is clearly insufficient to alter the clear meaning of "prevailing party" in the fee-shifting statutes. Given this meaning, this Court need not determine which way petitioners' various policy arguments cut. Affirmed.

CONCURRENCE: (Scalia, J.) The dissent stretches the meaning of "prevailing party" beyond its normal meaning, and assumes that the catalyst theory applies when the suit's merits lead the defendant to abandon its case and give the plaintiff the redress sought. This distortion of the notion of "prevailing party" produces an award of attorney's fees when the merits of the case have not been resolved, and the real reason for the defendant's abandoning its fight is unknown. Although the majority's decision may sometimes deny fees to plaintiffs with a solid case where the defendant moots the case by abandoning it, this outcome is preferable to the result that would be achieved under the dissent's approach, where the plaintiff with the phony claim would be rewarded for it.

DISSENT: (Ginsburg, J.) The majority's holding requires that to be a "prevailing party," a plaintiff must secure a court entry memorializing the fact that the plaintiff has received the relief sought. This insistence on a court document is contrary to courts of appeals' precedents applicable to numerous federal fee-shifting statutes and allows a defendant to escape a statutory obligation to pay attorney's fees, even thought the suit's merits caused the defendant to

Continued on next page.

"abandon the fray . . . to accord plaintiff sooner rather than later the principal redress sought." The effect of the decision is to reduce the incentive for enforcing federal law by private individuals or entities. The ultimate goal of a lawsuit is actual relief—a judicial decree is merely a means to that end. Therefore, if a party achieves that end, the usual understanding is that it is the "prevailing" party, and this is the meaning of "prevailing party" under a fair reading of the FHAA and ADA. Here, Buckhannon (P) achieved the relief it sought, and therefore should be considered the prevailing party. The legislative history supports this conclusion by referring to cases requiring an award of attorney's fees where a party has vindicated rights without formally obtaining relief.

▶ *ANALYSIS*

The impact of this decision will be limited in scope because an employer's change in conduct will not moot a case in which the plaintiff has a meritorious claim for injunctive relief, backpay, compensatory damages, punitive damages, or nominal damages. The greatest impact of rejecting the "catalyst theory" may be in actions against a state where the only relief available is a prohibitory injunction.

▬▬▬

Quicknotes

AMERICAN RULE The rule that attorney's fees are not recoverable, unless expressly provided by law or pursuant to a contract.

DECLARATORY JUDGMENT A judgment of the court establishing the rights of the parties.

INJUNCTIVE RELIEF A court order issued as a remedy, requiring a person to do, or prohibiting that person from doing, a specific act.

JUDGMENT ON THE MERITS A determination of the rights of the parties to litigation based on the presentation evidence, barring the party from initiating the same suit again.

▬▬▬

Arbor Hill Concerned Citizens Neighborhood Association v. County of Albany

Attorneys (P) v. District court (D)

484 F.3d 162 (2d Cir. 2007).

NATURE OF CASE: Appeal of attorneys' fees award.

FACT SUMMARY: [Facts not stated in casebook excerpt.]

🏛 RULE OF LAW
The critical factor in calculating attorneys' fees in civil rights cases, including employment discrimination cases, is the amount the reasonable client would pay.

FACTS: [Facts not stated in casebook excerpt.]

ISSUE: Is the critical factor in calculating attorneys' fees in civil rights cases, including employment discrimination cases, the amount the reasonable client would pay?

HOLDING AND DECISION: (Walker, J.) Yes. The critical factor in calculating attorneys' fees in civil rights cases, including employment discrimination cases, is the amount the reasonable client would pay. The fee for attorneys who work out of their district, which is historically known as the "lodestar," is not strictly the hourly rate charged by attorneys in the district where the district court sits. A district court may use an out-of-district hourly rate, or some rate in between, in calculating the presumptively reasonable fee it if is clear that a reasonable, paying client would have paid those higher rates. The presumption is that a reasonable paying client would in most cases hire counsel from within his district, but the presumption may be rebutted. The district court should bear in mind all case-specific variables that have been identified as relevant to the reasonableness of attorneys' fees in setting a reasonable hourly rate. Finally, the meaning of the term "lodestar"—the true sense of which is "a star that leads"—has, in the context of attorneys' fees, shifted over time. This opinion abandons its use, in favor of the reasonable-client standard.

▶ ANALYSIS

The rule established by this case could be problematic when applied to cases that attorneys take on a contingency-fee basis. A reasonable client would not pay anything for the services of an attorney if the case were accepted on a contingency-fee basis and lost. While the court boils down the complicated issues to simple terms, its holding may not be easy to apply.

Quicknotes

CONTINGENCY FEE AGREEMENT A fee agreement between an attorney and client that is dependent upon the ultimate disposition of the case and comprises a percentage of the party's recovery.

Managing Risks in Employment Discrimination Disputes

Quick Reference Rules of Law

PAGE

1. **Settlements and Releases.** A release that does not conform with the Older Workers Benefit Protection Act (OWBPA) cannot waive age-discrimination claims. (Oubre v. Entergy Operations, Inc.) — *110*

2. **Arbitrating Discrimination Claims.** An ADEA claim can be subjected to compulsory arbitration. (Gilmer v. Interstate/Johnson Lane Corp.) — *111*

3. **Arbitrating Discrimination Claims.** An arbitration agreement that unilaterally forces employees to arbitrate claims against the employer but does not require the employer to arbitrate its claims against the employee is unenforceable as unconscionable under California law. (Circuit City Stores, Inc. v. Adams) — *113*

Oubre v. Entergy Operations, Inc.

Employee/accepter of severance package (P) v. Former employer (D)

522 U.S. 422 (1998).

NATURE OF CASE: Appeal from summary judgment in an age-discrimination action.

FACT SUMMARY: Oubre (P) agreed to sign a release as part of a severance package from Entergy Operations, Inc. (Entergy) (D), but the release did not conform with the requirements of the law and Oubre (P) sued, but did not return the money received as part of the deal.

> ## 🏛 RULE OF LAW
> A release that does not conform with the Older Workers Benefit Protection Act (OWBPA) cannot waive age-discrimination claims.

FACTS: Dolores Oubre (D) worked at a power plant run by Entergy (D) until 1995, when she was offered a voluntary severance package. She accepted, received over $6,000, and signed a release of "all claims" against Entergy (D). The release did not comply with the requirements of the OWBPA because Oubre (P) was not given enough time to consider it and was not permitted a period of time in which to change her mind. The release also made no direct reference to age-discrimination claims under the Age Discrimination in Employment Act (ADEA). Oubre (P) later filed suit claiming constructive termination of her employment based on her age. The district court granted Entergy (D) summary judgment, holding that Oubre (P) had ratified the defective release by keeping the money she had received. The court of appeals affirmed and Oubre (P) appealed.

ISSUE: Can a release that does not conform with the Older Workers Benefit Protection Act waive age-discrimination claims under certain circumstances?

HOLDING AND DECISION: (Kennedy, J.) No. A release that does not conform with the Older Workers Benefit Protection Act cannot waive age-discrimination claims. Generally, a contract tainted by mistake is voidable at the option of the innocent party. Often, the innocent party can elect avoidance, but must tender back the benefits received, or ratifies the contract. In 1990, Congress passed the OWBPA, which set specific standards for knowing and voluntary waivers of rights against age discrimination. This law sets up its own statutory regime, separate and apart from general contract law. There are no exceptions or qualifications to the rules set forth in the OWBPA. Allowing waiver where the requirements have not been fulfilled would tempt employers to risk noncompliance. Accordingly, since Oubre's (P) release was non-complying, her age discrimination claims are not barred and she need not return the monies prior to instituting her suit. Reversed.

CONCURRENCE: (Breyer, J.) It is important to note that the OWBPA does not make the procedurally invalid release totally void and that any monies received may very well be deducted from an eventual damages award.

DISSENT: (Thomas, J.) The OWBPA does not address the common-law contract doctrines that insist on a tender back of benefits prior to avoiding a contract and therefore does not abrogate them.

▶ ANALYSIS

The majority opinion did note that cases could be complex to resolve under this rule. Since the release like the one Oubre (P) signed was effective as to some claims, a court might have a difficult time sorting out the actionable elements. The majority seemed mostly concerned with a rule that would prevent any evasion of the bright-line rule created by OWBPA.

■=■

Quicknotes

VOIDABLE CONTRACT A valid contract that may be legally voided at the option of one of the parties.

WAIVER The intentional or voluntary forfeiture of a recognized right.

■=■

Gilmer v. Interstate/Johnson Lane Corp.

Discharged older employee (P) v. Employer (D)

500 U.S. 20 (1991).

NATURE OF CASE: Appeal from reversal of denial to compel arbitration in an Age Discrimination in Employment Act (ADEA) action.

FACT SUMMARY: Gilmer (P) sued under the ADEA after his employer, Interstate/Johnson Lane Corp. (Interstate) (D), terminated his employment at age 62. Interstate (D) moved to compel arbitration pursuant to an arbitration agreement Gilmer (P) had entered into as a condition of his employment.

 **RULE OF LAW**
An ADEA claim can be subjected to compulsory arbitration.

FACTS: Gilmer (P) was required by his employer, Interstate (D), to register as a securities representative with, among others, the New York Stock Exchange (NYSE). His registration application contained an agreement to arbitrate when required to by NYSE rules. NYSE Rule 347 provided for arbitration of any controversy arising out of a registered representative's employment or termination of employment. Interstate (D) terminated Gilmer's (P) employment at age 62. Gilmer (P) brought suit under the Age Discrimination in Employment Act of 1967 (ADEA), and Interstate (D) moved to compel arbitration, relying on the agreement in Gilmer's (P) registration application and the Federal Arbitration Act (FAA). The district court denied the motion, the court of appeals reversed, and the Supreme Court granted review.

ISSUE: Can an ADEA claim be subjected to compulsory arbitration?

HOLDING AND DECISION: (White, J.) Yes. An ADEA claim can be subjected to compulsory arbitration. The FAA manifests a liberal federal policy favoring arbitration, and it is clear that statutory claims may be the subject of an arbitration agreement, enforceable pursuant to the FAA. Because neither the text nor the legislative history of the ADEA explicitly precludes arbitration, Gilmer (P) is bound by his agreement to arbitrate unless he can show an inherent conflict between arbitration and the ADEA's underlying purposes. There is no inconsistency between the important social policies furthered by the ADEA and enforcing agreements to arbitrate age-discrimination claims. Although arbitration focuses on specific disputes between the parties involved, so does judicial resolution of claims, yet both can further broader social purposes. Various other laws, e.g., antitrust, securities, or Racketeer Influenced and Corrupt Organizations Act (RICO) laws, are designed to advance important public policies, but claims under them are appropriate for arbitration. Gilmer's (P) argument that

arbitration will undermine the Equal Employment Opportunity Commission's (EEOC's) role in ADEA enforcement is also unpersuasive, since an ADEA claimant is free to file an EEOC charge even if he is precluded from instituting suit; since the EEOC has independent authority to investigate age discrimination; since nothing in the ADEA indicates that Congress intended that the EEOC be involved in all disputes; and since an administrative agency's mere involvement in a statute's enforcement is insufficient to preclude arbitration. Moreover, compulsory arbitration does not improperly deprive claimants of the judicial forum provided for by the ADEA: Congress did not explicitly preclude arbitration or other nonjudicial claims resolutions; the ADEA's flexible approach to claims resolution, which permits the EEOC to pursue informal resolution methods, suggests that out-of-court dispute resolution is consistent with the statutory scheme; and arbitration is consistent with Congress's grant of concurrent jurisdiction over ADEA claims to state and federal courts, since arbitration also advances the objective of allowing claimants a broader right to select the dispute resolution forum. Gilmer's (P) challenges to the adequacy of arbitration procedures are insufficient to preclude arbitration. His generalized attacks are out of step with the Court's strong endorsement of the federal statutes favoring this method of dispute resolution. There is no merit to his speculation that the parties and the arbitral body will not retain competent, conscientious, and impartial arbitrators, especially when both the NYSE rules and the FAA protect against biased panels. Nor is there merit to his argument that the limited discovery permitted in arbitration will make it difficult to prove age discrimination, because it is unlikely that such claims require more extensive discovery than RICO and antitrust claims, and since there has been no showing that the NYSE discovery provisions will prove insufficient to allow him a fair opportunity to prove his claim. His argument that arbitrators will not issue written opinions resulting in a lack of public knowledge of employers' discriminatory policies, an inability to obtain effective appellate review, and a stifling of the law's development, is also rejected. The NYSE rules require that arbitration awards be in writing and be made available to the public, judicial decisions will continue to be issued for ADEA claimants without arbitration agreements, and Gilmer's (P) argument applies equally to settlements of ADEA claims. His argument that arbitration procedures are inadequate because they do not provide for broad equitable relief and class actions is unpersuasive as well, since arbitrators have the power to fashion equitable relief, the NYSE rules do not restrict the type of relief an arbitrator may award and provide for collective relief, the ADEA's provision for the possibility of

Continued on next page.

collective action does not mean that individual attempts at conciliation are barred, and arbitration agreements do not preclude the EEOC itself from seeking class-wide and equitable relief. The unequal bargaining power between employers and employees is not a sufficient reason to hold that arbitration agreements are never enforceable in the employment context. Such a claim is best left for resolution in specific cases. Here, there is no indication that Gilmer (P), an experienced businessman, was coerced or defrauded into agreeing to the arbitration clause. Gilmer's reliance on *Alexander v. Gardner-Denver Co.*, 415 U.S. 36 (1974), and its progeny is also misplaced. Those cases involved the issue whether arbitration of contract-based claims precluded subsequent judicial resolution of statutory claims, not the enforceability of an agreement to arbitrate statutory claims. The arbitration in those cases occurred in the context of a collective-bargaining agreement, and thus there was concern about the tension between collective representation and individual statutory rights that is not applicable in this case. Moreover, those cases were not decided under the FAA. Affirmed.

DISSENT: (Stevens, J.) An antecedent issue that the majority avoids is whether the FAA even extends to arbitration clauses contained in employment contracts, regardless of the subject matter of the claim. Because arbitration clauses in employment agreements are specifically exempt from coverage of the FAA, Interstate (D) cannot compel arbitration pursuant to it. In addition, compulsory arbitration conflicts with the ADEA's purpose of eliminating discrimination by authorizing courts to issue broad, class-based injunctive relief. Because arbitration does not provide for such relief, it frustrates an essential purpose of the ADEA.

▶ *ANALYSIS*

The dissent argued that the FAA does not apply to all employment contracts and faulted the majority for skirting this issue. The majority declined to hear this argument because Gilmer's (P) arbitration agreement was with the NYSE, not his employer, and therefore was not an employment agreement. However, in *Circuit City Stores, Inc. v. Adams*, 532 U.S. 105 (2001), the Court held that the FAA exempts from arbitration only employment contracts of transportation workers. Although that case applied to state law discrimination claims, it clearly applies to federal claims as well.

■==■

Quicknotes

ARBITRATION AGREEMENT A mutual understanding entered into by parties wishing to submit to the decision making authority of a neutral third party, selected by the parties and charged with rendering a decision.

■==■

Circuit City Stores, Inc. v. Adams

Employee (P) v. Employer (D)

279 F.3d 889 (9th Cir. 2002).

NATURE OF CASE: Consideration of a contract issue on remand from the Supreme Court.

FACT SUMMARY: Circuit City (D) requires job applicants to sign a Dispute Resolution Agreement (DRA) in order for their applications to be considered. The enforceability of the DRA is at issue.

RULE OF LAW
An arbitration agreement that unilaterally forces employees to arbitrate claims against the employer but does not require the employer to arbitrate its claims against the employee is unenforceable as unconscionable under California law.

FACTS: St. Clair Adams (P) applied for a job at Circuit City. As part of the application process, he signed the Circuit City Dispute Resolution Agreement (DRA), which requires employees to submit all claims and disputes to binding arbitration. The DRA sets rules for procedure, discovery, allocation of fees, and available remedies. Circuit City (D) is not required under the DRA to arbitrate any claims against the employee. An employee who refused to sign the DRA will not be hired. [After Adams (P) filed a state claim against Circuit City (D) and three co-workers for sexual harassment, Circuit City (D) filed a petition in federal court to stay the state court proceedings and compel arbitration under the DRA. The Supreme Court held that the Federal Arbitration Act applied to the DRA and remanded for assessment of the legality of the agreement.]

ISSUE: Is an arbitration agreement that unilaterally forces employees to arbitrate claims against the employer but does not require the employer to arbitrate its claims against the employee, unenforceable as unconscionable under California law?

HOLDING AND DECISION: (Nelson, J.) Yes. An arbitration agreement that unilaterally forces employees to arbitrate claims against the employer but does not require the employer to arbitrate its claims against the employee is unenforceable as unconscionable under California law. Under California law, contracts are unenforceable if they are both procedurally and substantively unconscionable. Procedural unconscionability has to do with the balance of bargaining power between the parties and the extent to which the contract clearly discloses its terms. Substantive unconscionability concerns the terms of the contract and whether they are unduly harsh or oppressive. The DRA is procedurally unconscionable because it is a contract of adhesion, drafted by a party with superior bargaining power, and administered in a take-it-or-leave-it fashion.

The DRA is also substantively unconscionable because unilaterally forces employees to arbitrate claims against the employer, but does not require the same of Circuit City. The absence of a "modicum of bilaterality," which is required for contracts to be enforceable under California law, renders the contract unenforceable. But the DRA also restricts the employees' available remedies that are available to him by statute.

ANALYSIS

This case began in 1997 after Adams filed suit under California's Fair Employment and Housing Act, alleging he had been sexually harassed by three co-workers and faced retaliation and constructive discharge for complaining about the harassment. The company filed a petition in federal court to stay the state proceedings and enforce the agreement signed by Adams when he first applied for a position with the company in 1995. The district court granted the petition. The Ninth Circuit first found the company's agreement unenforceable in 1999, when the court said the Federal Arbitration Act was applicable only in commercial transactions. The Supreme Court found that the Ninth Circuit stood alone in its position. The Court reversed the Ninth Circuit in a five-to-four decision in 2001, saying the Federal Arbitration Act exempts only transportation employees, and remanded the case to the Ninth Circuit. The Supreme Court never reached the question of the specifics of the Circuit City agreement.

Quicknotes

ARBITRATION AGREEMENT A mutual understanding entered into by parties wishing to submit to the decision making authority of a neutral third party, selected by the parties and charged with rendering a decision.

HARASSMENT Conduct directed at a particular person with the intent to inflict emotional distress and with no justification therefor; a criminal prosecution commenced without a reasonable expectation of its resulting in a conviction.

UNCONSCIONABILITY A situation in which a contract, or a particular contract term, is unenforceable if the court determines that such terms are unduly oppressive or unfair to one party to the contract.

Common Latin Words and Phrases Encountered in the Law

A FORTIORI: Because one fact exists or has been proven, therefore a second fact that is related to the first fact must also exist.

A PRIORI: From the cause to the effect. A term of logic used to denote that when one generally accepted truth is shown to be a cause, another particular effect must necessarily follow.

AB INITIO: From the beginning; a condition which has existed throughout, as in a marriage which was void ab initio.

ACTUS REUS: The wrongful act; in criminal law, such action sufficient to trigger criminal liability.

AD VALOREM: According to value; an ad valorem tax is imposed upon an item located within the taxing jurisdiction calculated by the value of such item.

AMICUS CURIAE: Friend of the court. Its most common usage takes the form of an amicus curiae brief, filed by a person who is not a party to an action but is nonetheless allowed to offer an argument supporting his legal interests.

ARGUENDO: In arguing. A statement, possibly hypothetical, made for the purpose of argument, is one made arguendo.

BILL QUIA TIMET: A bill to quiet title (establish ownership) to real property.

BONA FIDE: True, honest, or genuine. May refer to a person's legal position based on good faith or lacking notice of fraud (such as a bona fide purchaser for value) or to the authenticity of a particular document (such as a bona fide last will and testament).

CAUSA MORTIS: With approaching death in mind. A gift causa mortis is a gift given by a party who feels certain that death is imminent.

CAVEAT EMPTOR: Let the buyer beware. This maxim is reflected in the rule of law that a buyer purchases at his own risk because it is his responsibility to examine, judge, test, and otherwise inspect what he is buying.

CERTIORARI: A writ of review. Petitions for review of a case by the United States Supreme Court are most often done by means of a writ of certiorari.

CONTRA: On the other hand. Opposite. Contrary to.

CORAM NOBIS: Before us; writs of error directed to the court that originally rendered the judgment.

CORAM VOBIS: Before you; writs of error directed by an appellate court to a lower court to correct a factual error.

CORPUS DELICTI: The body of the crime; the requisite elements of a crime amounting to objective proof that a crime has been committed.

CUM TESTAMENTO ANNEXO, ADMINISTRATOR (ADMINISTRATOR C.T.A.): With will annexed; an administrator c.t.a. settles an estate pursuant to a will in which he is not appointed.

DE BONIS NON, ADMINISTRATOR (ADMINISTRATOR D.B.N.): Of goods not administered; an administrator d.b.n. settles a partially settled estate.

DE FACTO: In fact; in reality; actually. Existing in fact but not officially approved or engendered.

DE JURE: By right; lawful. Describes a condition that is legitimate "as a matter of law," in contrast to the term "de facto," which connotes something existing in fact but not legally sanctioned or authorized. For example, de facto segregation refers to segregation brought about by housing patterns, etc., whereas de jure segregation refers to segregation created by law.

DE MINIMIS: Of minimal importance; insignificant; a trifle; not worth bothering about.

DE NOVO: Anew; a second time; afresh. A trial de novo is a new trial held at the appellate level as if the case originated there and the trial at a lower level had not taken place.

DICTA: Generally used as an abbreviated form of obiter dicta, a term describing those portions of a judicial opinion incidental or not necessary to resolution of the specific question before the court. Such nonessential statements and remarks are not considered to be binding precedent.

DUCES TECUM: Refers to a particular type of writ or subpoena requesting a party or organization to produce certain documents in their possession.

EN BANC: Full bench. Where a court sits with all justices present rather than the usual quorum.

EX PARTE: For one side or one party only. An ex parte proceeding is one undertaken for the benefit of only one party, without notice to, or an appearance by, an adverse party.

EX POST FACTO: After the fact. An ex post facto law is a law that retroactively changes the consequences of a prior act.

EX REL.: Abbreviated form of the term ex relatione, meaning upon relation or information. When the state brings an action in which it has no interest against an individual at the instigation of one who has a private interest in the matter.

FORUM NON CONVENIENS: Inconvenient forum. Although a court may have jurisdiction over the case, the action should be tried in a more conveniently located court, one to which parties and witnesses may more easily travel, for example.

GUARDIAN AD LITEM: A guardian of an infant as to litigation, appointed to represent the infant and pursue his/her rights.

HABEAS CORPUS: You have the body. The modern writ of habeas corpus is a writ directing that a person (body) being detained (such as a prisoner) be brought before the court so that the legality of his detention can be judicially ascertained.

IN CAMERA: In private, in chambers. When a hearing is held before a judge in his chambers or when all spectators are excluded from the courtroom.

IN FORMA PAUPERIS: In the manner of a pauper. A party who proceeds in forma pauperis because of his poverty is one who is allowed to bring suit without liability for costs.

INFRA: Below, under. A word referring the reader to a later part of a book. (The opposite of supra.)

IN LOCO PARENTIS: In the place of a parent.

IN PARI DELICTO: Equally wrong; a court of equity will not grant requested relief to an applicant who is in pari delicto, or as much at fault in the transactions giving rise to the controversy as is the opponent of the applicant.

IN PARI MATERIA: On like subject matter or upon the same matter. Statutes relating to the same person or things are said to be in pari materia. It is a general rule of statutory construction that such statutes should be construed together, i.e., looked at as if they together constituted one law.

IN PERSONAM: Against the person. Jurisdiction over the person of an individual.

IN RE: In the matter of. Used to designate a proceeding involving an estate or other property.

IN REM: A term that signifies an action against the res, or thing. An action in rem is basically one that is taken directly against property, as distinguished from an action in personam, i.e., against the person.

INTER ALIA: Among other things. Used to show that the whole of a statement, pleading, list, statute, etc., has not been set forth in its entirety.

INTER PARTES: Between the parties. May refer to contracts, conveyances or other transactions having legal significance.

INTER VIVOS: Between the living. An inter vivos gift is a gift made by a living grantor, as distinguished from bequests contained in a will, which pass upon the death of the testator.

IPSO FACTO: By the mere fact itself.

JUS: Law or the entire body of law.

LEX LOCI: The law of the place; the notion that the rights of parties to a legal proceeding are governed by the law of the place where those rights arose.

MALUM IN SE: Evil or wrong in and of itself; inherently wrong. This term describes an act that is wrong by its very nature, as opposed to one which would not be wrong but for the fact that there is a specific legal prohibition against it (malum prohibitum).

MALUM PROHIBITUM: Wrong because prohibited, but not inherently evil. Used to describe something that is wrong because it is expressly forbidden by law but that is not in and of itself evil, e.g., speeding.

MANDAMUS: We command. A writ directing an official to take a certain action.

MENS REA: A guilty mind; a criminal intent. A term used to signify the mental state that accompanies a crime or other prohibited act. Some crimes require only a general mens rea (general intent to do the prohibited act), but others, like assault with intent to murder, require the existence of a specific mens rea.

MODUS OPERANDI: Method of operating; generally refers to the manner or style of a criminal in committing crimes, admissible in appropriate cases as evidence of the identity of a defendant.

NEXUS: A connection to.

NISI PRIUS: A court of first impression. A nisi prius court is one where issues of fact are tried before a judge or jury.

N.O.V. (NON OBSTANTE VEREDICTO): Notwithstanding the verdict. A judgment n.o.v. is a judgment given in favor of one party despite the fact that a verdict was returned in favor of the other party, the justification being that the verdict either had no reasonable support in fact or was contrary to law.

NUNC PRO TUNC: Now for then. This phrase refers to actions that may be taken and will then have full retroactive effect.

PENDENTE LITE: Pending the suit; pending litigation underway.

PER CAPITA: By head; beneficiaries of an estate, if they take in equal shares, take per capita.

PER CURIAM: By the court; signifies an opinion ostensibly written "by the whole court" and with no identified author.

PER SE: By itself, in itself; inherently.

PER STIRPES: By representation. Used primarily in the law of wills to describe the method of distribution where a person, generally because of death, is unable to take that which is left to him by the will of another, and therefore his heirs divide such property between them rather than take under the will individually.

PRIMA FACIE: On its face, at first sight. A prima facie case is one that is sufficient on its face, meaning that the evidence supporting it is adequate to establish the case until contradicted or overcome by other evidence.

PRO TANTO: For so much; as far as it goes. Often used in eminent domain cases when a property owner receives partial payment for his land without prejudice to his right to bring suit for the full amount he claims his land to be worth.

QUANTUM MERUIT: As much as he deserves. Refers to recovery based on the doctrine of unjust enrichment in those cases in which a party has rendered valuable services or furnished materials that were accepted and enjoyed by another under circumstances that would reasonably notify the recipient that the rendering party expected to be paid. In essence, the law implies a contract to pay the reasonable value of the services or materials furnished.

QUASI: Almost like; as if; nearly. This term is essentially used to signify that one subject or thing is almost analogous to another but that material differences between them do exist. For example, a quasi-criminal proceeding is one that is not strictly criminal but shares enough of the same characteristics to require some of the same safeguards (e.g., procedural due process must be followed in a parole hearing).

QUID PRO QUO: Something for something. In contract law, the consideration, something of value, passed between the parties to render the contract binding.

RES GESTAE: Things done; in evidence law, this principle justifies the admission of a statement that would otherwise be hearsay when it is made so closely to the event in question as to be said to be a part of it, or with such spontaneity as not to have the possibility of falsehood.

RES IPSA LOQUITUR: The thing speaks for itself. This doctrine gives rise to a rebuttable presumption of negligence when the instrumentality causing the injury was within the exclusive control of the defendant, and the injury was one that does not normally occur unless a person has been negligent.

RES JUDICATA: A matter adjudged. Doctrine which provides that once a court of competent jurisdiction has rendered a final judgment or decree on the merits, that judgment or decree is conclusive upon the parties to the case and prevents them from engaging in any other litigation on the points and issues determined therein.

RESPONDEAT SUPERIOR: Let the master reply. This doctrine holds the master liable for the wrongful acts of his servant (or the principal for his agent) in those cases in which the servant (or agent) was acting within the scope of his authority at the time of the injury.

STARE DECISIS: To stand by or adhere to that which has been decided. The common law doctrine of stare decisis attempts to give security and certainty to the law by following the policy that once a principle of law as applicable to a certain set of facts has been set forth in a decision, it forms a precedent which will subsequently be followed, even though a different decision might be made were it the first time the question had arisen. Of course, stare decisis is not an inviolable principle and is departed from in instances where there is good cause (e.g., considerations of public policy led the Supreme Court to disregard prior decisions sanctioning segregation).

SUPRA: Above. A word referring a reader to an earlier part of a book.

ULTRA VIRES: Beyond the power. This phrase is most commonly used to refer to actions taken by a corporation that are beyond the power or legal authority of the corporation.

Addendum of French Derivatives

IN PAIS: Not pursuant to legal proceedings.

CHATTEL: Tangible personal property.

CY PRES: Doctrine permitting courts to apply trust funds to purposes not expressed in the trust but necessary to carry out the settlor's intent.

PER AUTRE VIE: For another's life; during another's life. In property law, an estate may be granted that will terminate upon the death of someone other than the grantee.

PROFIT A PRENDRE: A license to remove minerals or other produce from land.

VOIR DIRE: Process of questioning jurors as to their predispositions about the case or parties to a proceeding in order to identify those jurors displaying bias or prejudice.

Casenote Legal Briefs

Administrative Law .... Breyer, Stewart, Sunstein & Vermeule
Administrative Law .... Cass, Diver & Beermann
Administrative Law .... Funk, Shapiro & Weaver
Administrative Law .... Mashaw, Merrill & Shane
Administrative Law .... Strauss, Rakoff, & Farina
    (Gellhorn & Byse)
Agency & Partnership .... Hynes & Loewenstein
Antitrust .... Pitofsky, Goldschmid & Wood
Antitrust .... Sullivan & Hovenkamp
Banking Law .... Macey, Miller & Carnell
Bankruptcy .... Warren & Bussel
Bankruptcy .... Warren & Westbrook
Business Organizations .... Bauman, Weiss & Palmiter
Business Organizations .... Choper, Coffee & Gilson
Business Organizations .... Hamilton & Macey
Business Organizations .... Klein, Ramseyer & Bainbridge
Business Organizations .... O'Kelley & Thompson
Business Organizations .... Soderquist, Smiddy & Cunningham
Civil Procedure .... Field, Kaplan & Clermont
Civil Procedure .... Freer & Perdue
Civil Procedure .... Friedenthal, Miller, Sexton & Hershkoff
Civil Procedure .... Hazard, Tait, Fletcher & Bundy
Civil Procedure .... Marcus, Redish & Sherman
Civil Procedure .... Subrin, Minow, Brodin & Main
Civil Procedure .... Yeazell
Commercial Law .... LoPucki, Warren, Keating & Mann
Commercial Law .... Warren & Walt
Commercial Law .... Whaley
Community Property .... Bird
Community Property .... Blumberg
Conflicts .... Brilmayer & Goldsmith
Conflicts .... Currie, Kay, Kramer & Roosevelt
Constitutional Law .... Brest, Levinson, Balkin & Amar
Constitutional Law .... Chemerinsky
Constitutional Law .... Choper, Fallon, Kamisar & Shiffrin (Lockhart)
Constitutional Law .... Cohen, Varat & Amar
Constitutional Law .... Farber, Eskridge & Frickey
Constitutional Law .... Rotunda
Constitutional Law .... Sullivan & Gunther
Constitutional Law .... Stone, Seidman, Sunstein, Tushnet & Karlan
Contracts .... Barnett
Contracts .... Burton
Contracts .... Calamari, Perillo & Bender
Contracts .... Crandall & Whaley
Contracts .... Dawson, Harvey, Henderson & Baird
Contracts .... Farnsworth, Young & Sanger
Contracts .... Fuller & Eisenberg
Contracts .... Knapp, Crystal & Prince
Contracts .... Murphy, Speidel & Ayres
Copyright .... Cohen, Loren, Okediji & O'Rourke
Copyright .... Goldstein & Reese
Criminal Law .... Bonnie, Coughlin, Jeffries & Low
Criminal Law .... Boyce, Dripps & Perkins
Criminal Law .... Dressler
Criminal Law .... Johnson & Cloud
Criminal Law .... Kadish, Schulhofer & Steiker
Criminal Law .... Kaplan, Weisberg & Binder
Criminal Procedure .... Allen, Hoffmann, Livingston & Stuntz
Criminal Procedure .... Dressler & Thomas
Criminal Procedure .... Haddad, Marsh, Zagel, Meyer,
    Starkman & Bauer
Criminal Procedure .... Kamisar, LaFave, Israel & King
Criminal Procedure .... Saltzburg & Capra
Criminal Procedure .... Weaver, Abramson, Bacigal, Burkoff,
    Hancock & Lively
Employment Discrimination .... Friedman
Employment Discrimination .... Zimmer, Sullivan & White
Employment Law .... Rothstein & Liebman
Environmental Law .... Menell & Stewart
Environmental Law .... Percival, Schroder, Miller & Leape

Environmental Law .... Plater, Abrams, Goldfarb, Graham,
    Heinzerling & Wirth
Evidence .... Broun, Mosteller & Giannelli
Evidence .... Fisher
Evidence .... Mueller & Kirkpatrick
Evidence .... Sklansky
Evidence .... Waltz & Park
Evidence .... Weinstein, Mansfield, Abrams & Berger
Family Law .... Areen & Regan
Family Law .... Ellman, Kurtz & Scott
Family Law .... Harris, Teitelbaum & Carbone
Family Law .... Krause, Elrod, Garrison & Oldham
Family Law .... Wadlington & O'Brien
Family Law .... Weisberg & Appleton
Federal Courts .... Fallon, Meltzer & Shapiro (Hart & Wechsler)
Federal Courts .... Low & Jeffries
Health Care Law .... Hall, Bobinski & Orentlicher
Health Law .... Furrow, Greaney, Johnson,
    Jost & Schwartz
Immigration Law .... Aleinikoff, Martin & Motomura
Immigration Law .... Legomsky
Insurance Law .... Abraham
Intellectual Property .... Merges, Menell & Lemley
International Business Transactions .... Folsom, Gordon,
    Spanogle & Fitzgerald
International Law .... Blakesley, Firmage, Scott & Williams
International Law .... Carter, Trimble & Weiner
International Law .... Damrosch, Henkin, Pugh, Schachter & Smit
International Law .... Dunoff, Ratner & Wippman
Labor Law .... Cox, Bok, Gorman & Finkin
Land Use .... Callies, Freilich & Roberts
Legislation .... Eskridge, Frickey & Garrett
Oil & Gas .... Lowe, Anderson, Smith & Pierce
Patent Law .... Adelman, Radner, Thomas & Wegner
Products Liability .... Owen, Montgomery & Davis
Professional Responsibility .... Gillers
Professional Responsibility .... Hazard, Koniak, Cramton & Cohen
Professional Responsibility .... Schwartz, Wydick,
    Perschbacher & Bassett
Property .... Casner, Leach, French, Korngold
    & VanderVelde
Property .... Cribbet, Johnson, Findley & Smith
Property .... Donahue, Kauper & Martin
Property .... Dukeminier, Krier, Alexander & Schill
Property .... Haar & Liebman
Property .... Kurtz & Hovenkamp
Property .... Nelson, Stoebuck & Whitman
Property .... Rabin, Kwall & Kwall
Property .... Singer
Real Estate .... Korngold & Goldstein
Real Estate Transactions .... Nelson & Whitman
Remedies .... Laycock
Remedies .... Shoben, Tabb & Janutis
Securities Regulation .... Coffee, Seligman & Sale
Securities Regulation .... Cox, Hillman & Langevoort
Software and Internet Law .... Lemley, Menell, Merges & Samuelson
Sports Law .... Weiler & Roberts
Taxation (Corporate) .... Lind, Schwartz, Lathrope & Rosenberg
Taxation (Individual) .... Burke & Friel
Taxation (Individual) .... Freeland, Lathrope, Lind & Stephens
Taxation (Individual) .... Klein, Bankman & Shaviro
Torts .... Dobbs & Hayden
Torts .... Epstein
Torts .... Franklin & Rabin
Torts .... Henderson, Pearson, Kysar & Siliciano
Torts .... Schwartz, Kelly & Partlett (Prosser)
Wills, Trusts & Estates .... Dukeminier, Johanson, Lindgren & Sitkoff
Wills, Trusts & Estates .... Dobris, Sterk & Leslie
Wills, Trusts & Estates .... Scoles, Halbach, Roberts & Begleiter